THE NEW
and the Wisdom of Christ

By the same authors:

The Archetypal Feminine in the Mystery Stream of Humanity

Paths of the Christian Mysteries, From Compostela to the New World

THE NEW MYSTERIES
and the Wisdom of Christ

Virginia Sease and Manfred Schmidt-Brabant

TEMPLE LODGE

Translated from the German by Marguerite V. Miller and Douglas E. Miller

Temple Lodge Publishing
Hillside House, The Square
Forest Row, RH18 5ES

www.templelodge.com

First published in English by Temple Lodge 2005

Originally published in German under the title *Geheimnisse des Christentums, Alte und neue Mysterien* by Verlag am Goetheanum, Dornach 2002

© Verlag am Goetheanum 2002
This translation © Temple Lodge Publishing 2005

A catalogue record for this book is available from the British Library

ISBN 1 902636 74 0

Cover by Andrew Morgan Design
Typeset by DP Photosetting, Aylesbury, Bucks.
Printed and bound by Cromwell Press Limited, Trowbridge, Wilts.

Contents

Preface to the English Edition   vii
Preface to the German Edition   ix

Lecture 1, *by Manfred Schmidt-Brabant*
The Consciousness Soul and Christ Knowledge: The Cosmic
Pre-history of the Mystery of Golgotha   1

Lecture 2, *by Virginia Sease*
Prophecy in the Old Testament, the New Testament and
Anthroposophy   19

Lecture 3, *by Virginia Sease*
The Order of the Essenes, Jeshu ben Pandira, Jesus Christ and
the Third Millennium   31

Lecture 4, *by Manfred Schmidt-Brabant*
The Life of Christ Jesus in the Context of the Ancient Mystery
Religions   44

Lecture 5, *by Virginia Sease*
Transformations in Prayer and Meditation Resulting from the
the Mystery of Golgotha   61

Lecture 6, *by Manfred Schmidt-Brabant*
The World of the Gods in the Old Mysteries and the Spiritual
Hierarchies of Esoteric Christianity   74

Lecture 7, *by Virginia Sease*
The Development of Conscience in Pre-Christian Times and
Since the Mystery of Golgotha   90

Lecture 8, *by Manfred Schmidt-Brabant*
The Cosmic Being of the Isis Sophia—Christ Paths of the
Middle Ages: Monks and Knights—Grail Secrets, Templar
Destinies and Rosicrucian Deeds   102

Lecture 9, *by Virginia Sease*
Mystery Impulses in the Life and Work of Great Christian
Women   119

Lecture 10, *by Manfred Schmidt-Brabant*
Logos and Anti-Logos—Sorat, the Sun Demon, and the
Counter-world of the Trinity   133

Lecture 11, *by Virginia Sease*
Religion and Knowledge in the Age of the Consciousness Soul:
New Religions in the East and West   152

Lecture 12, *by Manfred Schmidt-Brabant*
The Creation of the New Christianity in the Supersensible
Cultus of the Nineteenth Century, and the Karma of Love as
the Earth's Future   164

Notes   181

Bibliography of Cited Materials from the Collected Works
of Rudolf Steiner Available in English   191

Preface to the English Edition

In view of the positive reception of the English translation of *Paths of the Christian Mysteries: From Compostela to the New World*, followed by requests for the subsequent lectures which appeared in German in 2002, this volume now also becomes available in English. In reviewing the original publication it became apparent that certain additions could augment the text favourably, especially for the English reader. These have been added. Also several minor errors in the footnotes have been corrected.

Again it is a pleasure as well as an obligation to express my profound gratitude to Marguerite and Douglas Miller for the careful textual scrutiny and the linguistic accuracy combined with sensitivity for the content which they brought to their task.

Also the publisher of Temple Lodge, Sevak Gulbekian, deserves a warm word of gratitude for providing an initial impetus for this translation.

Virginia Sease, Ph.D.
Goetheanum, Dornach, May 2005

Preface to the German Edition

This book follows on the publication of the 1999 volume, *Paths of the Christian Mysteries, From Compostela to the New World* [*Compostela, Sternenwege alter und neuer Mysterienstätten*]. The content here, as with the earlier volume, is the outcome of a course of lectures Manfred Schmidt–Brabant and I gave at the invitation of Manfred Kraus in connection with the Studienhaus Rüspe. These lectures were held in Rome in May 1999, with the theme 'The History of the Mysteries and the History of Christianity'.

The unexpected illness and the passing of Manfred Schmidt–Brabant in February 2001 prevented him from editing his lectures personally. I am, therefore, grateful to Elisabeth Bessau for reading and editing the lecture transcripts. I am also deeply indebted to Heinrich Muhler for transcribing the lectures from the tape recordings, and for the care he took going through them many times to assure their accuracy.

After the course was finished, we received many requests to have the lectures published. I am especially pleased that Manfred Schmidt–Brabant's work will be available as a result.

Virginia Sease, Ph.D.
Goetheanum, Dornach, September 2002

Lecture 1

The Consciousness Soul and Christ Knowledge: The Cosmic Pre-history of the Mystery of Golgotha

Manfred Schmidt-Brabant

We presented a general overview of the history of the Mysteries two years ago in Compostela.[1] Even then, it was already apparent that it might be appropriate to deepen those observations in a further course of lectures, pursuing what is generally called Christology, the Christ-being or Christianity.

As it turned out, the present course of lectures is being held within a special time frame. In 1901—a year after the beginning of the century, and it is now one year before the end of the century—Rudolf Steiner gave the lectures that he then published as his great basic text, *Christianity as Mystical Fact and the Mysteries of Antiquity.*[2] This is one element that will serve as a background for this conference. Another element is the great Christology course Rudolf Steiner gave in Rome almost 90 years ago—in March 1909. We will look in some detail at those lectures, which he repeated during the following year, 1910.[3] Thus, in a certain way, this course of lectures is situated within the time span of the twentieth century.

For a discussion like this, it is always necessary to find a sensible approach based on real human experience. Such an approach has been present throughout human history; for a human being to understand himself, he must take into account the age in which he lives as well as the state of his consciousness. It is human nature that, without this, he cannot have a complete existential experience of his place in the world. This has occurred in various ways throughout every age; but it was not as conscious in the past as it is today. In the old Mystery cultures, the human being experienced himself as a child of the gods or even an instrument of the gods. This was the case until independent thinking awoke in Greece. Over the course of the last two and a half millennia, this independent thinking has developed into the present state of consciousness, which can be characterized as follows.

A part of the soul that is most fully conscious is awakening in human beings. It is a part of the soul that the human being never before possessed in this way. We refer to it as the consciousness soul. In all previous states of soul the human being was directed outwards, sensing, perceiving, feeling, and then—even into the Middle Ages—thinking about the world, creating a soul-based image of the world. To be quite precise, a new age began in the year 1413. We call it the age of the consciousness soul; it did not, however, become a real issue until the twentieth century. It is characteristic of this age that the human being not only continues to direct his consciousness outwards, but that he turns it in on himself, on his own conscious activity, on his own existence. He asks himself 'Who am I?' with a very different power and autonomy than he had before. Everything that places him existentially and with certainty into the world is dependent on his answer to this question.

Who is this I? We will formulate this somewhat more precisely, because this is how the question is posed inwardly: 'Who is it within me that says "I am"?' If we formulate the question this way, the past three thousand years of history surface—the history of the Old Testament and of the New Testament. A history emerges at the beginning of which stood the figure of Moses who was met by a divine Being in the Sinai and was told by that Being, 'Proclaim to humanity that I am the I AM. *Ejeh Asher Ejeh*. If the Jews ask you, "What is the name of God?"—God is called I AM.' Later, individuals connected with Christian initiation knew that it was the Christ-being already revealing Himself in reflection through Jehovah so that Moses heard this I AM and became the first to proclaim the I AM.

Today it is quite understandable that a person in our culture—at the moment we are referring to the West, to the world of Christianity—says to himself: 'Self-knowledge is always knowledge of the Christ as well. If it is true that initiates throughout history always said that Christ has only one name and that is the name I AM, and if it is true that Moses already heard this I AM, then I will never arrive at real self-knowledge—and thus at a real foundation of existence in life—if I do not connect this self-knowledge with knowledge of the Christ-being.'

Here, of course, we find one of the most interesting questions a modern person can raise—we might even say, must raise: 'Am I really a Christian?' If I instinctively believe that the answer to this question is yes, how then am I a Christian? Is it by way of an outer confession, through membership in a church? That cannot be. That is a formalistic answer that might have its own justification. But when I say to myself as a human being, 'I do think I am a Christian', then in the age of the consciousness soul I must ask myself, 'What makes me a Christian?'

We will therefore pursue these observations so that we can arrive at a history of Christ knowledge, and thus at a history of self-knowledge for modern humanity. To that end, we will pursue a particular path. Rudolf Steiner drew attention to this path when he said that there is the external history that we write down—the history of nations, wars, the history of art, intellectual history. However, something else must be added in the course of time, and that is a history of the Mysteries, an account of the more hidden aspects of higher guidance connected with humanity's path of development. The being of the Christ can only be understood through this history of the Mysteries—actually a continuous history during which the Mysteries were sometimes active externally and sometimes more concealed. We need the history of the Mysteries for an understanding of the Christ-being.

Such a history of the Mysteries naturally confronts head on the external history of Christianity. Remembering this here in Rome is practically a matter of course. Two thousand years of Christian history are two thousand years of wrestling with an understanding of the Christ-being. Moreover, this understanding has been continually based on dogmas. Back then it was said: 'Enough talk! The Church proclaims a particular dogma. It shall be thus!' This did not stop the discussions, the riddles, the wrestling. They continued through the Middle Ages up into modern times. We stand before the multiplicity of three great denominations, each with a different kind of Christ knowledge; we stand before the many and varied independent churches, sects, counter-churches, each one proclaiming a different Christ. At this juncture, it is necessary to seek out a path that leads the human being's understanding into the history of the Mysteries so that he can enter there with this understanding.

Of course, there is an endless range of themes from both the outer history and the inner history, the history of the Mysteries. There are also many points of view to be found in the works of Rudolf Steiner. Here, we will take up a major aspect, and that is the fundamental question: 'How is the spiritual related to what belongs to the earthly-physical realm?' Precisely this question formed the background of the centuries old riddle: 'How was it possible for the Christ to have lived in Jesus? How was it possible that a divine being united itself with a human being?'

Initially that riddle was solved through a kind of dogma when two or three different Church Councils said: 'We maintain that Christ Jesus was truly God and truly man.' But it is characteristic of the consciousness soul that it is not satisfied with mere dogma, regardless of whether the dogma is true or false—that it wants to understand and penetrate the dogma. This motif, which emerges again and again in the most varied ways from the ancient Mysteries to the present, will permeate our observations here. How are what is spiritual and what is earthly—the divine and the human—related? How is the Christ-being related to the Jesus-being?

This is a concept that has been associated with this theme since the earliest Christian times, the concept of 'pre-history'. At the beginning of Christianity, among the Church Fathers in ancient times, a question had already arisen: Did the Christ-being actually exist before the turning point in time, before what we call the Mystery of Golgotha? In what way did He exist? And what was He prior to that? The result was an enormous epistemological discussion that has endured for two millennia.

Recently, a theologian from Tübingen published a comprehensive 800-page tome with the title *Geboren vor aller Zeit? Der Streit um Christi Ursprung* [Born before all time? The dispute about Christ's origins].[4] The author is well read, and the book is cleverly written, very like-able—he even refers to Rudolf Steiner in one place. But the nice thing is that he begins with a scene from Goethe's *Faust*. Faust returns home from a walk at Easter, still very enthusiastic about an experience with nature that is also a spiritual experience. He is again in his study. In order to continue the sacred mood, he begins to translate the Gospel of John; he translates the beginning of the Gospel with the words 'In the beginning was the Word'—*En archê ên ho logos* (Εν αρχη ην ο λογος), 'In the beginning was the Logos.' He tries to translate the word 'Logos' into his 'beloved German' and writes down quite correctly 'In the beginning was the Word.' But then he stumbles; we see Mephisto-pheles, who has crept in disguised as a poodle, growling at Faust insis-tently. One might say he exerts a Mephistophelian influence over him. Thus Faust says, 'I cannot value the *Word* so highly.' Then he says, 'In the beginning was the meaning.' No, the meaning is not it either. 'It should be, In the beginning was the power!' But it cannot be that either. And:

> The Spirit helps me! Suddenly, seeing advice to heed
> I safely write, In the beginning was the *deed*![5]

Under the influence of Mephistopheles, Faust has descended to the level of the physical world in his quest for the origin of the Logos.

This theologian, Karl Joseph Kuschel, cites this introductory motif in order to demonstrate how Christianity has wrestled for about two thousand years and up to the present time with the question: 'Had the Christ, the Logos, always been present? If He was there, was He a god?

Was He like God? Was He begotten of God?' There is an endless stream of literature on the subject.

We know that dogmatic positions have been taken again and again—as early as AD 325 at the Council of Nicaea—and as a result, we hear: Whoever says that there was a time in which Christ did not exist (*Anathema sit*), let him be condemned to damnation! The Council in Constantinople declared that Christ was born of the Father before all time began. Before the beginning of any time at all, the Christ-being was born of the Father. These dogmas were never able to stop the seekers after knowledge, even during those centuries. Thus the issue continued to occupy the Church Fathers throughout the Middle Ages. The result was that people were frequently declared heretics, because the Church said: 'We cannot recognize those who do not hold to the dogma, who arrive at a different view through their own understanding. They are heretics; we must exclude them from the Church.'

Kuschel reports that this question about origins is actually a fundamental question of religious life. It is still very difficult for the Catholic Church to speak about the pre-existence of every human being. We find it everywhere else—in Judaism, in Islam, in Buddhism. He offers several examples of how Buddhism holds that every human being has prior incarnations, as do the gods, of course. He notes that Judaism speaks of the pre-existence of the Sophia of God, of the pre-existing Son of Man, and also of the fact that the Torah had always been with God, before all time, and would later be revealed to humanity. Similarly, in Islam there is the pre-existence of the prophet Mohammed who was always with God. There is a first creation, and the Koran was also with God before all time.

Kuschel writes with a measure of correctness that the question of pre-existence is a primal religious question of humanity that 'goes far beyond what is Christian'.[6] Thus it also appears in Christianity and, of course, it plays an important role in anthroposophical Christology—a Mystery Christology—as the pre-history of the Christ in evolution, in time, in the cosmos. From the point of view of modern consciousness, it is understandable that even an open-minded theologian like Kuschel can base his work only on the written tradition. Like all modern theologians, he can no longer grasp that for centuries the early Christian Fathers—like Clement of Alexandria or Origen—had experiences that were quite different from an experience through the written texts. They were clairvoyant and had mystical experiences. And many Church Fathers— like Clement of Alexandria—had actually been initiated into the Old

Mysteries. Thus these modern theologians do not realize that super-sensible experiences and perceptions were still possible throughout the first centuries of Christendom; and from these experiences quite different answers could be found to questions like those about whether the Christ existed before the turning point in time and in what form.

With this observation we will find a connection to just such super-sensible experiences; however, they will be modern ones like those presented in the work of Rudolf Steiner. There are three areas of decisive importance.

First, we will find a connection to the anthroposophical understanding of the human being. People who no longer had supersensible experiences always had great difficulty with the question: How did the Christ live in Jesus? They could not find an answer based on an understanding of the human being because they gradually came to see the body more or less as a physical entity.

In the anthroposophical understanding of the human being we can distinguish clearly that the human being has a physical body, and in addition—invisibly—there is a life body, an ether body more related to the rhythms and everything that pulses within the human being. And then there is a soul body, an astral body, which is the carrier of every-thing related to our thinking, feeling and willing, our memories, emo-tions, and so forth. In addition, every human being has his true individuality, the ego. This configuration can be structured so that we speak of the bodily being, the soul being and the spirit being of the human being, and so that we constitute the human being of body, soul and spirit.

According to Church history, this trichotomy—the threefold mem-bering of the human being—was abolished by the Church in 869 at the Council of Constantinople. Until then, people were still able to make these distinctions based on old experiences: the bodily, not only the physical body, but the ether and the astral body as well; the soul quality of the human being (his individual soul existence); and the spirit quality connected to the ego and extending into the soul quality. As perception of the reality of the human being disappeared in the course of the first millennium, people no longer understood it and said: 'Because we are Christians, we believe that the human being has a soul, but not a spirit.' The soul has some spiritual qualities; for example, it can think. The tri-chotomy was abolished, and along with it the real understanding of the human being. As a result, the individual's relationship to Christ was rendered impossible or at least made extremely difficult. Thus, in the anthroposophy of the twentieth century we take up anew what had remained hidden or unrecognized over the course of long centuries: the true inner nature of the human being.

The second thing we will take up is the newly understood body of knowledge within anthroposophy concerning angels, the teaching about the hierarchies. By hierarchies we mean not only the angels but all the loftier spiritual beings. Through them we establish a connection with the earliest origins of esoteric Christianity, because teaching about the hierarchies goes back to Dionysius the Areopagite, an initiated pupil of Paul.

We will refer especially to a third thing that has led to our speaking concretely within anthroposophy about the history of the Mysteries, the history of evolution, the history of the cosmos. This third thing is the fact that the time we experience here in the physical realm in the blink of an eye has its own reality in the true supersensible realm and, in Richard Wagner's words, it 'becomes space'. Of course, we can reach forward into the future, but the past has vanished into what is physical. We can look into time and it presents itself to us as a gigantic cosmic memory. Using an old Mystery expression from Asia, we speak of the 'Akasha Chronicle'. An initiate can read the Akasha Chronicle. Everyone can learn to read it if he practises certain exercises—he can at least learn to read in the Akasha Chronicle of his own being—because everything that is ether, everything that is time, has an intrinsically permanent quality. In this way, we will take up Rudolf Steiner's descriptions of the pre-history of the Mystery of Golgotha based on an Akashic Chronicle that has existed as long as there has been time.

Of course, a modern person will say: 'Rudolf Steiner talks about his research. Must we then believe it?' But here is the decisive answer of our time for the consciousness soul: You are not required to believe it; you are not even supposed to believe it. You are supposed to think it. His indications should be used as a model for thinking in order to understand the real situation. This is extremely important for the following reason. When an initiate speaks about supersensible situations, he has to clothe them in the language of the physical world. It is a language appropriate for the laws that govern this world of objects; it is confined to a particular area— German, French, English, and so forth. The initiate has to translate what he sees in the spiritual world directly into something that can be expressed physically. There is absolutely no point in a person taking these physical expressions only at face value and going no further. Looking at these communications has a purpose only when we try to comprehend their

thought content, their knowledge and spiritual content, and connect it
with our own soul. Because then the individual will experience that the
spiritual–thought element in the initiate's report leads to the source of
what is seen clairvoyantly—perhaps as inward-sensing feeling at first and
then, eventually, as knowledge: 'I must reproduce this knowledge for
myself.'

When the spiritual researcher says the word 'angel', so many traditional
ideas manifest in us that we can hardly avoid them, even if we think of the
noblest angel we have seen here at the Vatican Museum. Angels—aren't
those the beautiful human figures in white robes, delightful ladies? These
are images, and we must take hold of the thoughts contained in such a
presentation and say: When the ancients painted angels in white robes,
they wanted to indicate the angels' purity. The angels stand above all
earthly temptations. When the ancients put palm fronds in the angels'
hands, it was to indicate that they are connected to the forces of life, that
they live in the realm of life, in the etheric. Above all, when we hear in
modern spiritual research about the angels, we should understand that it is
not just a matter of saying, 'There was an angel.' Rather we must ask,
'What did it do? What are its processes?' The spiritual element that I can
grasp is found in these processes.

All of this is needed in order to understand Christology from the
standpoint of the history of the Mysteries. For this history of the Mysteries
not only has a different content, but a different internal structure as well.
In external history I can say there was a time when rulers lived who led
wars, who increased their lands or decreased them, who experienced
certain things. One thing follows another, and when there was an A, B
followed, and when there was a B, C followed. In any case, I can try to
portray history this way.

This is not possible with the history of the Mysteries. There I have to
look at the totality of time; I have to understand that time is an organism.
Something that happened here does so because something else happens
over there; but this other thing happens because a third and fourth thing
are connected with it. In my own organism I know how my liver, gall
bladder, kidneys, lungs, and so forth are cogently interrelated to form a
unified organism, just as in a history of the Mysteries everything that
happens is cogently interrelated in a mighty, supersensible, cosmic
organism. In earlier times, a pious but quite correct expression for this was
'God's plan for salvation'. In a manner of speaking, God set forth the
whole creation process in a great plan of salvation where everything that
happens is related cogently and organically. In his study of these many

problems, Kuschel writes the following about the pre-existence of Christ: every glance at the beginning brings a vision of the whole as well. In the context of the history of the Mysteries, when I ask about the beginning I am simultaneously asking about the whole.

We will contrast the history of the Mysteries with the history of Christianity or at least pick up several themes from this comparison. The history of Christ-knowledge has always been a battle between orthodoxy and heresy, or heterodoxy as it was later called. From the first century on, the pious fathers frequently insulted one another, often in the nastiest way, each blaming the other for deviation and error and so forth. There were synods called 'robber synods' because they beat one another up during the meeting. When the Church later became the state Church, the deviants also became 'enemies of the state'. This is what we need to understand about these early times. In the first centuries, people were still connected with Mystery traditions; and they were gripped by Christianity so existentially that they made their whole existence dependent on what they understood of it. If someone said something different about the Christ, they experienced it as painful, like an attack on their own existence. In any case, this is how it was during these early times. Modern Church historians say it was a good thing that these enormous struggles took place at that time. We know that everything that deviated from the norm was later designated as Gnosis, but that developed only very slowly. Today, Church historians say there is a healthy, justified Gnosis and a heretical Gnosis. The healthy, justified Gnosis is the one in which people repeatedly encounter new aspects of the Christ secrets based on their own supersensible experiences.

There came a time when Christianity became a state religion, and during that time a feeling prevailed in the Church that found expression in the words *Extra ecclesiam nulla salus*—'There is no salvation outside the Church.' This was a strong conviction. 'The poor people who don't hold to the orthodoxy of the Church are lost! They will go to hell, their souls are lost. Therefore, I must do everything I can to help them when I see one of them deviating from the orthodoxy, and unable to be a part of this Church that alone can bring salvation. If need be, I will have to burn him at the stake, since the body is not so important; the main point is that his soul be saved.' This was the way things were until the time of Thomas Aquinas. We need to understand that people who belonged to the Church were deeply convinced of the necessity of saving souls through an institution that alone brought salvation.

Then things changed once again; the Church became like an imperialistic state. Only then did it become truly the case that the heretic was an enemy of the state, a terrorist so to speak, an opponent who must be destroyed—not saved. When we read about heresies and the persecution of heretics, we find these three stages: the simple directness of the first centuries; the feeling that souls are to be saved and that we are right to save them; and in more recent times, the Church becoming imperialistic, so to speak—and the persecution of anyone who thinks differently as an enemy of this imperial realm, as a troublemaker, as someone who could threaten its power.

If we now consider concretely the events that led up to the Mystery of Golgotha, something like a great picture of the whole of evolution must also stand at the end. Rudolf Steiner speaks about God's plan for salvation, and about the Trinity's plan for salvation as well. He describes this all-encompassing plan in his book *Occult Science, An Outline*, and says that our earth is only a kind of intermediate stage in a development that comes from the past—from the prior stages of the earth; he also says that the earth will continue in three more evolutionary stages, seven in all.[7] He asks the question that is also the question of modern science: Where did the universe come from and where is it going?

As contemporaries, we all live with a certain image that is constantly being embellished; this is the image that the universe was created through a primal bang. There was an unimaginably dense accumulation of matter that actually only existed as a kind of point; it suddenly exploded and expanded within a very short time—all of this was worked out in millionths of seconds. The whole universe slowly developed from this primal bang. Today, by observing its outermost edges, we can still determine how the whole thing continues to expand. But that will soon come to an end according to the newest astrophysical research. Then everything will slowly collapse in on itself again through millions and millions of years; at the end will come a general thermal death, entropy. Everything will disintegrate; everything will come to equilibrium; there will no longer be tensions between hot and cold and so forth. Instead, everything will be dissolved into a common state. In our time, we live with this image; our science lives with this image. The extraordinarily strong influence of this picture works right down into the events of daily life; we cannot always keep this in check.

Not only Rudolf Steiner but also the whole Mystery tradition contrasts another image to this. In that image, the whole universe emerged from the Divinity—God created, exhaled, the universe, and it will return again to God. A short meditative text by Rudolf Steiner says:

Primal Self,
From which everything arose,
Primal Self,
To which all things return
Primal Self,
That lives in me—
Towards you I strive.[8]

There is a certain resonance here with the feeling of India. The human being senses: 'I am a part of what was exhaled and what returns again.'

This is presented in a somewhat more differentiated way in *Occult Science, An Outline*. Rudolf Steiner says that a universe of wisdom emerged from divine wisdom. A cosmos of wisdom emerged from the divine. This cosmos of wisdom is to transform itself into a cosmos of love.

We could also say: God—about whom we have heard that the Sophia, wisdom, was with Him before the beginning of everything—exhales the universe and it becomes a universe of wisdom. Now a point is reached where this cosmos of wisdom transforms into a cosmos of love and returns to God.

Rudolf Steiner has formulated wonderful descriptions for this at the end of the book *Occult Science, An Outline*: 'From the stage of earth onwards, the "wisdom of the outer world" will become inner wisdom in the human being. And when it has been internalized there, it will become a seed of *love*. Wisdom is the prerequisite of love; love is the result of wisdom reborn in the "ego".'[9] As human beings, we stand at something like the turning point of this great cosmological process—about which the outer world knows only the 'big bang' and entropy, and which we understand as the breathing out into wisdom, the breathing in again into love—and, therefore, he then says: 'And the "cosmos of wisdom" develops into a "cosmos of love".'[10]

Love should arise out of everything that the ego can unfold in itself. Through its own revelation, the lofty Sun-being appears as an all-encompassing paradigm of love which will be characterized through the portrayal of the Christ evolution.

Now I have these questions: 'Within the context of evolution, who am I, and who is this "I AM"?' It is true for every moment of life that I stand within a stream in which wisdom transforms into love. In every moment of life I may have the feeling that I can resolve to undertake this transition only with my ego, only if I unite myself with the true 'I AM', with the Christ-being. Rudolf Steiner depicts the development of this Christ-being and says that the Christ-being also underwent an evolution.

There are three great evolutionary stages that precede the earth's current condition. In anthroposophy we speak about there having been an ancient, primeval, first stage of the world, the Saturn stage; it consisted only of warmth and time. Time begins; differentiated warmth fills the cosmos. Then comes another stage, the so-called Old Sun, where air and gaseous elements form out of the warmth; light is formed. A third stage, Old Moon, condenses further into water. Here, everything arises that we refer to as chemical processes until, finally, solid mineral matter develops on the earth along with everything we refer to as the sense of connectedness, that is to say an evolution, an evolving of natural phenomena into the cosmos we have today.

Rudolf Steiner directs our attention to the second stage of this development, to Old Sun. In particular, he directs it to supersensible beings, to the hierarchies, to angelic beings. He points out how everything we today call sun and planets coexisted there under completely different conditions; he points to how the sun did not yet hold its pre-eminent position at the centre of the planetary system, but how it—along with Venus, Mars and the other planets—was in a state that was still indefinite, not solid. And he points to how Christ was the regent of the sun, the Sun-spirit Christ. Rudolf Steiner also describes how something immense took place on this Old Sun. Rudolf Steiner himself says that we must always use human words to characterize certain things; but these human words merely hint at something powerful. What took place is what is referred to in esotericism as 'the Sun sacrifice of the Christ'.

This Sun sacrifice took place in two phases; it played out in two ways. There was something about this old cosmos that could be called the expression of the creative Trinity; the second part of this trinity, the Son Being, the Logos, the Cosmic Word, reaches into the Old Sun age in a very particular way. Rudolf Steiner said that today the stars of the zodiac stand at the place where earlier there were twelve ancient deities that appeared as an expression of the Logos, as an expression of the Cosmic Word. They were twelve Cosmic Initiators in whom was contained everything that existed in the ancient time. In this Logos, this Cosmic Word, lived everything that had ever existed. The first part of the great Sun sacrifice occurred when the Christ-being opened Himself to this Logos, this Son Being, so that it connected itself perfectly with Him. Although the Christ was a being of the hierarchies, He became a vessel for the Son, the Logos. From this Sun age on, we can, of course, differentiate—in terms of this development—between the Son, the second principle of the Trinity, and the Christ, but they have become a united whole.

A second thing occurred. At that time, the gods lived in various ways within these developing etheric realms. They lived in what was the warmth ether, the light ether, the air ether. Lofty spirit beings, among them the Christ, lived more in the ether element of light, not in the denser ether elements of the air, not in any condition of the air. Because of the nature of His being, the Christ was actually meant to live only in these higher etheric conditions. But the second part of the Sun sacrifice was that He united Himself with the denser sorts of ethers; He united Himself with an element to which the better gods—one could say—did not connect. He united Himself with everything that later would become earth.

Here we see a colossal event, in the truest sense of the phrase: a union of heaven and earth takes place. The Christ-being goes to the very heights and opens Himself to the Logos, takes up the Cosmic Word, becomes a part of the Trinity. At the same time, He descends and enters the elements that are becoming denser, preparing Himself in the process to be able to inhabit a human body sometime later.

This was the Being who appeared again and again to the initiates of the pre-Christian era as the Jehovah-being. Jehovah was something like the mirror of the Christ-being for the human world. At first, people were still not able to experience the Christ directly. Rudolf Steiner once said that Christ would have unhesitatingly identified Himself with Jehovah, one of the elohim, one of the gods. When Moses saw Jehovah in Sinai and heard from Jehovah, 'Ejeh Asher Ejeh', 'I am the I AM', it was actually the mirror of the Christ-being who spoke to him there.

Thus we see how something founded on Old Sun is deeply connected with our own human existence. What was founded was the way the spiritual and the physical are connected, and the possibility that a being can be both truly human and truly god. We hear later in the Gospels how the Christ said to humanity: 'You are gods',[11] and you are also human beings. Basically, the entire development of the modern Mysteries, the New Mysteries, begins when the human being learns to recognize in himself, 'I am spirit being and I am earthly man. I have a human part and I have a divine part.' Only one being is 'truly god and truly human'; but every one of us can say, 'God and man, divine and human, are in me.' The whole secret of the 'I AM' in human beings, the whole problem of 'Who am I actually—in this time, in my life, in my biography?'—depends on the response to this question of God and humanity.

While something like a cosmic preparation occurred during this Sun period, a second preparation takes place on the earth itself. The earth bears its own quite specific stamp. Here something has come from primal evolution that belonged to the human body, and something has come that belonged to the ego. There is a single question at the starting point of the whole of evolution—it is depicted this way in *Occult Science*: 'How did the three bodies achieve a level of development in which they could take an ego into themselves, and how did this ego itself come about and achieve the capacity to work within these bodies?'[12] It is all a matter of ego and body, spiritual and earthly, divine and human.

The course of this development was not at all smooth. The previous phase on the earth was the one in which the physical body gradually had to be given form. During this forming, there were constant points of crisis, catastrophic situations, during which everything could go wrong. It turns out that whenever such a crisis occurred—there were three great crisis points—something quite strange took place, something similar to the later Mystery of Golgotha, which is why Rudolf Steiner refers to them as 'preliminary stages of the Mystery of Golgotha'.[13] There was a kind of salvation or rescue mission. The actual Mystery of Golgotha concerns the rescue of the human ego, but at that time it was a matter of rescuing and saving the bodily arrangement that the ego needs in order to be able to live on the earth.

Now one of the most puzzling and, at the same time, most wondrous events takes place. The Christ-being is, as it were, summoned to carry out this rescue, this salvation, together with another being. In order to describe this being, we have to make use of some clarifying concepts. At an earlier time—we call this the Lemurian epoch—humanity appeared on the earth. God made a clod of earth and blew the breath of life into it— these are abbreviated images for a long development. But what came to earth as humanity, what is metaphorically called 'Adam' when it came into contact with the earth, was not all of the humanity at God's disposal. A portion of humanity stayed behind. In the symbolic language of eso-tericism, it is called 'the innocent part of the Adam soul'. It is the part that did not enter into incarnation and thus did not cause the Fall of Man, although it underwent all of the previous evolution. This being 'had lived through the times when the human sheaths were created; lived through the Saturn period during which the seed was prepared for what would become the physical body; the Sun and Moon periods when the etheric and astral bodies formed themselves; it also lived through the smaller phases that repeated the great epochs.'[14] This being was never incarnate, never accompanied the other part of its existence, the Adam part, never entered into incarnation. It experienced from the spiritual world how the whole development of the body threatened three times to fall into catastrophe. This being had sympathy for these catastrophic situations, drew the Christ into itself, and made it possible to rescue the process.

The first catastrophe would have been that the human senses did not respond selflessly, that the human being—as we know from Goethe's *Theory of Colour*—would always have been attacked by red, would literally have been drawn out of himself by blue. And the same would have been true for all other sensory experiences. He would have been incapable of having an undisturbed sensory perception; in some way or another, it would have always thrown him off balance. Thus the first preparatory step of the Mystery of Golgotha was the rescue of the senses—the calming, the humanizing of the senses.

Then another catastrophe threatened during the Atlantean period. For example, the human life processes we know as nutrition and so forth threatened to degenerate completely. As it is described, the human being would have been torn apart by disgust, loathing and greed—all of which we have in moderation. We do not immediately attack our food and so forth; we can control ourselves. We simply push away what we do not want so that we do not make ourselves sick. Nonetheless, if we observe carefully, we see that remnants of the life processes still threaten to go out of balance. The second sacrifice of Christ was necessary for this reason—so this innocent Adam soul could bring human beings into equanimity in our life processes. Thus we can still be carried away, but not too strongly. That is why I mentioned Goethe's theory of colour; the predisposition is still there. There are people who are hypersensitive, who are made sick by a colour, who cannot stand a certain colour. They dislike it. Here we notice a middle ground is created, but the predisposition is still there.

The threat is strongest in the third catastrophe. We move from the physical into the etheric, and then into the astral. The thinking, feeling, and willing of humanity threaten to fall completely into chaos. The dragon of physical corporeality threatened to take hold of thinking, feeling and willing. Thus this third sacrifice entered at the end of Atlantis, and it is still found in the Mysteries in all the images of dragon slaying. Of course, the Mysteries not only knew about the event, but they also perceived it as it occurred.

Naturally, everything we have looked at here—this pre-sacrifice, the great Sun sacrifice—lived in the consciousness of the Old Mysteries. It was proclaimed not only by the priests, but also in a way that was customary in the Old Mysteries. There are descriptions of how the people of those Mystery periods came into the spiritual world after death and experienced the Sun-being and His secrets. There are also depictions of how people at that time had the experience: 'I come from the Being of God. That is the source from which I can say, "I am."' This was the great proclamation in the old Mysteries; above all, it was proclaimed by one of the greatest of those initiates who endure throughout the ages. We address him by his name from the Persian period, the Zarathustra-being. It was Zarathustra who spoke to people about this Sun-being, and especially about the coming of this Sun-being.

The anticipation of the Messiah was part of all pre-Christian Mysteries. We speak about the anticipation of the Messiah based on the Jewish Mysteries; but there are extensive accounts of how the anticipation of a coming saviour lived in all the Nordic, the Western, the Celtic Mysteries—these accounts reached Asia, and moved through all of North Africa and the Middle East. The Mysteries, each in its own way, knew that a divine being would come and descend to the earth.

The Mysteries knew of an event that they told about in varying ways. That was what we call the Fall of Man. They knew that humanity was on a path of ruin, that it would go under if something fundamental did not take place. So all of the Mysteries looked towards a divine hero, a Sun hero, a Sun messenger—to a Sun-being that would come to rescue humanity and the earth.

Thus it was especially Zarathustra who, under many names, prepared and proclaimed the coming of this Sun god throughout the pre-Christian Mysteries. It was the Zarathustra-being who prepared the final step for the coming of the Sun god, the Christ. For many people this is still the strangest, most puzzling step, for it contradicts our sense of tradition. Two Jesus boys were born at the turning point of time, and further, these two Jesus boys become the elements that will form the sheath for the Christ-being. The Gospels speak clearly about this, and textual criticism as well as Church history have always addressed the fact that two sets of parents with two different family trees are described. In the Gospel of Matthew, a Jesus child was born to Mary and Joseph—at that time many people had those names; they were quite common names—and their lineage went back to Solomon. And in the Gospel of Luke, a Jesus child is born whose lineage went back to the priest Nathan, a contemporary of Solomon. Thus we speak of the Solomon Jesus child and the Nathan Jesus child.

Spiritual Science reveals how something is created that is infinitely—if one follows it with feeling, one might say cosmically—artful. One of the greatest initiates, Zarathustra himself, incarnates in this Solomon Jesus child. The family was royal, of royal lineage. There is much evidence that the parents were highly educated, very wise, and well aware of their place in the lineage of Solomon. The other child, from the Gospel of Luke, is the innocent Adam soul that is incarnating for the first time—the Nathan Jesus. The part of Adam that remained protected by spiritual beings in the spiritual world, the part that participated in, even arranged for, the Christ-being to enter three times into the development of the body—this is the Adam soul that incarnates for the first time.

Thus we can understand why two completely different perceptions are depicted; we find this in the Apocrypha as well. This Nathan Jesus is described as possessing infinite charm, infinite tenderness, infinite deli-cacy. Rudolf Steiner indicates we can probably say that the one was born in Bethlehem, and that the other Jesus child was in Nazareth after the flight into Egypt. He connects this with something we will discuss; he says Bethlehem was where the cult of Adonis was celebrated. The whole milieu of that age continued to be one of boundless Mysteries. There was a large, very widespread cult devoted to Adonis, the god who had been killed. Aphrodite loved him, and he was killed by a boar. Aphrodite goes into the underworld to plead for his life, but the underworld releases him for only half a year. Thus here is a god (he was connected with vegetation) who lives and appears in the upper world, then disappears again in death—a god who is born, who dies, and who is born again.

Rudolf Steiner formulates it in the following way: 'The god killed there as Adonis and resurrected from the dead is not thought of as embodied in flesh; instead, what we have as a god is first an image, an image of that angel-like being that was penetrated by the Christ at the end of the Atlantean period . . . and that then became the Nathan Jesus child. The fate of the Nathan Jesus is celebrated in the Adonis rite. The Adonis who dies and is resurrected was often celebrated there'—now comes the decisive point—and thus, in Bethlehem, the 'aura was prepared' into which this Jesus child could be born.[15]

Now to the other story. Of course, there were the kings—among them earlier pupils of Zarathustra—who said to Herod: 'The new king will be born here.' The angel warns the family; they go to Egypt—which is also a sign that their position in the world is completely different from that of the truly, lovingly humble and poor family of the Nathan Jesus. This is no problem for Joseph. They travel to Egypt, live in a Mystery centre there for a time, and return when the angel calls them back.

The other Jesus child grows up in Nazareth, an Essene colony. The

Essenes were people who had fully taken up the Hebraic Mysteries. What characterized the Essenes, above all, was a strict asceticism, but also a strict schooling in esoteric knowledge. Thus, these two boys live at the same time.

Now, the miracle takes place that was known throughout the Middle Ages—the uniting of these two Jesus children during their twelfth year. We know the outer history. The parents were in Jerusalem; the Jesus child wanders off. People look for him and find him in the temple. This is the very quiet Nathan Jesus. He stands there teaching and explaining the Torah to the rabbis—full of wisdom! What was happening? The Zarathustra ego had left the other Jesus child and had entered into the Nathan Jesus so that a unification of an ancient, innocent soul of humanity and an ancient, mighty spiritual egoity of the human being were present there.

It is amazing how much was known about this, even into the Middle Ages. Hella Krause-Zimmer has written a book about this entitled *Die zwei Jesusknaben in der bildenden Kunst* [The two Jesus children in the visual arts].[16] We look at these wonderful images—for example, the one by Borgognone in Milan, where the teaching Jesus is seated there and a second Jesus, who appears pale, is leaving. Rudolf Steiner says that this second one dies soon after because the ego has departed. One of the most wonderful pictures, however, is one by Ferrari in Stuttgart. Jesus stands there and teaches; the rabbis are there, and a second Jesus child with a halo is nestled close to him, merging completely with him as though to say: 'I am absorbed in you; I give everything to you.' Next to him we see Mary and Joseph, not in the least irritated. Joseph is very consciously listening to what the Jesus child preaches, quite evidently understanding what is taking place; like Mary, he is completely aware and not worried.

A vast amount of Mystery knowledge streamed into the Middle Ages. The Middle Ages could even still profess something, could still hear something, when the Apocrypha, the Egyptian Gospel, says that grace will come when 'the two become one'.[17] In our own time we know from the Qumran texts that the Hebraic Mysteries had waited expectantly for a kingly messiah and a priestly messiah, and that while they waited they had lived with the question: How will a kingly messiah and a priestly messiah work together? I will close my opening remarks on the prehistory of the Mystery of Golgotha with this description of the origin of the Jesus figure, so that we have a first, great image of the task of anthroposophy—to tie together, once again, the threads between what is spiritual and what is earthly, between the divine and the human, between heaven and earth.

Prophecy in the Old Testament, the New Testament and Anthroposophy

Virginia Sease

We now want to focus on the view that time is actually a stream and that human beings have always tried to find access to this stream.

Possibilities have been shaped differently in every age, and the shaping of possibilities also belongs to the history of the Mysteries of humanity. What was good for the development of humanity in one epoch was no longer suitable for its development in another epoch. The forces active in the world are in and of themselves neither good nor bad; it is a matter of when and where they are at work, and at which stage of development humanity finds itself. For example, astrology was quite appropriate as an art in the third post–Atlantean epoch; at that time, it would have been considered more of an art than a science. The life of humanity was regulated according to the wisdom of the stars, according to astrology. That was right for that time.

Human beings of that time were in the process of developing the sentient soul. That is the part of the soul, the aspect of the human soul's capacity, that is especially bound to events in nature. As a result, the human being is outside himself and connected with the surrounding world; the ego, left to itself, broods muffled within the soul.

In the development of humanity, it is noteworthy that not all people or groups of people develop at the same rate. The pace of development varies. This means that elements of the third epoch can be found in every subsequent epoch of humanity. The third epoch is called the Egypto-Chaldean-Babylonian-Assyrian epoch because these cultures achieved a high point in their development at that time. In regard to this matter of the configuration of the soul, we also find that there are even later groups of human beings who are at the stage of sentient soul development rather than at the next stage—the intellectual or *Gemüt* soul, or the consciousness soul development of the current time. It is very difficult to speak of this today, because it implies that not all human beings are at the same stage of development. An observation like this can be immediately interpreted as prejudice in many quarters. But this is not prejudice; it is the course of world history.

If we look back on this development of the sentient soul—every great period of development lasts for 2160 years, a cosmic number—then we can say its development occurred between 2907 and 747 BC. That is a very long phase of development. We see that certain forces prevailed in a powerful way in Europe, especially southern Europe. These are called the sibylline forces. At that time, in this third epoch, a deep wisdom emerged from the soul depths of these women, the sibyls. Their soul life was chaotic—that is a characteristic of it—but what sprang from this chaos was a wisdom that was also appropriate for that time. Later, however, with the blossoming of the intellectual or *Gemüt* soul—we think especially of Greece, of the Roman culture, and then of the European Middle Ages— these soul forces were no longer appropriate for the time. The muffled, inward brooding of the ego, the total surrender of the self to the phenomena of nature, was no longer appropriate for that age.

Now another soul quality needed to develop. This quality had and has as its task that the human being wake up, that the human being know 'I am here; out there is the world'—and that he experience the difference. As a result, it also becomes possible for the human being to achieve individual freedom. We experience this throughout the Greek culture, decisively in the Roman culture, and then, in waves, during the Middle Ages. Thus it became possible that the ego of the human being could now speak strongly and was no longer muffled.

We have a great record of the chaotic, sibylline forces; it shows how the world up to the late Middle Ages and the beginning of our own age found a final way to depict these forces. This documentation is, of course, the figures, the paintings in the Sistine Chapel.

We can clearly see the traditions and the importance of the sibylline culture in them. We can see how this lived in Michelangelo so that he could depict it in magnificent colours and without difficulty—by which I do not mean technical difficulty, but rather inner difficulty. This is why, so many centuries later, we can find our way into the feeling of the world of the sibylline forces and the world of the prophets.

Today a whole science of the sibyls exists called *sibyllistics* in the scientific world. Sibyllistics attempts to ascertain what this sibylline culture meant. Even the origin of the word 'sibyl' is unclear. It was already widespread in the pre-Attic age—thus prehistoric, early Greek. Historical sources exist, however, and a significant one is by Heraclitus of Ephesus. He takes 'Sibyl' to be a single figure and writes: 'Because she speaks mirthless and unadorned and unsalved words with raging mouth, Sibyl has been heard for a thousand years through the power of God.'[1]

There are controversies in sibyllistics. Which of the sibyls is the oldest? Many say that the oldest is the Delphic sibyl, while others assert that the oldest is not the one at Delphi but rather the Erithrean sibyl. Rudolf Steiner regarded the Erithrean sibyl as the oldest.

There are many traditions surrounding the Delphic sibyl in what has been passed down through mythology. She is said to have foretold the Trojan War long before the war itself; it is thought that many of her sayings were taken up by Homer. People say that she can be found in the Homeric songs. It is important to note that the Delphic sibyl was always regarded as the daughter of the seer Tiresias. When we look at these images, we note that Michelangelo depicted this Delphic sibyl with the wind blowing through her hair; the wind is even beneath her blue veil. The force of the wind is a characteristic of the Delphic sibyl. There is something like a scroll in her hand.

The Erithrean sibyl was named after the city of Erithrea. What is important about her is not that she foresaw the Trojan War but that she gave advice to the Greeks as they left for Troy. She is the one who prophesied the downfall of Troy and said other things as well—for example, Homer will write lies. She embodies a rather powerful sibyl. Michelangelo's presentation of her is very interesting. There is a naked boy above or next to her. This boy holds a torch and will light a lamp near her head. Here we also see that in her are very strong passions, a quality of the sibylline nature. She is able to see more with this torch, with the light of the lamp's flame near her head. This is also a symbol for earlier times, because when people were in that stage of development they were not closed off in the region of their heads, but rather expanded outwards, a bit like a lamp with which they could also find their way. Michelangelo's depiction is like a remnant of this fact from ancient times.

The Cumaen or Cimmerian sibyl is perhaps the best known. There are many traditions surrounding this sibyl. She appears and becomes well known immediately after the fall of Troy; thus she is somewhat younger. She is said to have prophesied especially in Italy. She comes from the city of Cumae in Campania. We see that the mouth of this Cumaen sibyl is half open. From this, we can imagine that she babbles unconsciously and that she brings forth her prophecy through babbling. There is a well-known legend about this Cumaen sibyl. When she was found, it could be seen that, powerful though she was, she was all shrunken up—she was in a bottle! The question was posed to her: 'What do you want?' And she

The illustrations of the sibyls by Michelangelo are in the order in which they appear in the Sistine Chapel.

Left: The Libyan sybil; Right: The Prophet Daniel

Page 23
Upper left: The Cumaen or Cimmerian sybil
Upper right: The Prophet Isaiah
Lower left: The Delphic sybil
Lower right: The Prophet Joel

Page 24
Upper left: The Erithrean sybil
Upper right: The Prophet Ezekiel
Lower left: The Persian sybil
Lower right: The Prophet Jeremiah

responded: 'I want to die.' In the *Aeneid*, Virgil depicts how the hero Aeneas is given advice about how to enter the underworld. Such advice comes from the Cumaen sibyl.

The Libyan sibyl has long been known; she appears in a tragedy by Euripides. When we look at the Libyan sibyl, we see how she makes a somewhat hasty gesture, as though she had to pass along something quite mysterious.

The fifth sibyl, the Persian one, also has other names. She is frequently called the Chaldean sibyl from Babylon and is also often referred to as the Hebraic sibyl. This is especially striking because she is supposed to have been Noah's daughter, and is even supposed to have written 24 books of prophecy. One prophecy is supposed to have concerned the birth of Christ as deity and how He would appear on the earth.

There are these five images by Michelangelo, but we know about more than five sibyls. Varro (116–27 BC)—a great teacher and the first librarian in the library at Rome—claimed that there were ten sibyls. This claim then continued throughout history. Occasionally, we still find ten images—even rather unexpectedly. Ten sibyls and ten prophets are depicted in the stained glass windows of the cathedral at Beauvais.

There is supposed to have been a second Cumaen sibyl, but there is controversy about whether or not she exists. This is a well-known story. This second Cumaen sibyl comes to King Tarquinius Priscus, the ruler of the Roman state at that time, and offers him nine books of prophecy. He thinks they are too expensive. So she goes away and burns three of them. Then she returns and offers him six books. Again they are too expensive. She leaves and burns three more of them. She returns for the last time and offers him the three books for the price of the nine. He does buy these three books. Of course, this can be interpreted in various ways. The three books that remained had enormous significance. They were under the care of the priests, and that naturally means that there were priests from that time—this was before Christ—who still had insights into the secrets of the Mysteries. During times of great need the Roman senate could also receive information from these three books. Later, they were burned and 14 books appeared that were to replace them. These were publicly burned in the fourteenth century after Christ so that—it was said—these traditions would not continue. It is a strange fact that, in this time, something actually not a part of the fourth cultural epoch is ostentatiously burned.

The other sibyls are: the Samian sibyl from the island of Samos in the Aegean Sea; the Hellespontine sibyl; the Phrygian sibyl; and the Tiburtine sibyl, who was especially venerated by the Greeks in Tivoli. These are the ten sibyls, but there are still more—like the Colophonic sibyl and even a European one.

As Rudolf Steiner approached the Mysteries of humanity, he found this whole chapter on the sibyls extremely important, a chapter filled with great significance and meaning. From the standpoint of intellectual history, it is also interesting that the Erithrean sibyl comes from Ionia. We connect the first philosophers with Ionia, the first of the Greeks who were to lead humanity to clarity of thinking. These sibyls have strange depths in their souls. This can also be seen in the way that Rudolf Steiner describes them: 'As though from chaotic depths of their soul life, these sibyls exude all sorts of things that they have to say to this or that folk group about the future of earth evolution, the terrible, but sometimes the good as well. The sibyls exude something far removed from everything we call orderly thinking, something that emerges as though from chaotic depths of the soul; almost every sibyl expresses this in a way that reveals ... they are stepping before humanity with a spiritually penetrated fanaticism and want to force what they have to say upon the human being ... they step forth, the people gather together, and like a forceful imposition the proclamations of the sibyls about human beings, peoples, earthly cycles, sound forth.'[2]

Then the beginning stages of philosophy appeared in Ionia—Thales, and later Aristotle, everything that really grows from an orderly soul life. This is where we experience the powerful contrast between what humanity needed for the development of the fourth post-Atlantean epoch and what holds humanity back. The one stream is represented by the fact that philosophy could develop this clarity more and more. But sibylline culture worked on like a shadow next to this philosophical development of clarity.

It is important that we thoroughly understand these sibylline forces. We are currently in a period—especially during the second half of the twentieth century—in which we can notice a flood of these forces, these mantic, prophesying forces. In particular, certain practices have developed that promote exactly these aspects of modern Wicca or witch culture. It is as though this has been more or less asleep down through the centuries— we say more or less because there were always times when things of this kind were expressed. Then—particularly during the second half of the twentieth century—these forces arise.

When we look back into the Greek period, what occurred through the sibyls was something that flowed from chaos and existed as a tangent to the other development, the development of the forces of thinking. At that time, these forces of thinking had to evolve to the point where a few people could bring some level of understanding to the Mystery of Golgotha. Rudolf Steiner mentions that the forces of the sibyls were so strong that they would have lasted until the end of earthly days if something had not entered into the situation—it is the Christ Himself Who rescued humanity from them.

We have heard about the three preliminary stages, the three pre-earthly sacrifices of the Christ-being. Each one was a major salvation of humanity. Here another kind of salvation occurs, and that is the salvation from these displaced soul forces. The Christ stream continued; in the New Testament there are many examples of how Christ prevented these forces from arising when He was confronted by them.

Prophecies of Jewish origins, the *Oracula Sibyllina*, were widely disseminated, but were revised from a Christian perspective and acquired a new content. This is important when we look at the prophets. In many of its descriptions, the *Oracula Sibyllina* has as a starting point the prophecies connected with the coming of the Messiah.[3]

I would like to cite a formulation from an oracle in which we can find the annunciation of the Messiah in a special way that speaks of the earth's renewal:

> But finally, in the course of time, the earth was renewed; an infant boy
> Came from the womb of the Virgin Mary to illuminate the world,
> Descended from heaven and took human form;
> Gabriel's holy form of strength appeared for the first time on the earth,
> And the voice of heaven's messenger spoke to the Virgin:
> 'Take, O Virgin, God into your virginal womb.'[4]

In this oracle, each sibyl speaks and each sibyl prophesies the coming of the Messiah; this oracle is relatively poeticized compared to earlier depictions.

Now we turn to Goethe. It is often said that there is nothing that is not in *Faust*! We recall the scene 'On the Lower Peneus' in the second act of *Faust II*. There is the Manto passage where Chiron, a centaur, arrives with Faust on his back; Faust is searching for Helen of Troy and Chiron brings him to Manto, a sibylline figure. He talks about Manto and says to Faust:

> She is to me the dearest of the sibyl's guild
> Not grotesque her motive, but charitably willed.[5]

From these few words—meager as they are—we can see that Goethe had a fundamental understanding of these things, and especially of what the sibylline forces involve.

In the paralipomena—drafts that were not included in *Faust*—Goethe sketched a scene in which Chiron accompanies Faust: '. . . here they come across a long procession of sibyls, in number far greater than twelve'—Goethe knew Varro with the twelve—'Chiron describes the first sibyls to march past as old acquaintances and recommends his protégé [Faust] to the contemplative, thoughtful daughter of Tiresias, Manto.'[6] It was noted earlier that the Delphic sibyl was actually supposed to be the daughter of the seer Tiresias. In the final version, Goethe connects this motif with Manto, but as the daughter of Æsclepius, the great healer.

The sibylline culture appears during the Christian centuries, often in interesting ways. The 'song' of Thomas of Celano is well known. He was the first to note the following, which is quite important in the requiem, the mass sung for the dead:

> Dies irae, dies illa,
> solvet saeculum in favilla,
> teste David cum Sibylla.

This was also cited by Goethe in *Faust*. It means:

> Day of wrath
> O day that leads this world epoch to ashen ruin
> According to the testament of David and the sibyl.

Music aficionados know this well from Mozart's *Requiem*, where *Dies irae, dies illa* is a powerful chorus.

Among those five sibyls found in the Sistine Chapel there are also the figures of six prophets, and a powerful seventh, Jonah, although he is separated a bit from the others. These six prophets are completely different from the sibyls in both character and depiction. They are calm, pensive, some have books; they are neither passionate nor wild, but sit there deliberately and meditatively.

The question is: Why was it that Michelangelo as well as people in Beauvais and other places associated the prophets with the sibyls? Of course, it is obvious that both foretell the future; it is logical, since they work prophetically. In part, this association goes back to Virgil, who wrote not only the *Aeneid* but also ten pastoral poems—the *Eclogues*. There are illustrations in the British Museum by Blake of Virgil's pastoral poems called *The Pastorals of Virgil*. They are powerful images.

The prophesying occurs only once through a sibyl—in the fourth poem, called the *Messianic Eclogue*. Virgil was also the guide through Dante's hell; he knew his way around with these creatures and with human beings. Rudolf Steiner underscored the fact that the mission of the prophets was completely different from the mission of the sibyls. The Hebraic prophets' mission was to bring clarity and transparency into the soul life of the human being, while the mission of the Greek philosophers was to bring clarity of thought. There was order rather than chaos. The prophet wants to leave the characteristics of sibyls behind; the prophet wants only what can develop and work in the clarity of the ego. The prophet wants to bring into proper alignment the forces that the sibyls brought to passionate expression.

The first of Michelangelo's six prophets is Isaiah. His name means 'Jehovah is salvation'. He was called to prophecy around the end of the seventh century before the turning point in time. Isaiah has a quite specific calling. He sees the throne of the Lord and around him are beings from the hierarchy of the seraphim. A seraph-being brings a glowing coal from an altar that Isaiah sees and purifies Isaiah's mouth with it, so that what he then speaks is the truth from the perspective of the cosmos as well. The seraphim—the highest of the nine hierarchies—are the spirits of love, and they have great tasks. Is there a greater love than that shown by a spiritual being who accepts the task of giving the possibility of speaking the truth to the human being who wishes to speak it? Isaiah also made prophesies about the Messiah and introduced a noteworthy image—the image of the lamb that later became so well known in the Christian tradition and remains so to this day. He brings the image of the lamb as the image for the 'suffering vassal of God' or 'servant of God'.

Daniel—his name means 'God is judge'—could interpret dreams. He nearly met a terrible end. He was in the Babylonian captivity and came then under the new regency of Darius the King. He did not want to accept anything from Darius; he remained true to Jehovah. He was thrown into the lion's den, but was saved from the jaws of the lion by an angel. This is a favoured theme in Romanesque art, especially in the capitals of architectural columns.

Ezekiel, 'May God make us strong', was the first prophet called during the Babylonian exile. His visions play an important role—he is the first to have seen the four faces. In one of his visions, he experiences himself taken hold of by a windstorm, a cloud and a fire. In them are four figures like human beings, each with four faces: human, lion, bull, eagle—with human hands, and bull's feet, and with four wings.

Michelangelo also depicts Jeremiah, 'Jehovah exalted', who sits there contemplatively, and Joel, 'Jehovah is god', whose demeanor hints at Jehovah's strict Day of the Judgment. Zachariah, 'The Lord has remembered', is absent from these paintings.

The prophets in the Old Testament always connected their prophetic gift with a fervid activity. They never sought to influence the human being; instead, when they spoke they turned their words into deeds. The fervour of their activity served to enkindle the development of the will. Of course, this is different from what the sibyls did.

Another stream runs parallel to that of the prophets; the Hebrews called it Bath-Kol. In Hebrew, Bath-Kol actually means 'daughter of the voice', a heavenly voice; according to the Talmud it is a kind of divine revelation. It ranked just below prophecy in importance.[7] First came the prophets, and then came this Bath-Kol voice, the daughter of the voice. It is not the voice itself but rather the daughter of the voice that speaks and comes to expression. This voice from heaven was audible to the ancient prophets. Then, it gradually became mute until it was heard again by Jesus during his wanderings.[8]

With the advent of Christ Jesus, ancient prophecy had fulfilled its mission. Old Testament prophecy lived with a view to the coming of the Messiah; it was fulfilled through the Mystery of Golgotha. The Easter Mystery actually brings us a prophecy for the future. Although the Easter event took place two thousand years ago, it is the beginning of a new kind of prophecy. ' "The One you seek is no longer here!" ... The empty grave and the resurrected Christ, that is the Mystery of Prophecy; and thus in the Easter Mystery we have the Mystery of Prophecy.'[9] It is not the kind of prophecy where the soul forces of the human being remain unredeemed, as it is with the sibyls. The Christ forced this kind of prophecy in humanity to retreat. This is something where we experience the future under the sign of the resurrection. It is among the new perspectives connected with the development of the Mysteries in our time.

I would like to mention an example of how the transformed forces of the sibyls, transformed by the Christ, appeared in later times. Rudolf Steiner stressed that the Maid of Orléans (1413–31) was actually a personality through whom Christ worked. What she experienced and achieved resulted from the new power of Christ. Although she had worked prophetically, nothing in her soul would have been influenced by those impenetrable, opaque sibylline soul forces; instead she was thoroughly penetrated by the Christ. She serves as a first example of how transformative forces could reveal themselves through the Christ forces in the fifth post-Atlantean epoch.

The Order of the Essenes, Jeshu ben Pandira, Jesus Christ and the Third Millennium

Virginia Sease

We now want to take a closer look at the Essenes, a special community that existed at the time of Christ's birth.

The Essene community has been of particular interest since 1947 when a shepherd boy made a surprising discovery in an abandoned cave in Qumran on the Dead Sea. The many urns the boy found there contained scrolls representing an Essene settlement's collection of sacred texts. The discovery consists of approximately 45 texts; some of the scrolls are almost 21 feet in length. It had been known for centuries that an esoteric community had lived in this area. Some in antiquity had spoken or written about it, especially Philo of Alexandria, who has long been recognized as a source of such information. Philo, a Greek-speaking Jew who lived in Alexandria, was not a member of this community, but he knew about them.

These Qumran scrolls brought completely new information to light. Historically significant discoveries are often accompanied by controversies about the meaning of the documents. This happened here as well. What came to light with this discovery, however, was a flourishing Mystery practice in the middle of Judaea that included a Gnosis, a secret teaching with initiation rites, and a sacramental element with a communion supper celebrated by community members; it also revealed that this community had a deep, esoteric understanding of Jewish scripture. All of this becomes clear from the writings that became available at this time. These texts describe a path of schooling that led to enlightenment, as well as a doctrine known in Manichaeism as the two principles: the principle of Light and the principle of Darkness. The writings of the early Christian Gnostics dealt in detail with these principles of Manichaeism.

This discovery in Qumran occurred only two years after another important discovery. A vessel was unearthed during excavations in Upper Egypt; when it was broken open it was found to contain the Coptic-Gnostic library of Nag Hammadi. There were no scrolls, but codices and books consisting of about 1500 individual papyrus pages. The find at Nag Hammadi dates to the early centuries of Christianity.

These discoveries are valuable because they offer insights that were only hinted at previously—by Philo of Alexandria, for example. Rudolf Steiner is a notable exception to this. Long before these discoveries were made, Rudolf Steiner spoke in detail about the content of both—about these papyrus pages from Nag Hammadi as well as the scrolls uncovered in Qumran. He spoke about them in lectures to the members, especially in the 1910 Bern lecture cycle on the Gospel of Matthew.[1] Andrew Welburn—an Oxford University professor with a connection to anthroposophy—has written an extensive volume entitled *The Beginnings of Christianity: Essene Mystery, Gnostic Revelation and the Christian Vision.*[2] It is well worth mentioning here that Welburn is not in the least bit hesitant to cite Rudolf Steiner's spiritual research. He confirms that everything Rudolf Steiner indicated about the Essene community at that time is in accord with the more recently discovered documents.

Rudolf Steiner emphasized that we can discern in the Essene community a return of the Mysteries to Palestine. What had been separate for millennia was brought together again in Palestine. Welburn asserts that 'the Essenes penetrated the central religious life of the Jews, in contrast to the baptist groups on the fringes of the Judaic region ...'[3] Around the turning point of time, there were many smaller or larger esoteric groups in this part of the world. They were often baptist sects, baptismal sects; this means that through baptism—through a full-body immersion in water—the human constitution was loosened. The soul essence and the ego loosened themselves from the physical and etheric bodies, and the ether body also expanded. This is similar to the experience a person has when nearly drowning; the person sees before him a panorama of his life up to that point. These baptismal sects used this sort of experience so that human beings could arrive at a kind of enlightenment.

Two prominent denominations existed at this time, the Sadducees and the Pharisees. The Pharisees were especially strict. They rejected the idea that any fact could have a spiritual explanation. The Essenes can be seen as a kind of counterweight to the Sadducees and the Pharisees, because they followed another approach. Rudolf Steiner confirms that it is important for the Essenes that their doctrines also provide a path to the Jesus child in the Gospel of Luke. This is an important aspect of our consideration of the kind of doctrine that was cultivated by this Qumran settlement, this Essene settlement.

Although Philo of Alexandria (*c.* 20 BC–AD 30) was not a part of the

Essene community, he wrote in detail about this group in *On the Contemplative Life*. Since he was not a member, it is all the more unusual that he somehow gained access—at least in some degree—to the customs and teachings of this community. Of special importance in Philo's account are two precepts, Mystery rules, by which these people, the Essenes, lived. Rudolf Steiner confirmed the existence of these two rules and also gave a deeper interpretation of them. They were connected to the rhythm of the day, so that before sunrise or at sunrise, when a person awoke and descended into his bodily nature, a prayer was said. It is a prayer of gratitude that the person has been able to return from the night and take hold again of the bodily nature, because it is only through this bodily nature, through the possibility of working on the earth, that the human being is able to develop himself. The remainder of the day was dedicated to the task of furthering the development of this soul. For example, a person fasted during the daylight hours; because eating was associated with the physical body, it could be done at night when the day was over. In the evening, when a person entered into sleep, he knew he was pursuing further spiritual paths through sleep.

Speaking was strictly limited. An important feature of the Essenes' relationship to speaking was that only the essential was spoken. A kind of asceticism was practised in speaking. The Essenes spoke, but only what was essential in service of their own soul's good and the good of the souls of others.

There was a congregation, for instance, in which a day—the seventh day—was set aside. We are not certain whether it was a Sunday. This seventh day was dedicated to coming together and to learning; the initiate teachers of this congregation spoke and elucidated the Mysteries. No one worked on this day, not even the animals. It is noteworthy that women also took part which is quite unusual for this time. The women were separated off by a curtain, but they were permitted to hear everything the men heard about the teachings. The Essenes knew about reincarnation and were also able to recognize that the eternal individuality of the human being is neither feminine nor masculine, that genders are a part of Maya, a part of the clothing necessary for a given incarnation.

This might lead us to think that the full meaning of their asceticism lies in eating and drinking only during the evenings, and then quite simply. But many Essenes had absolutely no need of food for days on end; Philo writes that they were nourished as though by 'the light of heaven'. Some Essenes fasted for three days, some for six. Philo notes that they not only devoted themselves to looking within, but 'also wrote songs and hymns in praise of God with the most varied meters and melodies to which they then gave a special elevated form through solemn rhythmic movement'.[4] This is striking because it sounds a bit like a first attempt at eurythmy.

Here we see a difference between the Essenes and other sects like the baptists, the Nasireans, and so forth, which were probably not as devoted to the arts. Asceticism existed among the Essenes; but it was a kind of asceticism that added something to nourish the soul in an entirely different way—in the way that the arts alone can nourish the soul, especially the arts connected with speech and music, and those connected with movement.

A visitor to the site of Qumran experiences an incredible dryness of the desert unlike any other dryness—even in the area around the Dead Sea—and sees the salt deposits. The Mojave Desert in California is quite hot and has all the characteristics of a desert—it is also below sea level and has salt crystal deposits—but, it can seem almost a humid oasis compared to the Dead Sea and the area around Qumran where the Essenes lived.

The greatest of the baptist sects was, of course, the baptismal mission of a great individuality, John the Baptist. John the Baptist travelled widely, but his centre was by the River Jordan, somewhat south of the city of Jericho. The road to Qumran goes past Jericho; and it is here, only nine miles north of Qumran, that John the Baptist was especially at home. John the Baptist was no doubt familiar with the Essenes. This is also suggested by science, by the Qumran research. Rudolf Steiner says John the Baptist was briefly connected with the Essenes and experienced how they anticipated the Messiah. This anticipation was the most important point of contact between John the Baptist and the Essenes; but, according to Rudolf Steiner, John the Baptist would never have exchanged the teachings of Judaism with the teachings of the Essenes.

In contrast to the Essenes, John the Baptist worked publicly. In order to be baptized, it was necessary to be a Jew—that was a precondition—but anyone could accept the doctrines of John the Baptist and practise them.

We see that the Essenes as well as the Therapeuts—another group that had much in common with the Essenes—actually form the transition to Christianity from the Mysteries of this and earlier times. There were other communities, not just the one in Qumran, although Qumran was the main settlement—and it is significant that these Essene communities represented something like the quintessence of a certain Mystery stream.

Among the Essenes, but also with the Therapeuts, the most important feeling revolved around the mystery of the blood. The mystery of the blood is the true meaning of all deeper Hebraicism, and it focused on the time when the Mystery of Golgotha was to take place, on the incarnation of Jesus, the incarnation of the Christ, on the Mystery of Golgotha itself. The Essenes—by which is meant the initiates among them—were able to trace their insights back to Abraham, and they perceived clearly how a seed had been implanted into the being of Abraham by a divine Being. This seed was so strong in its physical-etheric constitution that it could be carried over into the physical-etheric constitutions of all the people who lived in the Jewish nation as his descendents—throughout the subsequent generation and those that followed.

What, in fact, was this seed that could be carried on by subsequent generations? Before Abraham, all inspirations, visions, illuminations came as impulses from the spiritual world. The human being—in our terminology—had no say in it; they came as divine gifts. Abraham had worked through his constitution in such a way that when this seed, this predisposition, was given to him, he could exercise it to form his own thoughts, lift himself up to God. Thus he was not only a passive recipient but could turn his gaze upwards from out of his own inner self. This was an especially important moment in the development of humanity.

It was also a prominent aspect of the Essene path of schooling which attempted to purify the individual through spiritual exercises so that everything accumulated since the time of Abraham could be stripped off, left behind—as though swept away. It was a stringent soul cleansing. This difficult mystic path took place in 42 steps. The 42 steps are related to the 42 generational steps back to Abraham. The Essenes followed these 42 steps backwards in their initiation—in their initiation teaching and their initiation rites.

The secret of Abraham was one of the secrets they knew. But through their initiation, they also knew of another secret. They knew, in fact, that when a divine being wished to descend, or was about to descend, in order to enter the human realm from the heavenly realm, this being had to do so through 42 steps. The downward path to become a human among humans also consisted of 42 steps. This was how they anticipated the Messiah. Moreover, it was even necessary to prepare two lineages for an event as powerful as the incarnation of the Christ-being. One lineage served more to prepare the physical body, the etheric body, the life body. We find this secret in the Gospel of Matthew; it is the path through the 42 generations back to Abraham. The step in which Solomon appears is one of these 42 steps; hence these steps are also called the 'Solomonic line', and the child is called the 'Solomonic' child. The genealogy in the Gospel of Matthew begins with Abraham and continues through 14 plus 14 plus 14 generations, and ends with Jesus.

In the other lineage described in the Gospel of Luke, we see how the astral body was prepared—the soul capacity for what was, in time, to enter as the great ego. This line does not come downwards through 42 steps; instead, in 77 steps, in seven times eleven steps, it takes us to the very threshold of the spiritual world. This genealogy actually begins with Jesus and goes upwards towards heaven. With Abraham, the genealogy goes from heaven down to earth, from Abraham to Jesus; but here it goes from Jesus heavenwards and concludes 'He was a son of Seth, He was a son of Adam, He was of God'. With that, the lineage of Jesus is completed in reverse. '. . . He was of God' refers to the Adam-soul that was left behind, as we have already heard. We are familiar with Michelangelo's wonderful depiction of this in his *Creation of Adam*.

The Chaldean Mysteries follow the incarnations of the Zarathustra-being—the lofty initiate from the beginning of time, the pupil of Manu, the great leader of humanity. They anticipated the Zarathustra-being would descend again into an incarnation during the time when this did, in fact, occur. The Chaldean Mysteries were widespread in the third epoch, but its teachings were still present in later times. The Essene school also anticipated the descent of Zarathustra. There were the 42 steps back to Abraham on the one hand; the other anticipation pointed to Zarathustra.

There has been much research about the esoteric aspect of the Essenes, especially since 1947. Today, for example, we are in a completely different position than the people who heard Rudolf Steiner's lectures in 1910. They had only a few indications passed down from Josephus Flavius, Philo and, of course, Rudolf Steiner's own descriptions.

Let us turn our attention now to the individuality who lived at that time under the name Jeshu ben Pandira. 'Jeshu' is equivalent to 'Jesus'; 'ben Pandira' means 'son of Pandira'. It is a quite peculiar phenomenon in the esoteric tradition—especially during the last two centuries—that many esoteric streams, even Helena P. Blavatsky, have actually confused Jesus Christ with Jeshu ben Pandira. Jeshu ben Pandira lived under the direct influence of a great teacher of humanity. Such a teacher of humanity is often given a special designation in esotericism to make clear the distinction between that teacher and the more normal sort of great and important teacher: he is called a Bodhisattva.

The name 'Bodhisattva' is taken from the Eastern tradition. There are always twelve Bodhisattvas, and they are the great teachers of humanity. According to Rudolf Steiner, they live in constant view of the Christ, and the Being of the Christ always flows into them. This can be presented in an image: twelve Bodhisattvas surrounding the Christ—beholding the Christ—and His Being flowing into them, the qualities of His Being streaming into them.

Each of these twelve Bodhisattvas has a special earthly mission to complete, and each receives this earthly mission from Christ. The Bodhisattva can view this task as completed only when his mission is fulfilled. Then he is no longer a Bodhisattva; he is elevated to the rank of Buddha, and no longer descends to earth. How is his mission achieved? The Bodhisattva must acquire for himself the capacity he is to develop for humanity; it first becomes his own human capacity. The final step is the attainment of the rank of Buddha.

The Bodhisattva is never fully immersed in human corporeality. When we say that Jeshu ben Pandira was the Bodhisattva or under the influence of the Bodhisattva, it means that to a certain degree an incorporation was present. An incorporation signifies an overshadowing that partially permeates the individuality, whereas an incarnation means that the Bodhisattva has entered the individuality fully, also physically. A complete incarnation will occur only as the final step from Bodhisattva to Buddha. That was the case with the Gautama Buddha, about 600 years before the turning point of time. We know about Prince Siddhartha who was popularized in Hermann Hesse's novel *Siddhartha*. This Bodhisattva completely united himself with a human being in the moment when he received his enlightenment under the bodhi tree. As the Gautama Buddha, he lived and taught for decades afterwards. We find his teaching written down later in the *Dialogues of the Buddha*. The Bodhisattva returns completely to the spiritual world between two incorporations and lives there with the other Bodhisattvas in community with the Christ.

What was it that had been attained by the Gautama Buddha? He not only spoke about his teachings—the teaching of love and compassion— but also experienced this teaching. In addition, he prepared a path for humanity known as 'the eightfold path'. It consists of eight great qualities that the human being must attain—right thinking, right judgement, the right word, right action, the right point of view, right habit, right memory, and right attitude of contemplation.[5] He attained all of this and was then able to experience his mission as fulfilled. The being of the Gautama Buddha is very powerful. Like all Bodhisattvas, he was always deeply connected to the Christ, and after he was no longer on the earth he fulfilled other tasks in harmony with the Christ.

Every Bodhisattva who ascends to the rank of Buddha must immediately find or identify his successor. We know one of these successors as Jeshu ben Pandira. Approximately three thousand years after our time, he too will have fulfilled his mission and will then ascend to become a Buddha. The Buddha who is now at work is known in Eastern teaching as the Maitreya Buddha. Rudolf Steiner adopted this terminology and, in anthroposophy, we know this Buddha as the Maitreya Buddha as well.

Jeshu ben Pandira lived from 125 to 77 BC. At the time Jeshu ben Pandira underwent his overshadowment by the Bodhisattva, this Bodhisattva had already experienced approximately four incorporations after the incarnation of the Gautama Buddha. There has been an incorporation of this Bodhisattva about once every century since then—approximately 19, according to Rudolf Steiner. The Bodhisattva's mission unfolds over a period of time. Rudolf Steiner describes precisely how we can recognize this incorporation. Before an individual takes this Bodhisattva into himself, no one can see that this person has been selected to receive such an incorporation. Everything—childhood, adolescence—is normal. Then, between the thirtieth and thirty-fifth years, the person experiences something entering him and changing him; he then knows what his mission is, what he has to fulfil. Afterwards, after this event has taken place, this mission is perceptible to clairvoyant vision.

Jeshu ben Pandira is mentioned in the Talmudic literature, although infrequently. He is most often treated quite negatively in Jewish tradition. He was charged with being a heretic, a blasphemer, and he met a terrible end. He was stoned and, after he had been killed, he was hung from a tree as a symbol of his disgrace. Jeshu ben Pandira had a particular task with the Essenes at the time: to show what the Christ would be like when He incarnated. Jeshu ben Pandira had pupils among the Essenes—five in particular—who had already experienced enlightenment, who had passed through the 42 steps from Abraham, and had been prepared. Each of these five pupils took up a particular aspect of Jeshu ben Pandira's teaching. One of them, Matthai, prepared for the Gospel of Matthew. He actually wrote the document by which the teachings of Jeshu ben Pandira could be acknowledged as pointing to the coming of the Christ.

Now we come to the question of subsequent incarnations—later embodiments as they are also called—following the incarnation as Jeshu ben Pandira. In 1911, Rudolf Steiner said something remarkable that has puzzled many people. He said: 'One of [Jeshu ben Pandira's] embodiments is also set to take place in the twentieth century. It is not possible to say anything more specific at this time about the reincarnation of this Bodhisattva.'[6]

We have spoken about the sibylline forces from the third cultural epoch, about how these sibylline forces prevailed in the depths of the soul. We have spoken about how these forces then surfaced, and how they were compelled to retreat by the Christ Himself, by the invisible work of the Christ on the human being. It is a fact that not everything is visible; an effect always emanates invisibly from the Christ. These forces are transformed. We have already spoken about the Maid of Orléans in whom these forces were transformed to a high degree. Rudolf Steiner describes her as a Christ-penetrated sibyl: 'It is the time ... when the fifth post-Atlantean epoch arrives; when the power of the Christ has to reach the point where it rises up more and more out of the subconscious foundations of the soul. We see how gently, how tenderly, how immersed in the most noble human soul qualities the sibylline force of the Maid of Orléans appears to be.'[7] This is as far as the transformation had gone by the time this Maid of Orléans made her prophecy about the conflict between the English and the French.

There are still remnants of old magical practices in our own time; in a certain sense the fifth cultural epoch is a reflection of the third cultural epoch. We can see the relationship between the third cultural epoch—the Egypto-Chaldean-Assyrian-Babylonian epoch—and the fifth cultural epoch, described by Rudolf Steiner as the Anglo-Germanic epoch. These characterizations are not meant in an exclusionary sense, but are intended only as indications about which human groupings have specific tasks in connection with the development of the consciousness soul. The fourth cultural epoch—Greece, Rome and into the Middle Ages—stands alone, so to speak. Much of what was present in the third epoch—even in terms of the magical element and so forth—remained as though in a deep sleep during the fourth epoch, and then reawoke in the fifth epoch.

Here, I would like to mention one of the Mysteries passed down from the Mystery tradition of the Old Testament: the so-called Bileam or Balaam Mystery. The Revelation of John contains an epistle addressed to the community of Pergamon; the altar of Pergamon in the Berlin Museum is from the same city. In this epistle to the Pergamon community, John sounds a powerful warning against Bileam. John the Evangelist, the Apocalyptist, takes up this Mystery and writes his admonition. Bileam was a seer from the city of Pethor on the Euphrates and a great opponent of Moses. This means he was an opponent of the words 'I am the I AM'. He was a powerful opponent of the voice Moses experienced as the voice of God. Bileam was therefore an opponent of the Christ-being who had spoken through that voice. Bileam misused the magical power of language. Unlike the unconscious activity of the sibyls, he worked as a soothsayer, a conscious misuse of his gifts as a seer. When we experience the misuse of language today—the consumption of language—there is a direct connection to this Mystery from the time of Bileam. Its seed is to be found there. In the Emil Bock text, the words of John the Apocalyptist (John the Divine) read:

> But I must nevertheless reproach you. Some of you cling to the teachings of Bileam ... to set a trap for the sons of Israel ... Strive for the transformation of the senses. If you fail to do this, I will fall upon you without warning and will fight against you with the sword of my mouth.

In esoteric terminology, the sword of the mouth is the 'double-edged sword', the sword of the Word.

> Whosoever overcomes will receive from me the hidden Manna and a white stone with a new name engraved upon it which no one knows but the one who receives it.[8]

A new name is, of course, the true ego of every human being; it is the name which the individual alone receives. And it is also the true name of the Christ Himself.

The Bodhisattva Jeshu ben Pandira and his task for humanity during approximately the next three thousand years stand in contrast to the Bileam forces. This task corresponds to the task of the Buddha. The task of the Gautama Buddha now no longer belongs to him—he has fulfilled his mission; humanity itself must now fulfil this task. During the next three thousand years or so, every human being must make his own way along the eightfold path so that he is practised in 'right thinking', moves onwards to the 'right judgement' that results from 'right thinking', and to the 'right word' that comes from 'right judgement'. The 'right action' should be objective, and the 'right point of view' should be related to the individual's destiny in life. Then these qualities should become 'right habit'. 'Right memory' helps the human being to be consistent, while 'right attitude of contemplation' frees him from influences that come from his past. This is how these steps are to be completed.

Only when the eightfold path is developed in human beings will a spiritual organ—now latent in them—no longer be dormant, but will become active instead. This is the spiritual organ described as the 16-petalled lotus flower. It is located in the region of the larynx and will be developed by way of the eightfold path. With the development of these spirit organs, the spiritual world has brought things halfway; but the human being must develop the other half himself. In regard to the 16-petalled lotus flower, this means that the spiritual beings have already developed eight of these petals in seed form, but the human being must develop the other eight. This is taking place now and during the next three thousand years.

We might think: 'Three thousand years is a long time. I don't need to worry about any of this right now. I still have time.' On the other hand, we could also think about Rudolf Steiner's indication that we have an incarnation perhaps every eight hundred or a thousand years. We could even imagine that a person might be an exception to this rule and return to life earlier. Spiritual pupils are often the exceptions; they come sooner and have little time to rest between incarnations. Nevertheless, if we take stock honestly of what we are and what we must become, and think, 'OK, maybe if all goes well, I will have six more chances to practise this,' then there is really not a lot of time. If one of these lifetimes is short, there is even less time.

During his period of development with humanity, Jeshu ben Pandira has as his goal that human beings not only think something, but think something so that it enters directly, morally into their deeds. Take the following example. Today, a person can be very bright, very clever—there are many clever people—and that person can, for example, think about what is good. This is not a problem. And yet this person is not a moral person. He can generate all sorts of thoughts, but that is no indicator of his moral character. The meaning of the evolution of humanity—especially from now on—will be found when the human being not only has ideas about what is good, but when these ideas also become the impetus for his moral conduct. During Jeshu ben Pandira's approximately 19 earlier incarnations—about which Rudolf Steiner did not speak specifically—he had the task of setting this in motion; and this is a particular reality in our own time.

In this regard, Rudolf Steiner mentions that language will have a much greater effect in the future, one connected with the region of the larynx. He says '... today there is still no human language that works so magically that, when someone expresses a moral principle and it sinks down into someone else, that person feels it directly as moral and can do nothing other than carry it out as a moral impulse.' And then he identifies the goal: 'During the next three thousand years, the human race must become as though saturated with magical morality [magical in the sense of transformative] ...'[9] Jeshu ben Pandira is the bearer of the morally active Word, the 'bearer of what is good through the Word.' Like every Bodhisattva, he has a specific task in relation to the Christ-being. We saw how it was his task two thousand years ago to instruct those in the Essene community who were sufficiently enlightened, teaching them about how the Christ will come to earth and how He might be recognized. That was his task. If the given dates are correct, he died 77 years before the birth of Jesus. Now it is his task to make the full import of the Christ understandable for modern times. That is a profound Mystery secret of our time.

Rudolf Steiner describes in a striking way how a change occurred for the Christ-being in the circumference of the earth, where the Christ can be found since the Mystery of Golgotha. This change has been taking place since approximately the sixteenth century, when the seeds of materialism were becoming increasingly strong. Human beings brought this materialism with them into the realm that follows death. Since the Mystery of Golgotha, since the resurrection, the Christ-being has been in the circumference of the earth as an angel in order, one might say, to have a form in which to manifest. The darkness grew for this angel-being in which the Christ, the Resurrected One, lived. In the nineteenth century, the situation became something like a death by asphyxiation in this dark materialism. This experience of dimming, darkening, of death by asphyxiation, was like a second crucifixion for the Christ—this time not on the earth, but in the supersensible realm. Since the twentieth century, the fact that the Christ underwent this second crucifixion and overcame it has given human beings special possibilities; these are similar to the new possibilities given humanity by the Christ-being through the Mystery of Golgotha. These possibilities have developed over the course of two thousand years. Since the twentieth century, something new has been possible as a result of the Christ-being's experience of this death by asphyxiation, namely, that human beings are able to see more than just the physical; the scales are gradually falling from their eyes, and they receive insights into the world bordering ours, the etheric world. Thus, more and more people will have the possibility of experiencing the Christ-being in the etheric.

The Christ-being will not live physically on the earth again; His mission here was completed. However, the Christ always has new tasks— also in relation to the development of humanity. Humanity is now increasingly in a position to experience the Etheric Christ. The task of Jeshu ben Pandira, this Bodhisattva, is to clarify this path for human beings. And when he has his subsequent incorporations in the coming centuries, this will constitute his task.

There is still no larynx able to bring forth the language human beings must bring forth if this Bodhisattva is to become a Buddha. This will be a language penetrated by what is good to a degree that the human being is not yet able to attain. Of course, it is natural to ask: Is there an example of such a language today? Has anyone ever experienced something like this, something in this direction? Most of us, for example, never heard the language of Rudolf Steiner; nevertheless, if we talk with older friends, we hear that the quality of this language—spoken with a faint Austrian accent that softened it—made such an impression that those who heard it never forgot it.

I would add here that I do not intend to imply that Rudolf Steiner is the Maitreya Buddha. I am only speaking about the quality of his language. During the last years of the great poet Christian Morgenstern's all-too-brief life, he was a pupil of Rudolf Steiner. A very sensitive person and a great artist, Christian Morgenstern also experienced Rudolf Steiner's language through his artistic sensitivity. He once wrote of that language:

> He spoke. And as he spoke, there appeared in him
> the zodiac, cherubim and seraphim,
> the solar star, the planets wandering
> from place to place.
>
> All this sprang forth with his sound
> lightning fast, a cosmic dream, newly found,
> all of heaven seemed in prayer called down
> through his own word.[10]

Perhaps here we can gain for ourselves some sense of how this future language will be formed.

The Life of Christ Jesus in the Context of the Ancient Mystery Religions

Manfred Schmidt-Brabant

We will begin our considerations with two motifs from Rudolf Steiner that are related to the many aspects of our theme. Rudolf Steiner says that there is no wisdom in the world sufficient for a real understanding of the events that took place in Palestine at the beginning of the Christian era for humanity and the whole world. This one sentence should not cause us to abandon our work, because another sentence accompanies this one: 'Loftier capacities will arise for humanity, and with each new capacity we will see the Christ in a new light.'[1] It is in this sense that this course on the history of the Mysteries is intended. Indeed—in all modesty—it could be said that this is a course on the Mysteries themselves.

A description like this one by Rudolf Steiner is based on a certain fact of the human constitution, namely, that we carry the outcome of human history in our whole being. All of the history of the Mysteries has worked its way into the development of the members of our being. We carry the consequence of the history of the Mysteries in the physical body; we carry it in the ether body, in the astral body. And our ego has gone through various incarnations as well. Each of us took part in the history of the Mysteries: the Mysteries in Greece, in Egypt, in Persia, in Rome, in the medieval Mysteries. It is a little-known fact that human beings have the capacity to look back again and again on these past incarnations, hence on our experiences in the time stream of the Mysteries.

When we are presented with a straightforward description like the one Rudolf Steiner gives us of the Mystery content of the past, we might feel a bit like someone who has lost his memory in an accident. Such a person no longer knows his name or who he is; he is present in the moment, but his whole past has disappeared. We can show him objects, take him places, and ask: 'Do you remember this place?' Perhaps he says: 'Yes, it has a strange effect on me.'—'And, this person here, do you remember him?'—'No, I don't know who he is, but his presence moves me somehow.' We question him this way and we have some success. By presenting images from his earlier life, we help such a person to remember his past once again.

This is the situation for all of us as human beings in the present time. To begin with, we have lost the memory of our incarnations. This was not so in ancient times; but our entrance into a denser and denser corporeality has gradually cut us off from what ancient Egyptians, for instance, could still remember. In making such an observation now, we might again arouse in ourselves the feeling: 'Yes, that seems familiar to me; these images from the ancient Egyptian Mysteries or from other periods seem familiar to me.' In recent times, memories of previous lives have been surfacing in people again. We must not delude ourselves that the details of everyday life will appear to us; instead, we might look for basic things—the feeling for a life in Greece, or one as an Egyptian or Palestinian, or in the centuries after the birth of Christ. Rudolf Steiner speaks about these times past, especially in the lectures he gave to theosophists in Rome. In another place, he says that practically all the people in his audience were incarnated during the first Christian centuries, or in the twelfth or thirteenth century. He admonishes the audience: Remember!

A second consideration can be added to this. One of the participants in our course wrote me: 'When we take up the subject of the history of the Mysteries, shouldn't we also examine the horrendous events of the present?' In fact, these occurrences cannot be understood without looking at the history of how they too developed. The Serbs make frequent reference to the battle at Kosovo Polje (the Field of Blackbirds); they base their whole national identity on that battle. It was the war with Islam that occurred in 1389. The mighty and terrible clash of Catholic Christians, Orthodox Christians and Islam in the current Bosnian crisis is a consequence of the history of the Mysteries, a consequence of the history this course will examine. I offer this as a reminder that we are not looking at a dim, grey past. We are looking into our own hearts; we are examining our own existence. This is a bit like the feeling of someone from our childhood telling us things that we may remember only vaguely.

When we look today at the life of Jesus in His own time, we often overlook the fact that they were still widespread then. The Mysteries no longer reigned as they did in older times when the Mysteries defined all aspects of life. And yet a far-spread world of the most varied Mystery religions came from these Mysteries, and all this suffused the profound magnificence of the temples. Rudolf Steiner says about this:

People today have no idea of the incredible splendour and glory that existed during the first Christian centuries. They have no idea of the incredible splendour and glory in all manner of heathen temples. These temples contained images of the gods that were artistic renderings—right into the details of their form—of what had lived in the Old Mysteries. In these ancient times there was no town or countryside that did not have its full share of artistic and mystical elements; and out on the fields where the farmers grew their grain there were small, individual temples, each with its own image of the gods.

There follows a quite important sentence that leads us into the present time:

And no land was tilled without that work being brought into a living connection with the forces seen to flow from the cosmos, descending from above with the help of the magic powers to be found in the special way these images of the gods were formed.[2]

It could be said that these images of the gods had a magical power to bind the spiritual to the earthly. A special element lived in this whole world where the Mysteries echoed, but where they were also still active. In order to understand this, we must turn our attention again to the Old Sun period of the earth when something took place through the Christ-being; Rudolf Steiner calls it the great Sun sacrifice. The Christ-being surrendered Himself completely to the Cosmic Logos, to the Son Principle and was simultaneously immersed in the denser etheric sheathes that later made it possible for Him to come into contact with humanity.

There was another spirit in addition to the Christ. This was not the spirit of the Sun, but the spirit of Venus whom we later came to call Lucifer. According to Rudolf Steiner, Lucifer was, at first, like Christ; they were like brothers, except that Lucifer's signature was entirely different. He was not only the spirit of infinite wisdom and light; he was also the spirit of infinite pride. While the Christ opened Himself in devotion to the loftiest divinity, Lucifer closed himself off, basking in his own light. The result was that the Christ-being ascended—He united Himself with the loftiest divinity—and Lucifer's path descended to the earth. Rudolf Steiner says that all later development depends on this moment.

We must properly understand this moment. Much of what occurs in the cosmos is based on the loftiest wisdom; thus not only did Lucifer fall, but countless other beings fell with him. This was often depicted wonderfully during the Middle Ages in images of the fall of the angels; in miniatures and so forth, the angels were shown tumbling from their seats in heaven. Some remain sitting, others tumble off their seats—this is a very real imagination. This fall was a sacrifice. Rudolf Steiner repeatedly says that it was a sacrifice for the luciferic beings to have remained behind in order to prepare the path to the Christ. Lucifer and many luciferic beings became the great divine teachers in the Mysteries. In Lemurian times, and then especially from Atlantis on, luciferic beings and Lucifer himself were the divine teachers in the Mysteries. Rudolf Steiner depicts how these divine teachers appeared in the later Mystery religions. He says that Wodan, Thor, Zeus, Apollo and Mars were luciferic gods who taught in the Mysteries.

Because Lucifer is the great spirit of wisdom, everything that flowed into the time around the Mystery of Golgotha was penetrated with luciferic wisdom. The Christ-being is the God of love; Lucifer is the spirit of wisdom. This is how the coming of Christ was anticipated in all the pre-Christian Mysteries. Lucifer brought humanity a particular gift—the powerful force of the ego. He gave this powerful force of the ego to human beings, but so that they received it too early. The image we find in our language speaks of 'the Fall of Man'. The human being received the ego too early; it became a precocious egoism. Nevertheless, the human being received this egoity from Lucifer and it was developed in the Mysteries. The Mysteries came from the ancient, primal past and created a vessel into which the Christ-being could descend. This cosmic image serves as a model for what should happen in every human being—that every person form his ego into a Grail chalice in order to take up the Christ-being in it.

All these Mystery religions existed on various levels. There were, of course, highly spiritual connections. There were still complete initiations in the Mysteries well into the first centuries of the Christian era. But there were also corrupted, decadent Mysteries that arose from what had happened during the old Atlantean epoch. Atlantis was the time of the great oracle sites, the time when everything had a Mystery character, and there was nothing profane about these things yet. At that time, all the secrets of the Mysteries were strictly guarded in the sense that the human being underwent a lengthy preparation until he was capable of receiving the secrets step by step.

The secrets of the Mysteries were a kind of magical power. A person who experienced a Mystery secret was then in a position to become effective. He did not receive an intellectual answer, an intellectual content; he received a magical power. At that time, the soul life of human beings was still closely connected with nature. As a result, someone who received Mystery content could work in the realm of nature.

A disaster befell the whole of the Mysteries in the middle of the Atlantean times. Secrets of the Mysteries were betrayed to human beings who had not yet been prepared. This was a complicated matter; one might call it a second Fall of Man. Even some initiates were pulled into this betrayal. And many lower, demonic spiritual beings—even angel beings—cooperated in the fall of magical treasures from the Mysteries into the hands of unprepared human beings. This is described in *Occult Science, An Outline*.[3] Rudolf Steiner describes there how evil spread through every kind of Mystery with one exception. The Sun Mysteries under the leadership of Michael remained untouched by this betrayal. Towards the end of the Atlantean epoch, unprepared human beings used this magical power with the result that the whole continent was destroyed in a gigantic water catastrophe, as well as through air catastrophes that manifested in powerful tornado-like winds. Old Atlantis sank because of the misuse of these magical powers. Not so long ago, the famous island of Poseidonis with its golden city was located where the Atlantic Ocean is today. It was an island the size of a continent, and it was the last to sink. Plato reports that it sank in one night with 60 million people drowned and killed.

When we hear something like this, we might ask ourselves: 'How does that touch me? Was I also among them—perhaps not those who perpetrated the misuse, but among those who were lost in the catastrophe? Did I live before the catastrophe and even experience the great golden city of Atlantis?'

The Mysteries had spread throughout the area around Atlantis; and Atlantean Mystery sites at 'varying levels of development' were later found in Europe, Asia, Africa, but—according to the incisive word of Rudolf Steiner—also 'at varying levels of decay'.[4] Then we see Mysteries of the most diverse quality brought from the Atlantean epoch into the map of our own history—the Mediterranean region, the Middle East; good Mysteries and evil Mysteries.

Their effects endured right into the present. We live in a time when people, prompted by their consciousness souls, are once again seeking a connection with the Mysteries. In large measure, the whole 'New Age' movement is involved with taking up old content—but without understanding what this content is. Thus those lower spiritual beings who participated in the collapse of Atlantis, who were active in the decadent Mysteries around the turning point in time, arise and once again manifest here and there among human beings. We need—Rudolf Steiner calls for this—a demonology for our time, in the true, modern sense of the word.

This world into which both the noblest and also the most decadent Mysteries were carried over was the place where the Jesus child grew up from His twelfth year—when the unification took place—until the baptism in the Jordan. The Gospels justifiably do not speak at all about this period of His life, but Rudolf Steiner describes it at various times and places. What he says is summed up in *From Research of the Akasha. The Fifth Gospel*.[5] This *Fifth Gospel* depicts how the young boy grows up and becomes a young man. We must always keep in mind that the one who grows up, and who becomes an adult—a 21-year-old—is Zarathustra in the soul-sheath of the Nathan Jesus child. Rudolf Steiner says that 'a lofty, clairvoyant power' lives in that child.[6]

According to Rudolf Steiner's description, Jesus made many journeys through Palestine and the surrounding regions in the practice of His profession. We can come to a general idea of this: a cabinet-maker, a woodworker, someone who works with wood and who—as was possible at that time—moves 'from place to place'.[7] But Rudolf Steiner depicts in a wonderful way the impression this Jesus made on people, how they loved this Jesus Who had a very simple nature, how He sat with them and spoke with them, and how, when He departed, they believed He was still there and would always be among them.[8] It was in this way that the Zarathustra-being—now growing up—moved through the world of the Mysteries at the turning point of time.

This Jesus undergoes certain things that we must come to experience again, like an echo of His experience. The old prophets were constituted so that the spirit of God still spoke in them. Rudolf Steiner describes how the prophets felt that the spirit of God spoke in them and how people also experienced that these prophets were filled by the spirit of God. But this gradually disappeared, and the time came when the prophets no longer had the feeling: the spirit of God speaks from me. Instead, they only heard the voice, the 'Bath-Kol', the voice of the spirit, or the 'Daughter of the Divine Voice'. But this 'Bath-Kol' remained the source of a mighty proclamation. Infinite cosmic secrets streamed through it into the Hebraic Mysteries.

Then the ability to understand this voice ceased. Here was the first great experience Jesus had on His journeys—the inability of the Hebrew initiates to understand the voice of the 'Bath-Kol'. However, Jesus Himself—Zarathustra—heard the 'Bath-Kol'. He experienced it, and noted: This 'Bath-Kol' no longer reaches into the heights as before. To make a long story short, the existence of a mighty Mystery came to an end—there were initiates who no longer heard the voice, and those who still heard the voice but did not understand it; and there was the cosmic voice itself that no longer reached to the throne of God in order to mediate what came from Him.

That was the Christ-being's first great experience of sadness. His second experience of sadness was when He perceived that many of the old temples and altars were rife with lower—we would say decadent—cults. He perceived that the temples no longer displayed divine images but idols instead; rather than gods, evil forces were honoured. We could make a list of evil idols, but I will mention only one of them. A mighty idol made of iron stood in Jerusalem; its location is still known today. This iron idol—large, many feet high—was Moloch. A fire of live coals burned in it and children were thrown alive into this fire as sacrifices to Moloch.

Now we think of the Jesus-being who perceives this and much else, who perceives how demons move into these decadent cults, how the true priests have long since fled. He sees how demons have crept into the adherents of these cults and how, as a result, the most frightful illnesses spread. All of this is depicted by Rudolf Steiner with an extraordinary fullness of soul—the misery of the people that Jesus experienced along with them; the dreadfulness that He experienced first hand.

Then a quite significant moment occurs. Again Jesus comes to one of these abandoned temples and altars, and people stream to it hoping that a priest has returned who would once again bring blessing upon them. But in the face of the demonic world, Jesus falls as though dead, as though unconscious; He is carried away to the spiritual world, into the realm of the Sun. In this realm of the Sun, He once again hears the voice of the 'Bath-Kol', now powerful and as though transformed. And the so-called Cosmic Lord's Prayer, the primal Lord's Prayer of the old Mysteries, streams towards Him from this 'Bath-Kol'. It goes like this:

Amen.
The Evils hold sway,
Witnesses of emancipated egohood.
Selfhood guilt incurred through others
Experience in the daily bread,
Where the will of heaven reigns not
Since the human being took his leave from your kingdom
And forgot your names
You fathers in the heavens.[9]

The profound importance of this cosmic Lord's Prayer to Rudolf Steiner is shown in the fact that he spoke it at the laying of the foundation stone for the first Goetheanum.

We have heard how this Jesus boy—in Whom the Zarathustra ego lived—grew up in Nazareth surrounded by the colony of Essenes; and now we see how this Jesus associated with these Essene circles. He was not a member of the Essene sect, according to Rudolf Steiner, but He was recognized by them as an initiate. He was allowed access to all the Mystery secrets, since initiated Essenes very likely had insight into who He was.

From His twenty-fourth to His twenty-ninth year, Jesus regularly visits the Essenes, probably most often in Qumran, in the large cloister complex there, but in other places as well. There he meets John the Baptist who also wanders through the region and often visits the Essenes. Although John is also not a member of the sect, he like Jesus is recognized and honoured as an initiate.

These Essenes clearly recognized the whole dilemma of the time. They perceived the fading away of the 'Bath-Kol' voice as well as the diminishing capability of the Hebrew initiates. Naturally, they also saw the proliferation of decadent cults around them. As early as the time of Jeshu ben Pandira, they decided to distance themselves from this decadent world by means of the deepest asceticism, the strictest self-discipline, and the greatest purity, as well as intensive study of the holy books. As a result, they succeeded in isolating themselves from the ruination that had entered into humanity, first through Lucifer and, subsequently, through Ahriman. The Essenes were thus free of luciferic and ahrimanic influences.

But then Jesus had a mighty experience. He returns to Qumran and sees how Lucifer and Ahriman are lurking at the gates of Qumran but cannot enter this place of purity, of asceticism, of self-discipline. These spirits flee from the cloister gate and go out into the world. Jesus recognizes that the Essenes are locking out Lucifer and Ahriman but, in doing so, they are driving them out into the rest of humanity. This becomes an enormous problem for Jesus. What good is individual purity if the evil we overcome in ourselves is chased out into the world and fills other people? We will meet this theme later when we discuss the Grail secrets; it reappears with the initiation of Parzival.

This is one of the deep, painful experiences undergone by the Jesus-being. In all of this, something comes to expression that was, in fact, the basis for the Cosmic Lord's Prayer. Rudolf Steiner says this was long a prayer in all the Mysteries because the Fall of Man was experienced in all these Mysteries; human beings had separated from the gods, had forgotten the names of the gods, and the Mysteries experienced how evil began to hold sway as a consequence of this Fall of Man. The Cosmic Lord's Prayer is the cosmic prayer about the tragedy of the Fall of Man.

What was at the heart of the Fall of Man? The ego was supposed to have come face-to-face with the world, objectively and freely; and the astral body was to have taken care of everything to do with the soul. However, through the Fall of Man, the ego entered too strongly into the astral body; as a result, egotism came into being. When we are egotistical, it is always because the ego is active in the astral element and not free in the way it can be in pure thinking. As a consequence, a part of the human body began to change. Our physical body consists of two principal parts. The first is the invisible structure of the physical body. In esotericism, this is called the 'phantom of the physical body'—a kind of invisible form made of forces.[10] And the second part is the material substance that fills out this structure. There is a beautiful example that demonstrates this. If we hold a magnet under a piece of paper, there appears to be no visible effect. But if we sprinkle iron shavings on the paper and tap it a bit, suddenly the shavings arrange themselves along the magnet's invisible but clearly present lines of force.

Originally, only the finest substance was to have been integrated into the human physical body. Legend says that the substance of the human physical body should be no denser than the fragrance of a rose. Through the Fall of Man, however, increasingly condensed and coarse matter was added to the human being. The result was that this phantom deteriorated until the more delicate senses began to constrict—just as a lightweight framework starts to buckle when we hang heavier and heavier weights on it. The physical body began to lose the form that had been planned for it. The form intended by the gods was directed towards thinking so that the human being could experience his ego though thinking based on the structure of wisdom in our physical body. However, because of the Fall of Man, the inner structure of the physical body deteriorated more and more. The evolution of the earth threatened to prevent humans from developing their ego any further. All of humanity faced the danger of perishing as ego-humanity. Seen from the perspective of the cosmos—as it is described—the aura of the earth had become grey, cloudy and dark.

This was also known in the Mysteries. Thus the hope arose that a messiah, a divine being, a saviour, would come to rescue a humanity that was perishing as a result of the Fall of Man and its effects on the physical body.

All this is still part of the pre-history of the Mystery of Golgotha—it took place prior to the moment that would become the pivotal point in the whole evolution of the earth and humanity. Rudolf Steiner refers to what is called the baptism of Jesus in the Jordan as the greatest event in earth evolution.

Virginia Sease has drawn our attention to the baptism communities. Baptism brought about an initiation through water, a very special form of initiation. Rudolf Steiner says that humanity was prepared over several epochs until a baptist—based on his own state of initiation—knew: Now the moment has arrived. John is the most prominent and important of the baptists. The baptismal submersion in water caused a kind of shock-induced separation; the soul-spirit element would be freed for an instant and then people would have three distinct kinds of experience.[11]

The first experience is: There is a spiritual world. Many people have a sudden feeling of this as a result of a shock or the well-known near-death experience. The second experience is: My ego belongs to the spiritual world. The person suddenly senses: I am not standing opposite the spiritual world; I am a part of this spiritual world. The third, decisive experience of this initiation by baptism is: The 'I AM' lives in this spiritual world from which I am born as spirit. What people in the most ancient Mysteries experienced—that they entered the spiritual world, perceived the I-AM Being, the Sun-being, and knew: I come from this—now occurred much later, at the turning point of time, through the water baptism by John.

The *Fifth Gospel* depicts wonderfully how Jesus arrives at this baptism.[12] After all His terrible experiences, He returns home where He still lives in the deepest and closest relationship to His mother. Again, He relates all His experiences to her: from the decadence of these dreadful cults to the horrible disaster of the Essenes driving evil into the world—He empties His heart out to His mother. It is as though His whole being passes into her during this last conversation with her before the baptism; as though, now through this conversation, through the passing of His being into her, the Zarathustra ego is released. His being passes into her and—one could say—what is left behind is essentially the Nathan-Jesus child, except that the Zarathustra ego had been active in this sheath since the Nathan-Jesus was twelve years old. After this conversation, Jesus sets off. He is without an ego; the primal soul of humanity lives in Him and He feels Himself drawn to the baptism site at the Jordan, to where John is. This is one great mystery of this event.

Now we arrive at the second great mystery. The earthly Adam-soul lives in this John; John the Baptist is the oldest soul in all of humanity. In a wondrous moment in world and spiritual history, we see how this innocent part which had remained in the spiritual world and was incarnated in a human body for the first time as Jesus is now drawn to the other part of its being, the earthly Adam-soul; they meet one another.

The spiritual world sounds its call to humanity three times. Rudolf Steiner says that, as a rule, the spiritual world addresses such a call to humanity three times and if the spiritual world is not heard, it withdraws for a period of time.[13] The first call to humanity was the call from the Sinai: 'I am the I AM.'[14] What followed from it were the Ten Commandments. It is difficult to imagine today what it meant for the human experience of the ego that God said to the human being, 'Thou shalt not kill. Thou shalt not steal.'[15] It was as though the finger of God were pointed at the ego. That is the secret of the Ten Commandments and the secret of the Sinai; and this is the first great call to humanity. The second great call comes from John: 'Repent ye: for the kingdom of heaven is at hand.'[16] Stop using the Mysteries only for egoistic purposes, as was so often the case. 'Repent ye!'[17] Look again to what should exist in the human being; the true 'I AM' is imminent. This call of John before the baptism in the Jordan came from his mighty knowledge. John the Baptist was one of the great initiates of humanity; later, many esoteric schools revere him for this reason.

Then something wondrous happens that can be only described from an external perspective. John performs the baptism of Jesus. We can imagine John immersing Jesus and, in this moment, in this moment of baptism, the Christ-being draws into the Jesus-being. It can be said that John the Baptist is the one who performs the act that brings about the indwelling of God in a human being. From out of the spiritual world the words sound, 'This is my much beloved Son; today I have begotten you.' This is literally what it says, not '. . . in whom I am well pleased.'[18]

Now, we are once again confronted with enormous riddles. Who speaks at that moment? Who begets the Son? The apocryphal gospels—as much documents of initiation as the other Gospels—sometimes present us with quite puzzling things. We hear in the *Romanum*, in the old Credo, born 'of the Holy Spirit from the Virgin Mary'.[19] In the *Apostolicum* [Apostle's Creed] it says: 'Jesus Christ [. . . who was] conceived by the Holy Spirit, born of the Virgin Mary'. And in the *Niceum Constantinopolitanum* [Nicene Creed], the third great Credo, it says: 'And was incarnate of the Holy Ghost and of the Virgin Mary and was made human.' This third Credo sounds a bit strange. The Hebrew Gospel—one of the great apocryphal gospels, but also one of the most puzzling—contains the following: 'When Christ wanted to come to human beings on the earth, the Father God chose a mighty power in heaven called Michael, and entrusted Christ to the care of this power. And the power came into the world, and she was called Mary, and Christ was seven months in her body.' This is Mystery language; in fact, the Hebrew Gospel is full of Mystery language. It is in this gospel that Christ speaks after the baptism: 'Even so did my mother, the Holy Spirit, take hold of me by one of my hairs and carried me away to the great Mount Tabor.'

Rudolf Steiner describes this event in full detail. In the Credo for the Christian Community, he expresses it this way: 'The birth of Jesus upon earth is a working of the Holy Spirit, who, to heal spiritually the sickness of sin within the bodily nature of humanity, prepared the son of Mary to be the vehicle of the Christ.'[20] This needs to be read over and over in many different forms; I quote here from the beautiful little volume about the Credo by Adolf Müller, *Werdestufen des Glaubensbekenntnisses* [Evolutionary steps of the confession of faith]: 'The Holy Spirit [i.e., the third part of the Trinity] works so that the Logos can seek a dwelling within the human being.'[21] When we speak about the hierarchies, we will come to speak again about the Trinity.

The central event of the whole of evolution, the baptism, in which a divine being united itself for the first time with an earthly human being, is followed by the three great years. Profound riddles and mysteries are described in the Gospels. We must always keep in mind that the Gospels are initiatory texts, initiation texts. They are not intended to be biographical—although biographical incidents are used gradually to reveal the elements of Christian initiation. It is also enlightening to recognize that the Gospels are intended for all future cultural epochs. The Gospel of Matthew was the initiatory text for the fourth post-Atlantean epoch; the Gospel of Mark is the Gospel for our time, the fifth post-Atlantean epoch. In the future, the Gospel of Luke will be the initiation text for the sixth epoch; and the Gospel of John will not really be understood until the seventh post-Atlantean cultural epoch when it can serve as an initiatory text.

The process of incarnation occurs throughout these three years. Rudolf Steiner says, 'At first, the Christ-being was only loosely connected with Jesus of Nazareth; but, through a continuing development that lasted until the crucifixion, this Being united Itself more and more closely with the physical body of Jesus.' In the end, the Christ became fully human through the death on the cross. 'A god entering into a human body was not only a significant matter for humanity, it was also a matter of significance for the higher hierarchies.'[22]

An event central to the life of Christ Jesus occurred during these three years—the initiation, the awakening, of Lazarus. Jesus Christ was often in Bethany with Martha and Mary, and their brother Lazarus. One day, the Christ arrives and is given the news: 'The one you love so much has died.' The Christ reacts without consternation or sadness—as the Gospel makes quite clear; instead, He remains quite composed. Rudolf Steiner says that the entire story is an image concealing a profoundly meaningful event. Throughout all the old Mysteries it was customary for the candidate for initiation to sink into a deathlike sleep. This was necessary in order to loosen the higher members of his being—especially the ego and the astral body, as well as parts of the ether body—which were the focus of the initiation. Within the innermost secrets of the Mysteries, it was customary to put the candidate for initiation into a deathlike sleep by various means. Then, in the spiritual world, the initiate would carry out what was needed for the soul to be filled by the spirit and opened to the spiritual world. As a rule, this 'death sleep' and the whole initiation process lasted three days. Then the soul returned, and the 'death sleeper' awoke having been initiated.

Now the Christ performs in public an event that had previously only taken place within the deepest secrets of the Mysteries. Rudolf Steiner depicts this quite unambiguously at the beginning of the twentieth century in his book *Christianity as Mystical Fact and the Mysteries of Antiquity*.[23] This awakening of Lazarus was an initiation—the first Christ initiation. Lazarus, afterwards called John, is the first human being initiated by Christ. The fact that this person who had been initiated by Christ could describe the Christ Mysteries in the most intimate detail—in the Gospel of John and in the Book of Revelation—is the direct result of his initiation by the Christ-being Himself. It has been noted frequently— Rudolf Steiner remarks on this as well—that the Hebrew initiates immediately grasp what had happened, and that they say, 'What are we going to do' about this Jesus.[24] It was like a betrayal of the Mysteries when what had taken place in the most hidden inner sanctum was performed by the Christ in a completely public way. The Mysteries had been made public. Even though certain limits to this public aspect were later set within esoteric Christianity and esoteric schools, the public awakening of Lazarus still exemplified a major element in the whole transition from pre-Christian times to Christian times. What previously could only happen in a place hidden from humanity now occurs in full view of all humanity and—this is the decisive factor—*for* all humanity.

With the crucifixion, the Christ's deed of becoming human was ended; with it, this enormous experience also comes to an end for the spiritual world. Previously, no god had ever experienced death; death was the lot of humanity. The entire world of the gods and all of spiritual history changed because of the fact that the Son of God, the Logos, had come to the point of death. With the crucifixion of a god—Rudolf Steiner says this in *Occult Science*—'all Mystery wisdom ... had to take a new form'.[25]

Three great events characterize the Mystery of Golgotha: the resurrection, the ascension, and the outpouring of the Holy Spirit at Whitsun. The resurrection signifies that physical corporeality was restored when a god dwelt in a human being. Since the time of Golgotha, the physical body has once again been constituted so that it serves the original objective of the gods—making ego development possible for the human being. According to Rudolf Steiner, the restoration of the phantom is 'for all humanity' and it can be imparted to every person who is able to 'establish a connection to the Christ'.[26] This is true for people of good will. We still need to discuss the path to the Christ. I began with the questions that a person in pursuit of self-knowledge must ask himself, 'Am I a Christian? And, if so, how am I a Christian?'

Rudolf Steiner connects the resurrection with the baptism in the Jordan using a phrase that was later misunderstood and applied quite differently. He says the baptism in the Jordan is actually the *Conceptio Immaculata*, 'the immaculate conception'.[27] This uniting of Christ and Jesus took place in complete purity, in *Immaculata*. This is part of the resurrection. The *Conceptio Immaculata* of the baptism in the Jordan is closely connected to the resurrection. The point of the immaculate indwelling of the Christ in a human body is that He did not have any contact with the denser substances that had gradually been sullying the physical body since the Fall of Man. In esotericism, these substances are referred to as 'ash'. We are all filled with ash; ash is the technical term for the fact that we have bodily nature comprised of substances that are too dense. From the beginning, the Christ never came into contact with this ash because He did not go through the Fall of Man; as a result, it was possible for Him again to penetrate the phantom, the physical body, from within.

Now we can come to an understanding of the second event of the Mystery of Golgotha—the ascension. According to Rudolf Steiner, Christ underwent a further development as a result of having undergone

an earthly incarnation. This led Him into a new region of the spiritual
world, an event the apostles experienced as the ascension. Here it is
interesting to see how Rudolf Steiner transforms the ancient Credo. In its
oldest form it states, 'Ascended into heaven and sitteth at the right hand of
the Father.' The *Apostolicum* says, 'Ascended into heaven and sitteth at the
right hand of God, the Father almighty.' The *Constantinopolitanum* says,
'entered into heaven and sitting at the right hand of the Father'. Rudolf
Steiner says: 'Since that time He is the Lord of the heavenly forces upon
earth and lives as the fulfiller of the fatherly deeds of the ground of the
world.'[28] This is the description of the reality that was earlier called
'... sitting on the right hand of the Father'. During this course, we will
speak about the enormous changes that occurred in the world of the
hierarchies as a result of the Mystery of Golgotha—changes that extended
to the Trinity.

Finally, there is the third great result of the Mystery of Golgotha, the
outpouring of the Holy Spirit. This means that since the first Whitsun
every human ego has been able to unite itself with the Holy Spirit—the
third part of the Trinity. Esoteric Christianity expressed this in an unusual
way. In earlier times, people experienced the confession of faith as con-
taining the whole history of salvation; everything is said there that we, as
human beings, need to know. There was a tradition in esoteric Christianity
that was reported by Pirmin, the founder of the cloister on the Reichenau
in southern Germany. It says the Holy Ghost descended in fiery flames at
Whitsun, and every apostle spoke a portion of the confession of faith:

Peter:	I believe in God the Father Almighty, creator of heaven and earth.
John:	And in Jesus Christ, His only begotten Son, our Lord.
James spoke:	Who was conceived of the Holy Spirit, born of the Virgin Mary.
Andrew said:	He suffered under Pontius Pilate, was crucified, and was buried.
Philip spoke:	He descended into the underworld.
Thomas said:	On the third day, He arose again from the dead.
Bartholomew said:	He ascended into heaven, sits at the right hand of God, the Father Almighty.

Matthew said:	From there He will come to judge the quick and the dead.
James, the son of Alphaeus spoke:	I believe in the Holy Spirit.
Simon the Zealot said:	A holy catholic church.
Judas, son of James, spoke:	The communion of saints, the forgiveness of sins.
Thomas added:	The resurrection of the flesh and the life everlasting.[29]

There is primal, ancient knowledge reflected in such a story. The apostles were the representatives of humanity. All of humanity was seen assembled in the apostles, and there was the feeling that the Holy Spirit was coming to these human beings so that each one would receive a part of the truth. When they all spoke, the whole truth would manifest. We will find this again in the New Mysteries. It is a fundamental principle of the new social order of the Mysteries that when many people speak together, the whole truth is expressed.

Let us turn our attention to one last image. I have already said that when the Mysteries no longer existed in their old strength, there were still noble Mystery religions, and the gods continued to live in these noble Mystery religions. We must keep in mind that the Mystery of Golgotha was perceived by the whole ancient world of the gods. Rudolf Steiner says that great gods, good gods—but also demons—perceived what took place. The good gods allowed inspirations about the Mystery of Golgotha to come to those who served in their temples. This is the beginning of the great stream we refer to as esoteric Christianity. It would be nonsense to say that human beings at that time would have thought there was no longer an Isis or Osiris, no Apollo, no Zeus. They simply said that the Christ stood above them all.

Thus the early Christians who still looked to the gods heard teachings about the Mystery of Golgotha from them. This is how we will come to look back on Paul, Dionysius, the Gnosis, Clement of Alexandria, and Origen. The gods themselves interpret the secret of the Mystery of Golgotha for human beings.

Since that time, we have been constantly developing our understanding through thinking, our Mystery understanding. We will live more and more in a growing Mystery understanding of the Christ, of the Mystery of Golgotha. Both Virginia Sease and I are clear about the fact that we can offer you only the smallest fragments in these lectures. But, still, they are little pieces that can grow in your souls, just as they grow in ours. In all humility we can say: No worldly wisdom is sufficient to understand these mighty things. And yet every soul must take the steps necessary to approach this understanding.

Transformations in Prayer and Meditation Resulting from the Mystery of Golgotha

Virginia Sease

We have had the mighty image before our souls of how Jesus entered a temple during one of His journeys, fell into a transported state and experienced what the voice of the 'Bath-Kol' wanted to say; and how He then experienced the Cosmic Lord's Prayer. And we have heard how the 'Bath-Kol' had long been silent because the priests could no longer hear this cosmic voice of wisdom. We have also looked at the image of how—perhaps not consciously, but unconsciously—people, the masses, experienced the fact that the priests could no longer apprehend the voice of heaven.

Today, two thousand years later, human beings find themselves in a completely different situation. It could be said that the spiritual world speaks and that human beings wish to hear it. Countless people live with the feeling that there might actually be something to hear. Many different voices exist. At first, we are not able to say with certainty which spirit voice is speaking, which among the many voices is perceived by modern human beings. What comes from supersensible realms enters directly into us. Today, the great challenge for humanity is to learn to discern which voice people hear when they think they perceive one. Is it perhaps a more luciferic kind of voice which brings a message for humanity that says, 'The earth is not so important; flee into spiritual realms'? Or is it a voice more from the ahrimanic side that says, 'Seek your salvation on earth; make the earth into a kind of paradise'? People today are able to hear both these voices almost effortlessly. Or is the voice one that truly belongs to human beings, the voice we can describe as the Christ voice? Each of us must learn to recognize the differences among these voices.

We learn this discernment through the right kind of prayer and the right kind of meditation. Both prayer and meditation have a long history in human development. I want to turn our attention briefly to the great stages of their development and look at the events surrounding Jesus at the turning point of time.

Today there are many schools of meditation. Ten years ago, it might have been easy to list all the most prominent paths of schooling. Now the number of schooling paths is so overwhelming we are better off not even trying to list them all. But do we ever hear about a *school of prayer*? Practically never, except in the context of religion.

The mood of prayer in the great world religions was always cultivated with an attitude that can be summarized in the thought: I want nothing for myself personally; I should want only what the Divine wants. This was once the attitude of prayer in all great religions. But, during the third post-Atlantean epoch, this mood of prayer began to be edged out by other forces. We have already seen two types of these forces. We have seen the more negative ones in the attitude of the sibyls. And we have seen them in what can be summed up as the Bileam attitude—an attitude of magic that tries to possess the word by force. This existed strongly up to the time of the Mystery of Golgotha. What had been genuine prayer in earlier times often sank into the decadence of magical incantation. This magical charm was then placed in the service of idols. There were many such magical formulas until Jesus Christ taught His disciples how humanity is to pray. We can scarcely imagine how ubiquitous these magical formulas were at the turning point of time.

Magical charms were always formed around seeking fulfilment of an egotistical wish. With these egotistical pleas, the person prayed to acquire something advantageous for himself. This still occurs today; we think here of prayers we can call self-created prayers said by an individual.

These magical incantations underwent a transformation as a result of Christ Jesus' activity. A brief look at magical incantations will show what had to occur for such a change to take place. The foremost characteristic of these magical charms is their power to conjure. There are one- and two-part charms; the two-part charms were especially beloved in older times. The first part of the charm was always a kind of story about how a similar problem had been handled successfully—whether a healing, the expulsion of evil spirits, freeing a prisoner from his bonds, or the healing of an animal. It was a story in which success comes through the intervention of a particular divinity or procedure. Then, after the story, came the actual charm.

This practice was widespread in the northern regions of Europe. The magical incantation was a part of life there; every folk group lived with them; every nationality experienced something similar. In the northern regions, after people had been Christianized, mostly through coercion, it often happened that the essence of these magic incantations remained, but embellished with a Christian vocabulary. Often the magical formula was accompanied by certain actions, for example, gestures, handshakes and the laying on of hands. This was a definite part of the ritual.

Fortunately, we know something of how these heathen conjuring formulas made their way into folk usage. In the German tradition there are the Merseburg Charms, so-called because they were discovered in the cathedral library in Merseburg. These two Old High German charms from a ninth-century manuscript are significant because we can see in them how this heathen custom was cultivated in the northern regions. While we are fortunate that they were written down, what they represent is likely only the smallest fragment of this whole world of charms.

The world is divided into many and varied regions. In northern Europe—and this is characteristic—the use of alliteration made a strong impression on the senses of these people when they heard such a charm. While the impression of the will was conveyed in the northern regions through alliterative verse, people in the south were caught up by the rhythmic element. There the rhythm had more influence. I would like to read a few lines of a Merseburg charm so that you can hear the power of this alliteration. We can imagine these people standing outdoors in a grove, perhaps in a forest, while the priest spoke these words. We have described the mood of soul in the sentient soul epoch as being completely open, without barriers; thus they hear something that sounds like this— first in Old High German and then in English translation:

Phol ende Uodan vuoron zi holza.
dû uuart demo Balderes volon sîn vuoz birenkit.
thû biguolen Sinthgunt, Sunna era suister;
thû biguolen Frîia, Uolla era suister;
thû biguolen Uuodan, sô hê uuola conda:
sôse bênrenki, sose bluotrenkî,
sôse lidirenki:
bên zi bêna, bluot zi bluoda,
lid zi geliden, sôse gilîmida sîn.

Phol and Wodan rode in the woods,
There Balder's foal sprained its foot.
It was beguiled by Sinthgunt, Sunna her sister;
It was beguiled by Freya, Folla her sister;
It was beguiled by Wodan, as well he knew how:
Like bone-wrench, like blood-wrench, like limb-wrench:
Bone to bone, blood to blood;
Limb to limb—as if they were limed.[1]

This was not how all this came to expression in the Roman areas; nevertheless, there were still many Roman incantations in circulation. We have examples of them collected by B.M. Terentius Varro, a librarian in Rome who also created the list of the ten sibyls. He provided many examples of these Roman incantations, and stressed that there were often three aspects to them. One aspect was connected to the feet—feet touched the earth and, through the contact, pain was given over to the earth. Thus pain passes through to the feet and then is given over to the earth. This was how pain was relieved. The second aspect was saliva, which played a large role in magic. And a third aspect was that people were to practise asceticism when they undertook anything at all religious or cultic; asceticism increased the possibility of success. One of the pre-Christian incantations noted by Varro from around the turning point of time reads:

> 'I would rather cite,' said I, 'Sasernas' prescription for the malady from which Fundanius suffers, for his corns make furrows on his brow.'
> 'Tell me, pray, quickly,' exclaimed Fundanius, 'for I had rather learn how to root out my corns than how to plant beetroots.'
> 'I will tell you,' said Stolo, 'in the very words he wrote it, or at least as I heard Tarquenna read it: "When a man's feet begin to hurt he should think of you to enable you to cure him."'
> 'I am thinking of you,' said Fundanius, 'now cure my feet.'
> 'Listen to the incantation,' said Stolo.
> ' "May the earth keep the malady,
> May good health remain here."
> Saserna bids you chant this formula thrice nine times, to touch the earth, to spit and be sure you do it all when sober.'[2]

'When a man's feet hurt, he should think of . . .'; then the word 'you' appears in the verse, and where the word 'you' stands, the person speaking the verse should say the name of the spirit or god. He says, 'I am thinking of you. Cure my foot; may the earth keep the malady and may good health remain here.' Then there is a reference to how it should be practised: 'Chant this thrice nine times, touch the earth, spit, and be sure you do it all when sober.'[3] This was quite a widespread practice at that time.

We are trying to paint a picture here through which we can experience the world into which the influence of the Christ streamed. This picture can also show how the disciples who surrounded the Christ experienced His presence. But there are also hymns and verses from the Vedic stream.

This is interesting, because we might not have guessed that the Vedic stream of India would flow into Jerusalem—into the part of the world where the Christ events took place. The content of these traditions was seen as a kind of idol worship. Already in Old Testament times, Hebrews—they spread their influence widely—were collecting these traditions on their travels and bringing them back. This is one reason there are so many warnings about idol worship in the Old Testament. Of course, the Vedas had been passed down in a somewhat modified form. The *Rig Veda* is a collection of over one thousand old hymns used for cultic purposes. An important and well-known formula that Rudolf Steiner often brought into his early esoteric work stems from these Vedic hymns. In Sanskrit it reads, 'Tat twam asi', which means 'It is you'. It refers to two aspects that are important for our considerations here: spiritual schooling, and our experiences after death.

As the ancient initiates knew, the path of schooling takes us through the astral world where we experience a world of colour. We are immersed in a world of colour. Ascending higher—if we speak of this in stages—we arrive in the spiritual world, in the region of devachan. I will make no further distinctions here. The human being arrives in the spiritual world where he learns to understand the phrase, 'Tat twam asi'. He experiences his physical form as outside his selfhood. He says to this physical form, 'It is you.' Earlier, he had said, 'It is I.' Now he stands apart and says, 'It is you, my container for my earthly existence. You are not to be valued lightly, but honoured because you alone give me the opportunity to stand on the earth and evolve.' Every human being has this experience of 'It is you' about 30 years after death. He sees the primal image of physical corporeality after death—now not so much in connection with himself, but more generally. He looks upon the archetypal, primal structure of the physical body before corporeality had become so dense and dark. We are reminded here of what has been said about the esoteric image of ash.

The Vedic stream flowed into Israel, into Jerusalem, and became a fundamental element of spiritual life there. It was beneficial when put to proper use so that people did not scorn the physical body. Nevertheless, the ascetics' disdain for the physical body remained a problem for many esoteric communities around and before the turning point of time. There is even an inconsistency within the Essenes' community about the relationship to the physical body. On the one hand, in their esoteric teachings—their spiritual exercises and so forth—they experienced how the Abraham secret was carried by the blood and flowed into the 42 generations. This veneration of the physical foundation carried by the blood was one aspect of it. The other aspect, however, reveals the contradiction that existed among the Essenes, the Therapeuts, and other such groups of this period. Not only was their physical corporeality spiritualized by their strict asceticism, they sought to nullify, eliminate corporeality through this asceticism. This forms the basis for the powerful effect of the image seen by Jesus on His journey: the image of Lucifer and Ahriman, active through their influence in the physical body, being driven away from the gates of such a colony of Essenes.

Around the turning point of time, even pious Jews often made use of external measures to support their prayers. For example, they wore phylacteries—straps to which leather cases are attached. Sacred words, sacred texts were placed in these cases and worn on the forehead. They can be seen on pious Jews even today, especially in Jerusalem. In the Gospel of Matthew, Christ warns about this externalization of prayer when He speaks about the Pharisees and the scribes: 'But all their works they do for to be seen of men: they make broad their phylacteries...'[4] This is like a very condensed reference to many practices of the time. By contrast, the teachings of the Christ were in no sense to be practised externally. They point to how people should carry their religious life inwardly rather than outwardly—to how the individual should turn inwards and pray within himself, in his own soul. This represents an enormous change.

Some of the traditional prayers are found in the Psalms, for example. Many of these prayers have a long history; they were handed down over millennia, and they continue to be prayed. For example, the benediction by the priest was taken up later in the Christian tradition. Descriptions of the Psalms frequently indicate that they are to be sung, accompanied by a stringed instrument like a psalter. Often, an instrument with eight strings is indicated.

We also know about the tradition in which the Lord God speaks to Moses, saying, 'On this wise ye shall bless the children of Israel, saying unto them ...' and, 'The Lord bless thee, and keep thee; the Lord make His face shine upon thee, and be gracious unto thee. The Lord lift up His countenance upon thee, and give thee peace.'[5] Here a blessing becomes a prayer. What is characteristic of this prayer, however, is that it is not the individual, but Moses, who prays the prayer. Moses prays for human beings by means of this blessing. It is not the independent individual who can speak such a prayer—a prayer with a plea for peace, inner peace; rather it is spoken by someone who mediates between human beings and salvation—in this case, the initiate Moses.

An enormous step was taken by the Christ when He showed how the human being—alone, independent, without a higher authority—can pray. This was new in the esoteric tradition up to that time. In our age—since the turning point of time—a general principle for prayer has been established: the source of prayer cannot be the individual's egotism. Rudolf Steiner stressed that the essential attitude of every prayer is to be found in the words of Christ at Gethsemane: 'Not mine, but Thy will be done.'[6] This is the essential attitude, no matter what kind of prayer is offered.

If we look at prayer—in our time and since the turning point of time—a pattern emerges. We see how two streams of time come together. There is the stream of time from the past and the one from the future. When they converge, something like an eddy develops, similar to what happens when two streams of water converge. The convergence of these two aspects is decisive for the practice of prayer today. On the one hand, the stream that comes out of the past carries with it the legacy of our deeds. Everything from the past that comes to us out of our will, our feelings, our thoughts, can bring a flood of shame and remorse in us. If we are honest with ourselves, we do not often look back on our deeds and think 'I did that really well; what a great success that was.' Instead, an honest person more often thinks 'That was not as bad as it might have been; I was certainly given a gift of grace there.'

In this practice of prayer, we develop an attitude of reverence towards the divine because we have not strayed to the extent we might have. This attitude brings with it a feeling of intimacy with God. We have a feeling of warmth, of being warmed through by the divine, because we have the sense that something was present, something that supported us so that we did not have to travel down too many wrong paths. When we look to the future, we may feel anxiety or hope or expectation or fear based on the past. The important thing here is that we develop a feeling of devotion in ourselves. This is the feeling of devotion we experience through the words that Christ prayed in the Garden of Gethsemane, 'Not mine, but Thy will be done.' It brings us a light from the future. A real prayer moves between these two polarities: divine warmth, the devotion from the past, and divine light, the light of prayer from the future. Real prayer makes it possible for us to develop a feeling of devotion.[7]

Rudolf Steiner has clearly described the mystery at the heart of a real prayer.[8] A real prayer cannot be arbitrary. It must arise out of the wisdom of cosmic guidance, not randomly; it must be composed according to the laws of this wisdom. Rudolf Steiner worked intensively throughout his life with the Lord's Prayer. At this point, I want to summarize several aspects of his observations about the Lord's Prayer; in what he said we can see the Lord's Prayer brings everything together in accord with the rules of wisdom so that it becomes a genuine prayer.

It begins with the appeal: *Our Father, Who art in the heavens*; this points to the connection with the Father element, with the spiritual realm. Then come the first three petitions. They are associated with the three upper members of the human being that are yet to be developed. *Hallowed be Thy name.* Our gaze is directed to the Spirit Self, to Manas. The Apocalyptist wrote in an epistle to the congregation at Pergamon that he would give him '. . . a white stone in which is etched a new name which no one knows but he who receives it'.[9] We could say that this is taken up by Christ in this archetypal form: *Hallowed be Thy name.*

The second petition—*Thy kingdom come*—is connected with the Life Spirit in the human being; the third petition—*Thy will be done*—is connected with the highest level, Atma, Spirit Man. The third level will be achieved only in the future, when the human being is capable of saying *Thy will be done*—capable of really saying it without the implication: *Thy will be done as long as it is also my own will.* This third step will represent a complete transformation of what we experience, right down into our physical corporeality.

Now the prayer turns to the earthly realm: *Thy will be done on earth as it is in heaven.* Here our glance is directed towards the earth. The final four petitions—which relate to the four lower members of man's constitution—then follow. This begins with the physical body: *Give us this day our daily bread.* Next is the ether body—where we invariably affect one another in ways we are unaware of: *Forgive us our debts as we forgive our debtors.* This, in general, is the overall effect we have on our fellow human beings. It is a step we can take, one deeply connected with the social element. If we pursue this step, we will find ample evidence of how we may affect one another—agreeably or disagreeably—by means of what is physically invisible. This effect occurs through the etheric element, and we do not see it even though it streams outwards from us.

Then there is the prayer's petition connected with the astral body: *Lead us not into temptation.* It is always the astral body that wants to pursue desires. The final petition addresses the ego level: *Deliver us from evil*, from everything that seeks to destroy our ego nature. There are forces in the world that want to take hold of our ego, either to possess it or—even more seriously—to destroy it. We can see in these indications that this Lord's Prayer ends where the Cosmic Lord's Prayer begins.

There is a question that always arises in research about the life and work of Christ Jesus. It concerns how much He took from what already existed in the religious culture, and how much He changed, expanded, and embellished it in the Lord's Prayer. For example, the so-called 'Shema Israel' is often mentioned in this regard. 'Shema Israel' comes from the first two Hebrew words of Deuteronomy 6:4, where it states, 'Hear, O Israel: The Lord our God *is* one Lord.' In and of itself, the 'Shema Israel' was not a prayer, but it is woven into every morning and evening service in the Hebrew liturgy. Historically, Flavius Josephus attributes the 'Shema Israel' to Moses; it is likewise prescribed in the Talmud as a biblical commandment. The transitions to Christianity were gradual, and the 'Shema Israel' was probably still frequently used by the faithful during the first Christian centuries.

In addition, there is the 'Kaddish' prayer that exists in longer or shorter forms; it is a prayer of praise from the Jewish liturgy. It is known in Protestantism by the Greek term *doxology*. A doxology is found at the end of the Protestant version of the Lord's Prayer: 'For Thine is the kingdom, and the power, and the glory, forever and ever. Amen.' This ending to the Protestant Lord's Prayer is not found in the Roman Catholic version. The exact wording of the 'Kaddish' prayer is: 'May His great name be exalted and sanctified in the world that He created according to His will. May He establish his kingdom . . .' Then, as *responsum*, in response, from the congregation came, 'May His great name be blessed forever and to all eternity.' Claims are made that this was simply picked up by the Christ and that His work is therefore merely based on the Jewish tradition.[10]

Rudolf Steiner himself explains that the Lord's Prayer could be translated into thousands of languages and never lose even a bit of its effectiveness. Naturally, a mantra is most powerful in its original language—in this case, Aramaic. But even in translation the Lord's Prayer retains its enormous effectiveness. Rudolf Steiner also says that this prayer will continue to be effective thousands of years in the future. 'The Lord's Prayer is . . . a prayer by which the human being . . . is to be lifted up to a sense for the development of his sevenfold human constitution; and the seven petitions—even when they arise in the most naive people who cannot understand them at all—thus become an expression of the spiritual-scientific view of the human constitution.'[11] These petitions are effective even when the words themselves are not understood.

There are two prayers that Rudolf Steiner himself uses repeatedly—especially in his early esoteric work before the First World War, but also later in a somewhat altered form. I want to mention one of them in particular, a 'Prayer to the Helpers of Humanity'. Humanity is always accompanied—even before incarnation—by people who are more developed than the average person and, of course, accompanied also by spiritual beings—above all, the Christ-being Himself. In esoteric language, these helpers of humanity are called 'brothers'. Thus this prayer given by Rudolf Steiner is addressed to the brothers who have accompanied the whole development of humanity through the evolutionary epochs of Saturn, Sun, Moon and Earth.

These helpers are further divided into the 'brothers of the past', the 'brothers of the present' who help us currently and who are more developed than we are, and the 'brothers of the future', who are the leaders of humanity. They are called upon in an attitude of prayer. This is a prayer used by Rudolf Steiner in various versions, especially in the cultic, ritual work he undertook before the First World War. When the lines of this mighty prayer are read aloud, we hear how something powerful is brought down from the spiritual world through Rudolf Steiner.

> *Brothers of ages past*, may your creating become our wisdom; we receive the compass and the plumb line from your hands. May your accomplished work be strength for our soul, be strength for our hands.
>
> *Brothers of the present*, as you are wiser than we are, let your wisdom radiate into our souls so that we may become revealers of your thoughts of God.
>
> *Brothers of the future*, as you carry the building-plan in your will, may your strength stream into our limbs so that we may become a body for great souls.[12]

The following sentences are often connected with this:

> The cosmic structure must come to be;
> It must be built of human beings.

The other prayer Rudolf Steiner speaks of is the so-called Rosicrucian verse which he called the primal prayer of humanity. The prayer has three main parts which appear in their most concise form through the Latin words *Ex Deo nascimur* (From God we are born), *In Christo morimur* (In Christ we die), *Per Spiritum Sanctum reviviscimus* (We live again through the Holy Spirit).

The turning point of time brought an enormous change in meditation that can be summarized with the opening words of the Gospel of John: 'In the beginning was the Word, and the Word was with God ... and the Word was made flesh, and dwelt among us...'[13] With the Christ incarnation, the method of teaching in the esoteric schools changed. We may recall the various images, stories and parables through which Christ taught the apostles; He also spoke to the masses in images, and explained these images to them.

In pre-Christian times, the word was used for magical purposes—sometimes for good, often for evil. But in esoteric training the word was not used in schooling and initiation. Learning was done in silence; images were silently evoked within the soul of the person. Through imaginations—images in the soul—the pupil could even receive communications from the spiritual world if he were advanced enough. If there were words in mantric verses, it was not the meaning of the mantra but the sound that created the effect. The human being received the teaching through the sound, the tone and the rhythm he heard.

When a person meditates today, he meditates in words filled with meaning. In bringing his great esoteric teachings, Rudolf Steiner described how the modern esoteric teacher must speak so that the individual remains free. He said, 'The words in the esoteric lessons are selected so that they work in an entirely impersonal way as soon as they leave the lips of the teacher. They should create a garment in which the Logos, streaming through the world, can wrap itself. The words must be suitable for these flowing currents of the Logos. For this reason, they are set forth quite precisely.'[14]

There is a basic and fundamental attitude necessary for meditation. While the attitude for prayer is 'Not my will', the attitude for meditation is the individual experience of reverence for the spiritual in the human soul. It is an attitude of soul. This then leads to a state where 'the spiritual that rests in the depths of the human soul' is lifted into the consciousness of the human being. 'Thus the human being unites himself with his own spirituality.'[15] Calling forth what is spiritual, and uniting the human being with his own spirituality: this is the aim of meditation.

Meditative practice requires the quality of 'inner peace', for example. This may sound very easy, but we know how difficult it actually is to bring about 'inner peace'. We can begin a meditation—many people today practise some form of meditation—and other things begin to stream in at the same time. We can be meditating and suddenly we might notice that we are thinking about the appointment we have in two hours. In practice, meditation is not very easy. Patience is necessary, as well as commitment, so that we keep going with the exercise even when we have the feeling that we are not making any progress, or even quite the opposite—when we have the sense that we were better at it three years ago than we are now. It is also necessary that we have a love for meditation—that we approach it with the attitude: we want meditation; we love meditation; we do not grit our teeth and bear it, but do it out of love. Forcing ourselves to do it puts us at a distinct disadvantage.

Rudolf Steiner gave general indications on how to meditate. I will mention seven of them here. We can view the following as the first two; they are fundamental. First there are the basic exercises which are a continuous part of a meditative life. We discipline ourselves by means of them—through the concentration exercise, for example, or through the exercise of a free deed, or the exercise of equanimity or impartiality or positivity, and then the exercise of balancing all five of them. More details can be found in Rudolf Steiner's work—for example, in *Anweisungen für eine esoterische Schulung* [Indications for an esoteric schooling].[16] Equally fundamental are the exercises of the 'eightfold path' which then become a part of the soul. We discipline ourselves through the exercises of the eightfold path because the word 'right' is always included as a guide in each step. There is 'right opinion', the 'right judgement', the 'right word', the 'right way of acting', the 'right point of view', the 'right habits', and the 'right memory'—so that the individual does not forget what he has already achieved—and then the overarching 'right attitude of contemplation'. These two pillars—the basic exercises and the eightfold path—are there to accompany us.

There are also meditations in which a geometric shape is important, a triangle for example. Rudolf Steiner often used these in his early esoteric lessons. Their underlying purpose is to free the etheric body a bit by living into a shape like a triangle, a hexagon or a pentagram. This is necessary in meditation. Eurythmy, in which a person not only observes a geometric figure but moves and creates its form, is especially helpful here.

We can also take a word like 'stillness' or 'peace' as the substance of a meditation; here the meditant allows the word to move within herself.

Then we can allow a meditative formula that comes from one of the cosmic leaders of wisdom to live in our hearts—for example, 'In the beginning was the Word'.

Sixth, we can take up a verse that also has the potential to be a mantric form. We begin with the verse and experience its rhythm, the composition of its lines, its so-called concordances. Naturally, it must be quite a special verse; not just any verse has the potential to be a mantra.

The seventh general indication is concerned with building up an imagination. Rudolf Steiner gave many imaginations; for example, in *Occult Science, An Outline* he gives a detailed description of the Rosicrucian imagination and how a person might build up such an imagination—the black cross with the seven red roses in the meditation cannot be found in the physical world.[17] From these indications we can come to understand the various possibilities meditation offers as an individual path of schooling.

In closing today, I would like to draw our attention to the Ascension of the Christ. In the Christian tradition, the Ascension has always been recognized as a significant event. Through Rudolf Steiner's explanations of the Ascension, we are familiar with the deeper levels of its meaning that must be understood today. At the Ascension, the apostles see how the Christ vanishes from their view. He had been visible in the phantom body and then He disappears into the clouds. However, the apostles were clairvoyant enough to understand this event and to know what it meant. They saw the effect of His blood as it streamed into the earth; they also felt this effect because they could actually see how hardened the earth had become, how increasingly impossible it had become for people to keep their human, physical bodies alive on earth. Rudolf Steiner describes that this blood flowing into the earth was actually the physical effect of the Christ: '. . . from Jesus of Nazareth He had assumed . . . the three bodies . . . but the blood was completely His own, pulsed through by His spirit, by the fire of His cosmic, universal power of Love.'[18]

The apostles actually saw how the ether bodies of earlier human beings had wanted to flee; they no longer wanted to be connected with this encrusted condition of the earth. These ether bodies would flee towards the sun because they arose out of the Sun epoch of evolution. The sun was the dwelling place of the Christ before He descended to the earth. In the moment of Ascension, through the deed of Christ, the apostles perceived how ether bodies could remain connected with physical bodies; they saw how Christ could keep the ether bodies on the earth. This was something for all of humanity.

At the Whitsun event, with its oft-depicted image of small flames over each head and the outpouring of the Holy Spirit, the possibility arose that humanity could come to understand the Christ event—not all at once, but over the course of eons. This understanding is a consolation for every single human individuality; it is the Paraclete, the Comforter. The apostles were able to experience this at its beginning; it will also continue far into the future as a possibility for humanity.

The World of the Gods in the Old Mysteries and the Spiritual Hierarchies of Esoteric Christianity

Manfred Schmidt-Brabant

We have looked at the brief description by Rudolf Steiner that offers us a picture of the many temples, the many divine images, to be found everywhere throughout the whole Mediterranean region at the turning point of time. We must imagine that a city like Rome now has only the barest remnants of the greater and lesser temples, and the images of the gods that once filled it by the thousands. All these formed a living soul environment for the people of that time.

Rudolf Steiner's description concurs with that of the Neoplatonist Iamblichos, a patriarch of the fourth century who described this world of the gods. Iamblichos was head of an esoteric school and also had deep insights into what had been passed down from the old Mysteries. He identified '474 divine beings of various ranks', which he went on to enumerate. There are '360 divine powers' connected with the head organism of the human being, '72 planetary powers' connected with the chest organism, and '42 earthly powers' connected with what we would refer to today as the metabolism of the human being.

From the many lexicons of mythological and religious history, we can easily determine that Rome alone had 30 to 40 of the most diverse gods and goddesses. It would never have occurred to early Christians to say: 'These gods no longer exist.' Instead, they said something Iamblichos also said: 'These peoples all have different gods simply because one group of them selected 12 or 17 from among the 474, another group selected 20 or 25, and perhaps another group three or four, and so on.' Now comes the statement that is crucial to any understanding of the gods of these first centuries: 'And the loftiest, the most eminent of those who ever descended to the earth is the Christ.'[1]

This means that it never occurred to these early Christians to say Isis, Aphrodite, Venus do not exist. Instead—at least in the first centuries—they said that the heaven of the gods is quite diverse and from this heaven of the gods, people choose those deities appropriate for them, those suited to them. But, of course, according to the early Christians, the Christ-being reigned over all the others.

It was well known to the early Christians—we know this from their writings—that the Christ was recognized by other names in the early Mystery religions. Rudolf Steiner always pointed out that Osiris was actually the image of Christ as experienced in the Egyptian Mysteries; Ahura Mazda reflected the image of Christ in the Persian Mysteries.

People had very concrete ideas about these gods in the old Mysteries, ideas that presented the families of the gods and their destinies from a human perspective. In our materialistic age it easy to say: 'They had an anthropomorphic idea of the gods; they thought of them as being like humans.' It would be easy to conclude that the ancients thought: 'The gods are people like us— shaped like us, just a little bigger, a bit more powerful.' The fact is, exactly the opposite was true. People felt themselves to be like the gods. They said: 'The gods are actually the primal image of what we are, in reflection, here on the earth.' People experienced themselves as children of the gods, as born from the gods, as formed by the gods.

I am reminded here of Rudolf Steiner's description of the experiences people underwent when they were baptized by John: 'There is a spiritual world; my ego—I, as a human being—is a part of this spiritual world, this world of the gods.' Thus the form the ancient representations of the gods took was entirely the result of personal, supersensible experience. The depiction of these gods as either masculine or feminine was a part of this. At that time, people still had a primal sense for the cosmic qualities of masculine and feminine. People knew that a goddess might be said to have a different cosmic function than a god.

A number of years ago, Virginia Sease and I offered a course of lectures in Chartres about the nature of the divine feminine; they were later published as a small book entitled *The Archetypal Feminine in the Mystery Stream of Humanity, Towards a New Culture of the Family*.[2] We pointed out how Rudolf Steiner speaks with extraordinary love and intensity about the 'goddess Natura', 'one of the great feminine figures still present today'[3]; how he speaks about 'Mother Earth' as one of the feminine goddesses; and, in one of the most interesting passages, how he even speaks of the feminine character of the Holy Spirit. This theme arises repeatedly in theology, and there are certain books—especially in more modern times—which assert that femininity is actually among the attributes of the Holy Spirit. Some go so far as to say that the Holy Spirit is feminine. Rudolf Steiner confirms this, and adds how unfortunate it is today that we have lost all that was still known in ancient times.

Thus, each and every thing a person did in the milieu of the Mysteries at the turning point of time was connected with the gods. We remember from Rudolf Steiner's description of how temples with their statues of the gods were everywhere, and how a person felt magically connected in the course of his daily work with the activity of the divine through these temples and statues of the gods. A real blessing went out from such an altar—a real, magical effect. Today we can hardly imagine how natural it seemed at that time that the affairs of life were always accompanied by divine forces, by actual divine beings.

When we hear the word *Securitas* today we might think of the German insurance company. But in Rome, Securitas was the goddess of safety. A person would commend himself to Securitas, for example, by making sacrifices to her in order to assure his safety on a trip. Today, virtually no one sends off a little prayer to Securitas when he leaves his home and locks the door behind him. But she is still there; these gods and goddesses have not disappeared. Hygieia was the goddess of health; people turned to her whenever they fell ill, and they brought all their concerns about sickness and health to her. We are familiar with her now only through the word *hygiene*, the abstract concept. But this was how all of human life at that time was accompanied by the many divinities and gods. Or, to put it another way, the human being knew he was guided and protected by a world of gods that reached down into the world of human beings.

All of this sank from view in the culture at large. Not only did it sink below the surface, attempts were made to destroy it. However, it continued to exist below the surface into the Middle Ages. It can even be identified well into the modern age, in everything we refer to—in a positive way—as 'heathen custom', or, not so positively, as 'superstition'. One of the great twentieth-century German researchers of culture, Hanns Bächtold Stäubli, published an enormous work in ten volumes, *Das Handwörterbuch des deutschen Aberglaubens* [The concise dictionary of German superstition].[4] It is a vast, lexicon-like tome, with more than nine hundred pages per volume, and thousands upon thousands of entries on the connections between life and its elemental and spiritual background—about birth and death, the course of the day and year, house and home, plants and animals, the weather and the skies. And it only covers German superstition. Similar tomes on French, Italian and other superstitions could also be written.

Of course, the reasons for these superstitions are no longer understood today; for example when a black cat crosses your path—from left to right it is a bad thing but from right to left it is all right—or the use of the word 'abracadabra'. The Church also absorbed many of them into its practices. The ritual observances in the fields, the consecration of the plants and the like, arise from this Old Mystery wisdom. Two or three centuries ago, people still experienced a substantive presence behind the practice of a farmer's wife placing a little bowl of milk in the hallway for the good spirit of the house. She did this out of the genuine feeling: 'There truly are beings around us, lower spiritual beings, and we have to be on friendly terms with them.' This could be found in the soul life of many rural people well into the nineteenth century. Today, it has more or less died out and with good reason. Nonetheless, new paths to the world of these beings must be found.

The multitude of gods described by Iamblichos has a background in evolutionary history. If we go back in the evolution of humanity, we arrive at a time when early humanity—here we are speaking of the Lemurian epoch—was endowed by the spiritual world with individuality, with ego. This was the time described in the Bible through the great pictorial imagination that God 'breathed the living breath' into the human being.[5] God's breath is the image of the human being developed beyond a primitive stage of humanity—not merely a clod of earth, but a being endowed with individuality.

During this early time, the coexistence of the gods and humanity was self-evident. People were of one mind—they felt themselves to be part of the world of the gods. The whole earth was a single Mystery-being; nothing else existed. A 'Mystery' is always defined as the dealings between human beings and the gods, between the gods and human beings, as the reciprocal interchange between the spiritual world and the physical world. At that time, this interactivity was far-reaching and unstructured. We can say that the whole earth was a single Mystery continent.

A great epoch then followed which we traditionally call the 'Atlantean age'. It lasted for a long, long time during which the primal existence of the Mysteries was divided into realms classified according to the planets. There were Venus Mysteries, Mars Mysteries, Jupiter Mysteries, Sun Mysteries. It was not a matter of a whole continent; now there were regions—large regions—each governed by only one kind of Mystery. This can still be investigated in the history of the Mysteries. For example, the entire southern region of Spain was the domain of the Venus Mysteries. Jupiter Mysteries encompassed the whole region of northern Spain. There is much in the history of folk groups—in Spain, for example—that can be understood through the effects left by large Mystery regions of this kind.

Then came the post-Atlanean period, which was actually the first time folk groups and cultures were differentiated. Diverse peoples and cultures arose, along with a vastly more complex structuring of the whole character of the Mysteries. There were no longer regions, but towns centred on the temples, temple districts, that served particular Mysteries. A mighty process of individuation was necessary so that human beings who undergo repeated earth lives could always experience something new and different. If the whole of humanity had remained homogeneous, people would have been immersed again and again in the same relationships, and there would have been no opportunity for the ego to develop itself. But with this great individuation of peoples and cultures a diversity arose that still exists today; a person goes from one earth life to another, entering into another culture, another race, and often another religion. As a result, over and over again, he acquires something new for his individuality with each successive life.

It was during this individuation of peoples and cultures—and, thus, of the Mysteries—that the individuation described by Iamblichos took place. Now the distinct character of each culture formed the basis for its access to the world of the gods. Each culture chose from the abundance of what was available to it and selected what was appropriate. In fact, the inverse also took place—this individuation into folk groups and cultures came under the leadership of particular gods. The gods involved in the development of the cultures in the areas around North Africa or Scandinavia were different from those that played a role when the Persian people developed their culture.

An enormous diversity arose in this way, but in another way as well. At that time, human beings looked up to certain divine beings. They took on certain aspects of this divine being in their culture, in their unique physical traits, as well as in the language and customs that gradually developed. Another folk group might take up different aspects of the same divine being, so there were similarities as well as differences. The Romans looked up to a goddess and called her Venus; the Greeks looked up to different qualities of the same goddess, and they called her Aphrodite. The Egyptians looked to this same goddess from a completely different perspective and called her Hathor; and in Christian esotericism, we refer to this being as the archangel of Venus and call him Anael. Gender is another aspect of this diversity. We need to deal with these differences in an appropriately flexible way and understand them. Rudolf Steiner was once discussing something along similar lines and told the following joke. One person says about another, 'He is a vegetarian.' Someone else says, 'No, you are wrong. I know him, and he is a postman!' What Rudolf Steiner means is that we can experience different aspects of people; this was even more the case with the gods. People experienced different aspects of the gods.

This continued into the first centuries—at least in the West, in the Mediterranean region we are discussing—and then it faded away. Later, we will see why this happened. Now a turning point approaches that will become quite significant. Through the growing influence of the Christ impulse, a unity arises once more in the world of the gods. The world of the gods had become fragmented; we think here of the many gods in the Nordic Mysteries, in the Celtic Mysteries, and so on. Iamblichos and his contemporaries experienced the Christ as the Lord of the Powers of Heaven—and this will come to have an ever greater effect.

In the period of the old Mysteries, gods and the secrets of the Mysteries move from one culture into another. We know of stories in which gods are stolen, so to speak where the people of one city in Mesopotamia steal the statue of the goddess from the temple of another city and take it home with the feeling: 'Now the goddess is here with us.' Naturally, it is easy for a modern person to say: 'What a hare-brained superstition. If a god even exists, what does it have to do with a statue?' But a magical connection existed then; people felt there was something real connected with possessing the statue. By way of this statue, something like an invocation is sent to the divine being and, as result, the divinity was inclined to descend and work in the place where its statue stood.

One such grandiose, world-historic event played itself out in pre-history. We have already looked at the figure of Moses, a great spirit. In his previous incarnations he had been the pupil of the great Zarathustra whom we can call the great Sun-initiate. At a certain point in his development, Zarathustra acquired the capacity to give away his ether body and astral body to two of his most important pupils. He gave his ether body and the secrets of time to Moses; and he gave his astral body along with the secrets of space to the founder of the Egyptian initiation, Hermes. According to Rudolf Steiner, all of Zarathustra's wisdom, along with knowledge of all the older Mysteries, lived in Moses. Through them, Moses was initiated into many Mysteries; above all, he was deeply initiated into the Egyptian Mysteries. Destiny had led him to Egypt. He grew up in the temples there, and he was one of the highest initiates of Egypt. Now something came to pass that completely changed the whole situation in the Middle East. When Moses and his people left Egypt, he took many significant secrets of the Mysteries with him—most importantly, the secret of the Cosmic Word.

We must linger here a moment. With our modern intellectual understanding, we could easily say: 'What does it mean that Moses had learned something that he later took with him?' Realities still lived at that time in imaginative forms within the human being. By taking these secrets with him, Moses deprived the Egyptians of all knowledge of them. This is such a deep disruption that Isis—a being we have not yet spoken about—remains behind as a grieving widow because the Cosmic Word was taken from her. With such events as this, we must, of course, avoid all emotions based in modern-day, middle-class morality. We should not conclude that what Moses did is outrageous, or that he was a guest in Egypt and took everything from them. These are immense changes at the level of world and spiritual history. According to Rudolf Steiner, this resulted in the initiation secrets of that whole area being brought to the Jewish people by Moses.

When we speak about the organism of the history of the Mysteries, about 'God's plan for salvation', we should not forget that the gods—or God—were involved with the preparation of this whole lineage of the blood and the tribe; they took part in the preparation of the Hebrew people for the incarnation of the Christ. What takes place within the Hebrew people is part of the preparation for the Mystery of Golgotha. All the pre-Christian Mysteries are bundled up within the Hebrew people. At the same time, when Moses places the Mysteries within rather than outside the human being he radically changes the whole way the existence of the Mysteries was lived, and an enormous upheaval was set in motion. 'Thou shalt not make thee any graven image, or any likeness of any thing that is in heaven above, or that is in the earth beneath, or that is in the waters beneath the earth . . .'[6] This is the great teaching of Moses in the story of the golden calf—where people seek out the worship of external things. The mission of Moses was to make people aware that the true image of pure divinity lives within the inner ego. This marks the beginning of an age devoid of external images; simultaneously, it was a time that turned to the inmost core of the human being, because only the ego is capable of meeting the Christ.

At the same time, something like a powerful uprising of the old, decadent Mysteries took place. Before the Mystery of Golgotha, into the Middle Ages—and even into modern times—something like a powerful Mystery battle developed in which various forces stand in opposition to one another. There are two prominent streams of anti-Christian forces that already assert themselves in the pre-Christian era, and they are strongly present at the time of the Mystery of Golgotha.

According to Rudolf Steiner, one of these streams misuses ancient primal knowledge of the Mysteries in connection with folk and group egos. It is a wrong use of the folk ego when Mystery knowledge is allowed to benefit a single group. The second stream uses Mystery knowledge for personal, egoistic purposes in the service of the lower ego. This second stream becomes prominent in a city like Babylon. A lofty star wisdom had once existed in Babylonia, but when the Mysteries fell into decadence the priests gradually came to use this star wisdom more and more in the service of demons through magic, conjuring and casting of spells. In short, they placed the pure spiritual wisdom of heaven at the service of personal egoism. Babylon was notorious for this. Thus, John speaks in his Revelation about the 'Whore Babylon' in order to characterize a certain being. The whole earth is Babylon when it behaves as this city did then. A large part of what we objectively call 'black magic' came from Babylon. Black magic is the invocation of spiritual forces in order to serve personal egoism. One of the most difficult tests of conscience we as human beings can undergo comes when we ask ourselves, Might I be doing this? Do I use purely spiritual things for my own gain, for my own pleasure, for my delight, only for myself? Am I selfless, without a sense of egoism when I handle the spiritual content that comes to me?

Two examples of this corruption play a large role in the life of Jesus Christ. The first is the notorious infanticide instigated by Herod the Great. What actually lay behind this? Herod's family was not Jewish, not Hebrew. They were Arabs from Petra, and they had already brought all manner of decadent, depraved cults from there. Thus, Herod the Great was someone who, out of a half-mad obsession with power, performed evil rituals, black magic so that he could attain even greater powers. According to Emil Bock's descriptions, cruel rituals were carried out in which children were murdered, particularly in Bethlehem.[7] The murder of children for magic purposes continued throughout the Middle Ages and into the modern age; we may think of the French Bluebeard, Gilles de Rais, who murdered well over five hundred boys with his own hands in order to gain magical power. These are expressions of completely evil and decadent Mars Mysteries. Thus, behind the image of Herod's infanticide we find one of the great black magic corruptions still active today. The Three Kings arrive at the birth of Jesus, among them a reincarnation of Pythagoras who had been a pupil of Zarathustra. The kings come because they know from their initiation: 'In the infant boy lives our great and revered leader, Zarathustra.' Naively, they explain this to Herod. The angel appears to Joseph, warns him, and he flees with his family to Egypt. The image of this terrible infanticide remains today in the plot of the Christmas play, but the child was not discovered.

A second great corruption is also depicted in the New Testament. Herod Antipas, who lived somewhat later, unlawfully marries his sister-in-law, Herodias. John the Baptist severely criticizes this relationship because it is incompatible with traditional Hebrew law. Herod Antipas has John imprisoned, but does nothing more to harm him because he actually likes John and loves to talk with him. But John is imprisoned because he cannot be permitted to travel freely around the country, constantly complaining about the king. A great birthday celebration for the king takes place, and it happens that Salome, the daughter of Herodias from a first marriage, is to perform a dance. She performs the famous 'Dance of the Seven Veils'. The whole court is so crazed by it—including the king—that the king says: 'Demand of me what you will, even though it may be half my kingdom!' Salome goes to her mother and asks: 'What shall I ask?' Her mother says: 'Demand the head of John the Baptist!' Salome returns and says to the king: 'I demand the head of John the Baptist.' The king had given his word before the whole court, and could not go back on it. So John the Baptist was beheaded, and his head was carried in on a silver salver. Rudolf Steiner says that this is actually the counter-symbol of the Grail.[8]

Why would a whole court become crazed? And why would a king forget himself completely and promise everything? Certainly not because a scantily clad young woman was running around. At that time, in this climate, such undress was customary. All this happened because Salome performed a magic-sexual ritual that was another thread in these evil Mysteries. The 'Dance of the Seven Veils' is nothing other than the magic-sexual depiction of the seven indecencies of woman. These decadent Venus Mysteries exerted their power at that time, just as they do today. Fate punished Salome afterwards. She falls through a frozen lake, and the ice floes cut her head off.[9] But the consequences of what Herod the Great did with his murderous rituals, and the consequences of Salome's actions as a perhaps unconscious tool are still being felt right into the present time. We still stand in the midst of the history of the Mysteries. Nothing is in the past; all this is still taking place.

Then comes the next step. Here we must look at a person who is often somewhat misunderstood—Caesar, Gaius Julius Caesar. He is known as a great general. Many of us who learned Latin in school had to struggle with his *De bello Gallico*, but other aspects of his life are rarely considered. Caesar was the *pontifex maximus*, the highest priest in Rome—no small matter. The office was a reality, not merely an honorary title. Caesar stood fully in a Mystery reality and represented a quite specific aim in regard to the Mysteries as a whole. Only the commonwealth of Rome is to exist; all other Mysteries should be destroyed. As a result, by conscious order of Caesar, one of the most significant Mystery sites in Europe was destroyed. This was the Mystery site in France located in a place then known as Alesia, today as Alise-Sainte-Reine. An enormous hill, it is situated about 35 miles west of Dijon. The most important Mystery academy in Europe was located there. Thousands of people came from all parts of Europe to study Mystery knowledge, the primal knowledge of that time. This place was levelled by Caesar. Rudolf Steiner says: 'Over the course of just a few days, hundreds and hundreds of initiates were rushed from life into death' and, as a result, 'a wonderful, vital knowledge ... completely disappears from Europe.'[10]

The hill at Alesia can still be visited; it is a great, rounded mountainside with meadows. We can imagine how dozens, even hundreds, of homes, little temples, temple buildings of Celtic design, stood there. And we can imagine further how there had been a university town on this mountain, connected to the Mysteries.

What came from Caesar's doctrine was the conviction that only the Roman way of life should exist and nothing else. This is reflected in something Rudolf Steiner says. During this time, there were Mystery schools and initiates everywhere—in Greece, Egypt, the Near East; however, there were none in the Roman world. 'An abstract spirit had entered the Roman world ... [a spirit] that no longer [understood] ... the value of personality ... the value of what is essential; [it was] a spirit of conceptual abstraction.' Another school that would have a most fateful effect emerged from the milieu of this time and built itself up slowly from the fourth century on. It was a school which took up the battle against the whole ancient initiation principle, the battle against the initiation of the individual human being. It wanted to 'immortalize ... the Roman way'; 'the historic tradition' should enter in place of the individual.[11] A 'collegium' was created '... as heir to the Roman *Collegium Pontificum*'.[12] We arrive at this collegium, one might say, along a straight path. I have touched on Caesar. There were also others before him, but Caesar is the most serious destroyer; it begins with him. We see this continue in a collegium that must be described as working purely through black magic.

It continues to be active into the time of the Grail, when we find it located in Capua, the home of the infamous 'citizens of Capua'. It is difficult to determine whether this collegium was already meeting in Capua during the fourth century. Initiation science was eradicated, particularly in the Roman world; only knowledge of the outer, physical world was to remain.[13]

Here we are looking at the beginning of an evolution into which Christianity enters. The individual practice of Christianity and official church Christianity developed in this sphere. This is a time in which Christianity itself engaged in an extraordinary battle as well as in extraordinary disputes.

Rudolf Steiner depicts the world of many small temples and many priests, and shows how everything in this world is eventually destroyed—a process of grandiose proportions! He says: 'The Roman Caesars, in collaboration with the bishops and priests, took it upon themselves during these centuries ... to destroy these temples and shrines completely. During these centuries, an enormous wave of destruction washed across the world, a wave of destruction that is unique in the whole evolution of humanity: unique because of *what* was destroyed.'[14]

Thus, the old world of the Mysteries comes to an end in these centuries, and finally disappears when Christianity emerges as the state religion. What continue are small streams we refer to as esoteric Christianity. This esoteric Christianity can be traced back to two great and revered figures in our history, Paul and Dionysius the Areopagite.

Paul was born in Tarsus in AD 10; he was called both Saul and Paul from the time he was a boy. Paul was his name as a Roman citizen; Saul was the Hebrew name given by his Jewish family under Roman civil law. He was initiated in the two great and most crucial Mysteries of that time—the Greek Mysteries and the Hebrew Mysteries. Through this initiation he knew about the anticipation of a Messiah in the Mysteries. He also knew about the reason for the anticipation as well as about something that concerned all initiates—the corruption of the phantom. He was clairvoyant; he saw that the structure of human corporeality was crumbling. Humanity would not be able to develop further if the Messiah did not come.

The Sanhedrin commissions Paul to persecute this funny little sect that called themselves Christians and claimed the Messiah had been among them. He is on his way to persecute this group and undergoes the great experience outside Damascus which we connect with Paul. We generally refer to this as the Damascus experience and view it as something that is to be repeated later in individual human beings—in fact, something to be repeated more and more in humanity.

Paul reported something of his experience in his Epistles: 'I knew,' he says in the Second Epistle to the Corinthians, 'a man in Christ above 14 years ago, (whether in the body, I cannot tell; or whether out of the body, I cannot tell: God knoweth) such a one caught up to the third heaven. And I knew such a man ... How that he was caught up in paradise and heard unspeakable words, which it is not lawful for a man to utter.'[15]

What did Paul experience outside Damascus? He perceives something that, until then, had not existed, that had not even been possible in fact; he perceives the appearance of the Christ-being in the etheric realm. He experiences directly the meaning of the Ascension; from the earth, Christ had poured Himself into the whole ether aura of the earth. Had we observed the earth from the outside at that time as other beings experienced it, we would have seen that the aura of the earth was grey and black until the Mystery of Golgotha. After the Ascension, the aura of the earth began to light up in rainbow colours, like the rainbow colours of the future, perhaps like the colours we see in the image of the Resurrection in the Isenheim altar in Colmar. The image in the Colmar altar is a representation of the ether aura as it was experienced by Paul. But Paul sees more. He sees the restored phantom. He sees that something had happened that restored the physical body right to its very foundations. What does he actually see?

In the spirit there are no spacial dimensions. We cannot look into some kind of spiritual space and find the angels sitting there playing music—although it can be painted that way. Instead, a spiritual gaze is always directed into time, into the third heaven, back to the beginning of evolution when the hierarchies were beginning to create the physical body.[16] What Paul sees is how the hierarchies work to create the physical body; how the physical body is changed when the ether body is added to it; how the astral body is added to it; how, through many stages, it is built up further by various beings. He sees that all this is newly developed through the Mystery of Golgotha. He recognizes—we might better say, he knows—that he is looking at the Christ and is experiencing Him.

Now, on a journey to Athens, Paul meets a great and powerful personality, Dionysius the Areopagite. The Areopagus was a lofty part of the Greek polis as well as of Greek custom and culture; it was a small, select circle of men initiated in the Greek Mysteries. This Dionysius was the most eminent of them. Based on his insight, he immediately becomes a pupil and comrade of Paul. Everything Paul saw—the whole course of

evolution, the creative activity of the hierarchies—is passed on to
Dionysius the Aeropagite. Paul's vision, his capacity to perceive the
hierarchies, prompts the same vision in Dionysius. He becomes the great
founder of the Christian doctrine of the hierarchies as it still exists today in
anthroposophy.

We also speak of a Pseudo-Dionysius because the extant written
documents that give evidence of such a person date to the sixth century,
around 515. This can be proven philologically. But, of course, this cannot
be the same Dionysius mentioned in the New Testament. Rudolf Steiner
says that the secret knowledge in all esoteric schools was passed along by
word of mouth. Only at the end of a specific epoch were the contents
written down and made public. For this reason, Rudolf Steiner attributes
the doctrine of the hierarchies to the real Dionysius the Areopagite, of
whom he always speaks with the greatest respect. Rudolf Steiner also says
that all of modern spiritual science actually began at that time in the
esoteric school of Dionysius the Areopagite.[17]

This doctrine of the hierarchies is an entirely new ordering of the old,
chaotic world of the gods; it is a trinitarian ordering of the world of the
angels. The gods are presented in three times three hierarchies.

Rudolf Steiner included gods like Thor, Zeus or Apollo in these ranks.
The angels, the archangels of the folk groups, the archai responsible for
cultures, are the lowest ranks. The middle realm is comprised of the spirits
of form—the exusiai. Further on, are those beings related to all of the
forces in the cosmos, the dynamis; and then there are the spirits of wisdom
that penetrate everything. The highest hierarchy—at the very apex—is
the seraphim. It is said the seraphim receive everything from the Trinity
that can be called the plan for salvation, what evolution should be. Then
there are the cherubim, who disseminate the meaning of this plan, and the
thrones, who provide not only the physical substance of the world but all
substance.

With this, a totally new element of consciousness appears in humanity's
relationship to the gods. The individual human being now becomes
capable of comprehending order in the world of the gods; he becomes
capable of observing how wondrous changes occur. I spoke earlier about
the terrible destruction of the Celtic Mysteries in Alesia. This destruction
of Alesia was what broke the back, so to speak, of the Celtic peoples; in
fact, they gradually ceased to exist as a folk group after Alesia was
destroyed. They disappeared into other tribes, mixed in with the Ger-
mans; the folk group dissolved away. And the folk spirit of the Celts was
freed. This Celtic folk spirit became the guiding 'spirit of esoteric

Christianity'.[18] After the time of the Mystery of Golgotha, this archangel who had led the Celtic people becomes free and carries forward the ever-widening stream that is connected with the consequences of the Mystery of Golgotha.

These consequences of the Mystery of Golgotha take many forms. As Rudolf Steiner depicts it, many of the gods submitted themselves to the guidance of the Christ. The spiritual leadership of humanity submitted itself to the guidance of the Christ. In pre-Christian times there were beings who taught the chosen individualities in the temples the knowledge these beings themselves had brought with them from earlier planetary conditions. Now these beings submitted themselves to the guidance of the Christ. The spiritual leadership of humanity within the great centres submitted itself to the leadership of the Christ. Everything that had endured up to the time of the Mystery of Golgotha turns now to the Christ, submits itself to Him, recognizes Him. During the following centuries, the Christ passes through the Mysteries that still exist, and He reforms them in the sense of the Mystery of Golgotha. All that we experience as the building stones of esoteric Christianity—the Grail, the Templars, the Rosicrucians, many other great streams, the great orders, the great saints—are a result of the fact that the Christ gradually transformed the old Mystery knowledge, re-formed it, as Rudolf Steiner said.

A new spiritual order in the world of the gods was created through the hierarchies—this was a reality. At the same time, a change took place in the whole nature of the Trinity through the Mystery of Golgotha. Rudolf Steiner once said: 'That is why I must always say to you: the Trinity is actually situated above the hierarchies. But it reached that point only in the course of evolution.'[19] The whole Mystery of Golgotha altered the inner structure of the Trinity because, until then, no god had known death. In the divine, in the spiritual world, there is only change, transformation; death does not exist in these realms. Nevertheless, we look upwards to a primal divine being, to a 'spiritual' being above the hierarchies, whose nature, according to Rudolf Steiner, is of such 'sublimity' that 'the human capacity for comprehension is insufficient to grasp it.'[20] There is a primal divine being in the infinite depths of cosmic existence, a divine cosmic foundation, a primal self, that reveals itself in the Trinity, in the three means of revelation. In the Credo of the Christian Community given by Rudolf Steiner, there is a delicate sense that this being is in motion. The Credo says: 'An almighty divine being, spiritual-physical, is the ground of existence of the heavens and of the earth who goes before his creatures like a father.'[21] This is not the description of a resting, dead, static divinity, but a divinity who 'goes before his creatures like a father'.

During the last two thousand years, people have not only puzzled over the Christ-being, but over everything related to the Trinity. Rudolf Steiner says that the Father God lives in the blood; He leads human beings into material life. The Son God lives in the soul-spiritual realm; He leads human beings back out of material life. A third being, the Holy Spirit, is in a lofty position above birth and death; it emerges from the first two, and is connected equally to both the divine Father and the divine Son. Thus when we say *Ex Deo nascimur*, we understand: the transition from the supersensible to the sensory. When we say *In Christo morimur*, we understand: the transition from the sensory to the supersensible. And when we say *Per Spiritum Sanctum reviviscimus,* we understand: the uniting of both, the combination in which birth and death no longer exist, the resurrection through the spirit.

Over the course of the first millennium, there was an argument concerning the inner structure of this Trinity. The question was, 'Does the Holy Spirit proceed only from the Father or does it also come from the Son?' This is the famous *Filioque* debate: *filio que* means 'and of the Son'. The great schism in the Church precipitated by this question occurred around the year 1000. The Eastern Church, the Orthodox Church, decided: 'The Holy Spirit proceeds only from the Father.' The Western Church said: 'The Holy Spirit proceeds from the Father and the Son.'

What are the consequences of the Holy Spirit proceeding only from the Father? Everything spiritual in the human being becomes a matter of the blood, of material existence, of those very things into which the Father leads human beings. Only when the Holy Spirit also proceeds from the Son can the human being lift himself out of the blood ties and into his own individual existence again.

We live today in a time when the deification of the blood still plays a powerful role. I will not go into details here and will certainly not take sides; but when we look at how the principle of nationalities—the principle of the blood (between the Serbs, the Albanians, and others)—has played a murderous role, we can begin to grasp how world history is a result of the schism that arose in 1000. This is just one event that came in answer to the question 'Is the spiritual to which I turn a part of the world of the blood and physical matter?' 'Or is the spiritual a part of the world that, through death, leads me again out of blood and physical substance into individual existence?' These are the great conundrums which have placed the Trinity at the centre of a world-historical question.

Something else entered through the Mystery of Golgotha, namely, a structuring of the adversarial forces. As a result, we can now speak of a true middle way which represents the Christ, as well as of a luciferic deviation and an ahrimanic deviation. These beings already existed—Lucifer was there on Old Sun, Ahriman in ancient Persia. But their current role became possible when a middle way was created for human beings by the Christ. The middle way is the balance between spirit and matter, between the gods and human beings, between heaven and earth; it is the way that befits human beings and the gods. We can experience one great deviation—which we call luciferic—when this balance is left behind and the earth is forsaken, despised, because human beings want to rise above it. The other great deviation—the ahrimanic—is found when the spirit is forsaken; human beings turn only to the earth and live only in earthly things. For each category of the hierarchies there is a luciferic and an ahrimanic deviation. It is a split that goes through the entire world of the hierarchies. On every level of the hierarchies there are spirits with leanings towards the ahrimanic and those with leanings towards the luciferic. The Christ is always the middle way.

It is important in this discussion of the hierarchies to see that everything about them is in motion. If we observe the hierarchies throughout evolution, we see how angels rose to become archangels, and how archangels rose to become archai. It is not a rigid system, but a living condition of change. Humanity is placed into this living change so that it can become a tenth hierarchy through its own efforts. We are to join ourselves to the nine hierarchies and become a tenth hierarchy. We are not yet a hierarchy; the hierarchies are above us. We are the world of earthly human beings; but this world of earthly human beings can develop into the spiritual world as a tenth hierarchy. How is this possible?

This is the great secret of evolution that comes to us through the Mystery of Golgotha, through the Whitsun event, through the spirit of freedom and the spirit of love. It comes to us not only through freedom and love, but through human beings who develop themselves so they are able to comprehend the spirit of freedom and the spirit of love.

Isis Sophia is divine wisdom, is divine spirit. Human beings should and will turn to this divine spirit when they develop what is truly the spirit of freedom and of love.

Lecture 7

The Development of Conscience in Pre-Christian Times and Since the Mystery of Golgotha

Virginia Sease

Questions are often asked about what people felt in centuries past. Such questions seem natural today; but this would not have been asked in earlier times. For hundreds of years it was thought that people had always felt and thought the same way. So the question for us is: Is this really the truth? Alternatively, we can put the question this way: What did people in ancient Rome actually think and feel when they arranged to throw Christians to the lions? Did they feel anything? This is not only a valid question historically, but one that has been particularly relevant during recent decades: How did this manifest in the twentieth century? Did people have feelings or pangs of conscience when, as modern human beings, they committed atrocities? What, if anything, do they feel when they commit atrocities even today?

Rudolf Steiner points out how the human being changes over the course of time, how human qualities—even soul qualities—change. This fact is an essential background for understanding the question of how people in earlier times felt and thought. Soul qualities have missions. When we look at conscience as a quality of soul, we need to take seriously that it has undergone transformations, and that it has a significant mission for the past, the present and the future.

The phenomenon of conscience—which is closely connected to the Christ—was already present as a predisposition before there was a word to describe it. We have discussed in these lectures how humanity has undergone various stages and levels of soul development and how, on the whole, virtually everyone alive today is situated in the age of the consciousness soul. There are still some people who live secluded lives, who have not experienced the superficialities of our epoch— who, for example, would not know what to do with a can opener if they were given one. This, however, is not a cultural aspect of the consciousness soul epoch; it belongs, we might say, to some particular civilization. Generally speaking, all human beings—their actual soul development aside—are members of the civilization of the conscious-ness soul age.

Nonetheless, even today, some languages still have no word for con-science. Manfred Schmidt-Brabant and I had a remarkable experience of this in Japan. When you give a lecture there, you say a few sentences and then pause for the translation into Japanese. In the course of his lecture, Manfred Schmidt-Brabant made a brief statement like: 'Conscience is an important soul quality.' Then the translation began—it took a very long time and there seemed to be no end to it. This came up in the discussion that followed. 'Why,' we asked, 'did the translation of this little sentence take so long?' We learned that the Japanese language has no expression for this word 'conscience'. They had been puzzling over what this word could mean. Then Manfred Schmidt-Brabant said: 'Let me give you an example. You are alone in a room, and on the wall is a wonderful cal-ligraphy by a Japanese master. Somehow, you do something that destroys this work of art. What do you think and feel when you see what you have done?' There was great consternation. Finally, there was general con-sensus, and an answer was offered. They hoped no one would have seen the person doing this. Of course, the qualities of conscience exist in Japan, with individual variations; and conscience exists as an idea or soul quality. But there seems to be no word for it.

How conscience finds expression through language is not always as clear, as in the case of Japanese. Even in Romance languages, something has to be added to the word *conscientia* so that the difference between conscience and consciousness is somehow described. The words are distinguished by adding an attribute. It is not by coincidence that this word first surfaces in Old High German as *giwizzani*. This is noted in a glossary by Notker Teutonicus (950–1022). During the Old High Ger-man period, Notker Teutonicus collected so many words and their etymologies that it is possible to recognize in his work a spiritual history through the German language. In Old English and Middle English, the word for conscience, *inwit*, means 'knowledge within'.

We see how a general meaning for the word 'conscience' emerges over the course of centuries. We also know how the popular opinion of a word is coined and formed by luciferic beings at a lower level of development. The formulation, 'It is said . . .' indicates the general meaning as popular opinion, coined by these beings.

Two hundred years ago, Arthur Schopenhauer noted something amiss in the way conscience is most often interpreted. He writes: 'People of all religious faiths often understand conscience only as the dogmas and precepts of their own religion ... Their conscience consists of everything they know about the statutes and teachings of their church, together with the precept that they should believe and follow all of it.[1] And the case could be made that this is still true today.

The workers at the Goetheanum once asked Rudolf Steiner: 'What is conscience actually?' Rudolf Steiner described how the German word *Gewissen* [conscience] is related to *gewiß sein* [to be certain], and said that conscience is really the greatest certainty that can live in the human soul. However, the words *conscience* or *conscientia* approach the question from another side linguistically. They mean 'what is known together', *con scientia*, thus the words contain the meaning: an aggregate of earthly knowledge.[2] This is a rather different interpretation of the word.

According to Rudolf Steiner, conscience is a quality which is not born and does not die. It is something noble in the human being, deeply connected to the Christ Mystery. Human beings must go through various incarnations before they begin to have a feeling of conscience. Rudolf Steiner also describes how humanity is made up of young souls and old souls. No value judgement is implied in these designations. Being an old soul is not better than being a young soul; being fresh and new is not better than being old and tired. No difference in value is implied. We are to understand from this only that old souls have been on earth more often than younger ones and have had many incarnations. Thus, in a larger cosmic context old souls have more incarnations, young souls fewer.

The development of conscience is by no means complete. It exists in an almost latent state as a soul quality within us, but we can still experience it; with time, it will be experienced more and more. Thus the question of conscience is part of any discussion about the evolution of humanity.

Nature, as we know, progresses in leaps and bounds; its development is not constant. Natural occurrences can surprise us if we think things are supposed to go from A to B, then on to C, then to D, and so forth. The nature of human soul development is the same. Research shows that a drastic change took place in the Greek period during the fifth century before the turning point of time, during the very brief time between Aeschylus and Euripides. When Aeschylus died (456 BC), Euripides was 24 years old. I mention this to show they were almost contemporaries. Both were playwrights and both dealt with similar material. But there is a vast difference in the way they handled this material.

In Aeschylus' play about the familiar story of Orestes, Agamemnon returns home after the Trojan War and is murdered by his wife, Clytemnestra, who had not expected him to return. His son, Orestes, then avenges his father's murder by killing his mother, Clytemnestra. We could say Orestes had been advised to carry out this act of revenge; he thought the advice came from the divine world, from Apollo. But in the second part of the drama Orestes experiences clairvoyantly how his deed has a further consequence; as so often happened in the ancient Greek tragedies, he experiences the onslaught of the goddesses of wrath, the Erinyes, known in Roman times as the Furies. He experiences their wrath. Even though he had taken revenge under the guidance of Apollo, he also experiences the existence of a higher world order. The goddesses of wrath come at him out of this higher world order.

The course of events is different in Euripides. He also writes about Orestes, but there is no longer any mention of the Erinyes. Instead he writes about an inner power—something has shifted inwards. Euripides does not call it conscience, but he speaks of this shift. What has happened here?

In the brief time between the writing of these plays, the human being had become capable of experiencing the centre of his being more in his own ego. With the advent of the intellectual soul, he notices that his ego places him in himself. As a result, he is distanced from the influences the natural world has on him. In Greek mythology, especially in the most ancient myths, the transformational qualities of the spiritual world are also manifested. For example, when an evil deed has been transformed into a good deed it is not the goddesses of revenge who appear, but the Eumenides, the good goddesses.

In the course of time—we are now speaking about the third epoch— we find souls living together at various developmental levels. We think of the many high cultures of the third epoch—the Egyptians, the Chaldeans, the Babylonians, the temple cultures. We think, for example, of the artefacts from these cultures on view in the Louvre, art objects created with refinement and delicacy—jewellery, sarcophagi painted with thousands of images—and we recall the pyramids and the temple buildings, and so on.

In these things we can see how deep the influence of the sentient soul was. The human being perceived what was in the outer world, and then developed his own capacities—refined coordination of his hands and fingers—in order to shape it. This is true in the case of music, as well. Because of their direct effect on the human soul, music and the development of the various tonal modes had long been under the guidance of the highest teachers in the Mysteries. These teachers knew that care had to be exercised in the creation of tone intervals because other soul forces might accidentally be activated. And the punishment for playing a forbidden musical interval was death.

The situation in northern Europe is entirely different. We cannot speak about a northern culture during the period of the sentient soul culture in the same way we speak of its offshoots in the south. This is true even up to the turning point of time or into the centuries following. Something else was being developed there in an atmosphere protected from the outer influences of these other great cultures. The ego was forcefully developed in the sentient soul; the sentient soul is a very powerful soul. And as this ego in the sentient soul developed in the forests and valleys of northern Europe, it acquired a strong character.

Rudolf Steiner once mentioned how difficult it would be to imagine the incarnation of the Christ taking place in Europe.[3] Why? Because humanity in Europe had evolved the principle of individuality to such a great extent, and had developed a certain equality among people. We think here of the Nordic institution of the Thing (þing) and of self-government. The Christ-being could not have worked in the Nordic culture under these circumstances. But, afterwards, because of the ego development there, Europe had a particularly strong and complete understanding of the Christ as the bringer of ego consciousness, the consciousness of individuality. This was reflected centuries later in the strong development of mysticism in Europe. This mysticism represents an effort to find a direct, individual connection to the Christ.

Christ's appearance was anticipated in the northern countries of Europe even before He had descended into earth evolution; it was predicted clairvoyantly, and was anticipated in the whole of Druid culture. They prepared the ground so that when the missionaries arrived, they found a body of knowledge already present in the souls of the people. Nonetheless, the missionaries did not always have an easy time of it among the Germanic tribes. We recall that knowledge of the old gods and experiences of them remained in the south—in Greece and Rome—even after efforts at Christianization had begun; the same was also true in the north. It is interesting to see how, in the north, the early Christian saints often acquired qualities—or a blend of qualities—from the old Germanic gods, of European Nordic gods. These missionaries even had to develop a different vocabulary.

We can also note here that there is no word for conscience in Old Testament Hebrew. The word did not yet exist. Often the word 'heart'—*Leb*—was used as a kind of surrogate to represent conscience as it began to reveal itself. For example, we find it used when God speaks and the human being is to listen. The soul should hear what God speaks, not as a voice from within, from the interior, but as a voice from without. This outer voice then penetrates inwards.

We can find a harbinger of conscience in the biblical accounts about David. He experienced intimations of conscience when he was still a shepherd boy. This was approximately a thousand years before the turning point of time, thus very early from the standpoint of the development of conscience. We read about this in 1 Samuel 24:5–6. King Saul and David are enemies; Saul and his army advance on David. During the night, David and his followers hide at the back of a cave, and realize that Saul and his men are approaching. From his hiding place, David deftly cuts the corner from Saul's robe. At that moment, David's men see the opportunity he has, and say: 'Now is your chance.' But David does not kill Saul. 'And it came to pass afterwards that David's heart smote him because he had cut off Saul's skirt. And he said unto his men, The Lord forbid that I should do this thing unto my master, the Lord's anointed, to stretch forth mine hand against him, seeing he is the anointed of the Lord.' The next morning, David allows Saul and his men to depart. He emerges from the cave and confronts Saul, shows him the skirt of his robe, and also says that he had intended no harm.

This is an important moment in the development of conscience: something in David held him back. I think it is relevant here that David was a musician. We have heard how the pure Adam-soul was permeated by the Christ to restore order in the developing human bodies—the physical body with its sensory impressions; the ether body with its life organs; and the soul, the astral body—creating a balance among the activities of thinking, feeling and willing. This balance is always represented as Apollo with his lyre; he is the pre-earthly representative for this effect of the Christ. David's soul was balanced enough to resist the entreaties of his men. As a result, he was able to call forth a deeper force within himself that later developed into the force of conscience.

With time, the Christ impulse made it possible to grasp how divinity lives within the human being, how the human being has a drop of the divine in himself, isolated, individualized. Goethe formulates this quite beautifully: 'What the human being reveres as God is his own inner being turned outwards.'[4] Goethe comes very close to articulating this enigma. Christ Himself often invokes the forces of conscience. We read about this in His parables. The story of the adulteress is also particularly revealing. The Pharisees, the scribes, bring her to the Christ; they actually want to set a trap for the Christ to find out what He will do. They try to make an

issue of it, and say: 'According to the law of Moses, she should be stoned.'
What is the Christ's response to that?

Christ 'stooped down', the Bible says, 'and wrote . . . on the ground . . .'
Then He 'lifted up Himself and said . . . He that is without sin among you,
let him first cast a stone at her. And again He stooped down.' He calls for
self-examination, and speaks directly—one might even say simply—to
the forces of conscience in these people. Then the story goes on to
describe how the Pharisees depart, and Christ asks the woman: 'Woman,
where are those thine accusers? hath no man condemned thee? She said,
No man, Lord. And Jesus said unto her, Neither do I condemn thee: go,
and sin no more.'[5]

Rudolf Steiner offers the following commentary on this story.[6] Jesus'
act of writing the deed in the earth has a much broader meaning. It is
connected with the fact that Christ Himself will soon be united with this
earth. When the blood—the most intimate element of the Christ-
being—flows into the earth in the Mystery of Golgotha, He becomes a
part of the earth. And when Christ says the woman should sin no more,
this means for people in general: 'Sin no more; do not sin again!' What is
recorded in the Akasha will be compensated for by the individual through
his own karma. After death—when he sees what he has done—he will
know how to compensate for his actions in his subsequent life. But the
individual does this only in a personal, individual realm, not for the earth
itself. The Christ must rectify these deeds for the earth itself. Someone
who is quite clairvoyant may look into the Akasha, the cosmic memory,
but even that person will not be able to see how this takes place if he is
unable to view it through the Christ impulse. This law is not only
applicable to the period after the Mystery of Golgotha. Christ took up this
compensation as a significant deed for the earth but also for those who had
died in pre-Christian times. This is one level of what it means that Christ
descended into the realm of the dead. He took this on and then bore it
Himself.

All this must be rectified for the whole earth so that the earth can also
continue its progress; so that the earth is not burdened by the misdeeds of
people to such an extent that it is no longer hospitable for human souls; so
that human souls can return again and again in order to continue their
development; so that the earth itself is also in a position to make the
transition to the Jupiter condition.

The early Church Fathers had a concept derived from astronomy. In
astronomy it is called the 'restoration of a temporarily altered constellation
of stars'. These Church Fathers coined the word 'apocatastasis' from this.

Apocatastasis was interpreted—particularly by Clement of Alexandria and his pupil Origen—to mean that an apocalyptic elimination of everything evil will take place in the last days and, through it, a restoration of the creation will occur. Everything will be redeemed and will exist again in its original glory. It will be such a redemption that even the devil will be redeemed; everything will be made whole and good again.[7]

Over time, this conception of the restoration of the good had an enormous effect and became connected with the punishment by fire that the medieval Church later spoke of as *purgatorium*, as the refining fire. This fire will not be eternal; it will be a purifying fire. There is a later reflection of this idea among the Cathars in the thirteenth century who, facing the flames at the stake, went singing to their deaths because they believed: This fire is transitory; through this fire, everything impure in our souls will be burned away.

In Origen, this punishment by fire includes the pain experienced through a person's conscience. Here Origen—and Clement of Alexandria—refer to Paul, especially 1 Corinthians 3, where Paul says that the works of every man will be tested by fire. It will burn with what each has brought with him—'gold, silver, precious stones, wood, hay, stubble'. This is a doctrine of universal reconciliation.

Origen presents his thoughts in old images. Heinz Kittsteiner describes how Origen compares the fire with processes in the human organism. If a person were to eat something that is spoiled, this spoiled food will be burnt and eliminated by the fire that burns inside, by the inner fuel.[8] It is the same when reason becomes pathological. The pathology is burned away by conscience. Conscience and fire are connected by Origen, and his interpretation then lives on into later times.

In the Middle Ages, Thomas Aquinas took up the question of the inner power of conscience in his *Summa Theologica*. What is important for our discussion is that he already points to a completely different, expanded dimension of conscience: 'Properly speaking, conscience is not a power but an activity. This can be observed in the name as well as from what is ascribed to conscience in the vernacular. In the real sense of the word, "conscience" means the relation of knowledge to something specific.'[9] Thomas Aquinas' reference to conscience not as a power but as an activity is quite far-sighted.

However, since the Middle Ages the Roman Church has always dealt with conscience as a powerful force. This found its way into Church doctrine to such an extent that Pope Pius IX issued an encyclical in 1864, *Quanta cura*, that said it would be an error—the encyclical actually cites

Gregory XVI who referred to such thinking as 'insanity'—to think individual conscience is a civil right and, therefore, free.[10] That is a powerful statement on the part of the Church! Why did this statement appear shortly after the middle of the nineteenth century? At that time, just before the beginning of the Michael Age, people had begun to ask: 'What is the nature of conscience? Is the human being not the master of his own conscience? Will he have to give an accounting for his conscience to some higher authority?' *Quanta cura* was the response of the Roman Church.

One image for conscience that has a continuing presence throughout the millennia—even into the eighteenth century—has been handed down since earliest times, especially in the Hebrew tradition. We think here of Yahweh and the depiction of how Yahweh's strength was experienced by Elijah during the storm, the thunderstorm. The Lord commands Elijah to go forth and promises him that He will pass by: '. . . and a great and strong wind rent the mountains, and brake the rocks before the Lord; but the Lord was not in the wind: and after the wind was an earthquake; but the Lord was not in the earthquake. And after the earthquake a fire; but the Lord was not in the fire. And after the fire was a still small voice. And it was so, when Elijah heard it, that he wrapped his face in his mantle and went out, and stood in the entrance to the cave. And behold there came a voice unto him, and said, What doest thou here, Elijah?'[11]

The storm, the numinous element, the unpredictable, always broke over humanity as a punishment from God—or from vengeful gods. This was so even in Greek and Roman antiquity. Then, in time, the phenomenon of the storm was associated with conscience. At that time, people experienced the storm as happening because someone had done something forbidden. In imagining this early experience, we need to realize that lightning was the mightiest, most unpredictable manifestation of light at that time. Thunder was the most intense sound the human being could hear. Even today, it is still shocking when we are suddenly surprised by a thunderstorm. Earthquakes are also connected with storms. When we look at this in conjunction with the events of Good Friday, we can come to realize how powerfully nature spoke in that moment as well.

Another aspect of conscience appears during the Enlightenment; but before that came the age of the Baroque. This Baroque period—in the seventeenth century—signified a particularly important developmental step in the spiritual life of Europe, one we should not undervalue. A little later we will deal with the Baroque age from another perspective because it was a period of intense activity by the great individuality we know as Christian Rosenkreutz. This age stood completely under the sign of Christian Rosenkreutz, especially in middle Europe.

At that time, a personality lived in the Rosicrucian stream who has since been relegated to near-obscurity, Daniel von Czepko (1605–60). We find frequent indications about conscience in his writings. Conscience often appears as the strict educator of the soul and the spirit; the human being must become ever more aware of conscience. We see this, for example, in the dramatic baroque style of his age, even in the German orthography of his verse.

> Pains have my conscience wracked /
> Into a thousand pieces cracked:
> My soul is eaten at the core /
> Shrivelled, sere, and whole no more:
> Fear and horror within the fire /
> Grip my spirit upon its pyre:
> And my heart is turned to stone,
> Its power to cry for help has flown.[12]

Here we sense the beginnings of a consciousness soul capable of observing the soul itself—and its inner mood.

When we understand conscience in this way, we begin to see its enormous task for the present time and for the future. This task is far loftier than the development of individual human beings alone, although it cannot be completed without individual human development. The moral views we have in one life return as conscience in the next life, and the life after that. This may come as a bit of a shock; if we have a bad conscience, we can think: 'What happened to my moral perception in my previous life?' Today, when someone has a bad thought or bad feelings, even when he does not commit a misdeed, these thoughts and feelings precipitate out of him and create something like empty membranes around him. These cavities can be filled up when beings with an evil nature slip into them. Someone who is quite callous will be undisturbed by these beings in the membranes of his evil thoughts and feelings; they are simply there as his surroundings. Others who are a little more sensitive feel the presence of these beings as an aura around certain people. If such a person becomes even more sensitive, he can experience these beings as pangs of conscience.

After death, conscience actually becomes our self, our external surroundings. We live after death in the substance of our conscience. Of course, this is experienced in various ways depending on the quality of the conscience. Conscience is creative, indeed the most creative element the human being has. Consider the fact that no one can make another person do something; no one can compel another person to do something his conscience tells him not to. Mind you, this is so only if a person is free. Today, millions of people are not free. An obvious example of this is if a person's conscience says: 'Do not kill.' But, for example, that person is in the army and not free to follow this inner voice. As a creative quality in the human being, however, conscience is at work in a person's deeds.

Conscience has a lofty spiritual origin in the realm of the first hierarchy, especially in the realm of the cherubim. It gradually descended to the earth and united itself with human beings as an inner quality. An external image for this is the cherub who casts Adam and Eve out of paradise.

The human being will unite with the Christ in the future. We have seen how the Christ received the corporeality He needed to work on the earth. We have considered the 42 steps and the 77 steps; we have considered the pure Adam-soul that was held in reserve and how this soul comes to the earth; how the Zarathustra ego, this great individuality, withdraws at the baptism in the Jordan, and how the Christ-being penetrates the prepared corporeality. This corporeality was prepared for the incarnation of the Christ-being and offered to Him. It was presented as a gift.

Christ will remain the great impulse connected with the earth when earth evolution is complete. The earth will be able to reach the next level, the Jupiter stage of evolution, with the Christ-impulse. However, humanity must completely weave itself into the sheaths of the Christ-being in order to achieve this. This means that human beings themselves will have to build up, create, the sheaths of the Christ-being. The astral body, the ether body and the physical body of the Christ will be formed by human beings.

We have often spoken here about the secrets of the Old Mysteries. This, however, is a secret of the New Mysteries. One can *think* this secret. Since the Mystery of Golgotha, this secret has been in a formative stage, but it will be quite a long time before it is fulfilled. Everything the human being accomplishes in his soul by way of reverence, of wonder—earlier, in our time, and into the future—creates the astral body, this sheath for the Christ-being. Amazement, wonder at nature, at art, at other human beings—all these forces of wonderment will be taken up throughout time by the Christ-being, and will come together to form His astral body. We can see how important this is when we recognize what is happening to

hinder the formation of this astral body today. We see evidence everywhere of an increasing tendency towards contempt and derision among
people. We are all too familiar with these phenomena.

Furthermore, everything human beings can muster as love and
empathy in their souls, in their thoughts and their deeds will be brought
together for the ether body of the Christ. All this will flow together to
form this ether body. When the Gospel says: 'Inasmuch as ye have done it
unto one of the least of these my brethren, ye have done it unto me,' we
have a glimpse of what happens when something is taken away from His
ether body.[13] We also see how the counter-forces fight these creative
etheric powers, attack them through hatred—pitting nation against
nation, religion against religion, and so forth. Today, in many cases, in
many situations, even the predisposition to conscience is threatened with
extermination in the earliest stages of childhood.

This creative etheric power was foreshadowed by the Gautama
Buddha. The Gautama Buddha brought the great doctrine of the power
of love and compassion, which continues to work in a refined form. We
spoke earlier about how the human being himself must acquire these
qualities, these eight qualities formed of compassion and love.

Now we come to the physical body. The situation of its substance at
the end of earthly time will, of course, be different. The most creative
element must become active here. This is what the human being can
contribute through conscience, through the conscience '... that draws
into the human soul as though from a higher world ... to which the
human being submits, to which he attributes a higher value than his own
individual, moral instincts. The Christ unites most intimately with it; the
Christ takes His physical body from the impulses of conscience in individual human souls.'[14]

These insights must be brought together if the future is to be created
consciously. This is actually one of the great tasks of anthroposophy, and it
arises from the seeds of conscience. Conscience must be the freest element
in every human being. Every human being must decide: 'What am I
making of my life, of my insight, of my personal relationship to the Christ
impulse?'

Lecture 8

The Cosmic Being of the Isis Sophia—Christ Paths of the Middle Ages: Monks and Knights—Grail Secrets, Templar Destinies and Rosicrucian Deeds

Manfred Schmidt-Brabant

We have seen how Dionysius the Areopagite provided the pre-Christian world of the gods with a new trinitarian order through a Christian imagination of the hierarchies. And we have noted that Rudolf Steiner spoke about the change from the pre-Christian time to the post-Christian time, and pointed to how the Mystery of Golgotha brought the Trinity itself into a new relationship to the hierarchies.

There is a being in this heaven of the gods that serves as a bridge between the pre-Christian world of the gods and the Christian world— the Isis Sophia. Even her name points to the duality of her role—to the Isis of the old Mysteries and the Sophia of the Christian New Mysteries.

Isis was the object of infinite veneration; her cults and her temples were everywhere throughout Europe. It is a mistake to think that Isis was only an Egyptian goddess, that she was worshipped only in Egypt. There were Isis shrines all the way into the far northern reaches of Europe—and Isis cults were celebrated there, although not always under this name. It was said already in the old Mysteries that Isis has ten thousand names. In the old cultures, there was always one being who was venerated as an all-encompassing mother, a Mother of the Gods—a maternal being from whom heaven and earth and all the gods originated. For this reason, there is much that can be said about this Isis; and in antiquity a rich literature already existed about her.

I want to turn our attention to one image that Rudolf Steiner often discusses, and to which he attaches the deepest significance. It is the ancient Mystery legend about the statue of Isis in Sais. There in Sais stood the image of Isis, but it was veiled. On the pedestal beneath this great statue were the words:

I am what was, what is, what shall be.
No mortal has yet lifted my veil.[1]

The ancient Mystery legend tells how a young man was filled with the will to learn the secrets of Isis; how he wanted to ask about this secret of Isis; how he lifted the veil; and how he was found dead the following morning. He had died when he lifted the veil of Isis.

Rudolf Steiner speaks of this event in quite concise, succinct remarks. What was the secret of Isis that could not be revealed to the ordinary human constitution before the Mystery of Golgotha? He offers the answer: it was 'the secret of the relationship between the spiritual world and the physical, earthly world'.[2]

Isis was portrayed as seated with the Horus child on her lap. We could ask: 'How could an image of a seated mother, even a Mother of the Gods with her child on her lap, be mysterious?' We must bear in mind the completely different nature of the human organization at that time, when such an image could evoke certain imaginations in the soul, certain supersensible knowledge. But it was knowledge that the human being did not dare to receive without preparation. According to Rudolf Steiner: 'The Youth of Sais was prohibited from simply walking in and viewing the image of Isis directly.' The following statement was valid for all uninitiated human beings of that time: 'Take care that what lies behind the veil is not revealed to your soul without preparation.'[3]

It is difficult for those of us today who by rights live in an intellectual age to look at one of the surviving Isis statues and fully grasp that an external image once led people into the supersensible world. This fact must actually be stressed again and again in comprehending the old Mystery temples. When people stood there before a statue of Isis, of Anubis, or any other image of a god, it was not a dead work of art. Through what was represented in such a work of art, they saw the reality of a particular god.

In the first Christian centuries, this world of the gods was a reality for Christians who had been initiated. They knew: 'This Spirit-God-being exists.' These Christians had been initiated in Eleusis or in some other Mystery centre, but what differentiates them from non-Christian followers of the Mysteries is that they recognized the Christ-being as the over-arching principle. They knew that this powerful divinity, Isis, had herself come into a new relationship to the Christ through the Mystery of Golgotha; they knew that, through the Mystery of Golgotha, she had become the Sophia of the Christ, the wisdom of God. Wisdom, as the Sophia-being, was already venerated in the Old Testament. But now, for initiated Christians, the great Isis-being corresponded to what was felt to be the wisdom of God, the wisdom about which it has always been said:

'It was with God from the beginning.' Before all time wisdom was with God.

We recall that something lived in this early Mystery period of Christianity that we express differently today through the prosaic words: 'The whole cosmos of wisdom originating from the Father God is to transform into a cosmos of love.' We have heard the words that describe this: when 'wisdom . . . is internalized [in the human being], it becomes . . . love.'[4] Humanity was given the archetype for this process in the Being of Christ. Thus, the feeling lived in early Christians that the Isis Sophia is also the wisdom of the Christ. As esoteric Christians, they felt themselves to be pupils of the Isis Sophia. Rudolf Steiner says the Gospel of John is the textbook of the Sophia.

Two great impulses related to what has been depicted here move through the whole post-Christian period; they endure into the present. The one impulse can be described in the following way. The evangelist Mark, author of the Gospel, lived in Alexandria. There he met Ormuz, one of the highest priests of Isis. He converted Ormuz to Christianity. Both Mark and Ormuz were clairvoyant; both were, in their own way, initiates. In this way they became disciples of the Risen One Who, according to Rudolf Steiner, went through the Mysteries, reforming them.[5] Something powerful now emanated from both men. They transformed the ancient Isis cult—which is also the cult of Isis and Osiris—into an esoteric, Christian cultus. Rudolf Steiner says that the Isis cult has its origins in the Mysteries of Atlantis.

We should not imagine that Mark and Ormuz had written something out; their actions were carried out in the spiritual world. The imaginative world of the old Isis cult was transformed here into a new, Christian, imaginative world. The cultus consisted of enduring imaginations. What Mark—the author of the Gospel for our fifth post-Atlantean epoch—and Ormuz created became the source for all cults of esoteric Christianity, always with certain variations among them. It became the source for the Grail cults, for the Templar cults. At the beginning of the modern age, this source was restored by great Rosicrucian masters so that it could retain its efficacy in the present as well as into the future. It served as the foundation of what Rudolf Steiner himself created before 1914 as a cultic institution. The cultic element formed one side of what emerges from the Isis Sophia being, now in relationship with the Christ.

The other impulse comes through someone who is still known today, but he is not fully appreciated. He stands at the beginning of the Middle Ages, which I date to around AD 500—actually to 476, the end of the

Western Roman Empire, when the Goths marched in and broke up the empire. This was the Roman, Boethius. He lived from 480 to 525, and was chancellor under Theoderic the Great, the Ostragoth. Together with his father-in-law, Symmachus, Boethius led an esoteric Christian community. He had planned an enormous work in which Plato and Aristotle would be reconciled with one another and harmonized. In fact, only the beginning of it remains. However, until Boethius took this up, Plato and Aristotle had always been viewed in philosophy and intellectual history as opposites.

If we study the scholarship on Raphael's *School of Athens* in Rome, we will uncover contradictions in the various interpretations of it. Two large figures are depicted at the centre of the painting, one pointing up, the other down. One school of interpretation says these two figures are Peter and Paul. Paul points towards heaven; Peter points towards the earth. Another school of interpretation says that these figures are Plato and Aristotle. Plato points upwards to the world of ideas; Aristotle points towards the earth we are to penetrate with concepts. Rudolf Steiner says that neither of these is what Raphael intended. What Raphael depicts here are the typical gestures of the human being in pursuit of knowledge. The one figure gestures to heaven and strives towards it; the other gestures to the earth and strives towards it.

Boethius intended to unite these two, but never did. He belonged to the esoteric Christian community—it was a school of instruction as well—which has long been viewed in the history of esotericism as the link between the transformed cultus of Mark and Ormuz and the western world. Boethius is always cited as the one through whom these cults entered the West.

To understand this, we have to realize that Boethius was a highly respected philosopher in the court of Theoderic. Theoderic faced a significant task in regard to the Church and he brought a great force of will to it. During the first centuries there was a dispute between two great bishops, Athanasius and Arius, and their followers. At first, Arius was quite successful. He had a very specific interpretation of the relationship between the Christ—the Logos—and the Father God while Athanasius viewed the two as being a unity. Rudolf Steiner says something concerning Arius that I have found in the work of modern Church historians too. They say this Arius actually wanted to place Christianity at the level of the Mystery cults. This is precisely what Rudolf Steiner said as well.

The Germanic empires were all followers of Arius. An understanding for the old Nordic Mysteries still existed everywhere among the Germanic peoples, which is why the Christianity professed by Arius was met with a good deal of acceptance among them. But Athanasius prevailed. Arius was declared a heretic by the Council of Nicaea in 325, and his writings were burned. Since then, the convictions of Athanasius have been the basis for the confession of faith in the Catholic Church.

Everything was unstable after the fall of the Western Roman Empire. There was no longer an emperor; Theoderic still ruled as the king of the Goths. Interestingly, the same Church historian who reproaches Arius for approaching Christianity from the perspective of the Mysteries also writes disapprovingly of Theoderic, saying that had he succeeded the whole Roman Catholic Church would have been finished. Terrible intrigues were set in motion. Theoderic the Great hears lies about Boethius that concern assassination attempts against the king and all manner of plots. Theoderic has Boethius thrown in jail where he languished for a long time until he was eventually executed along with his father-in-law, Symmachus. Theoderic died a year later.

While he was under arrest—it is said to have been a year—Boethius writes one of the best known books in the Middle Ages, *The Consolation of Philosophy*. During his imprisonment, he writes: 'There is only one salvation for the soul of the human being and that is wisdom. Become a pupil of wisdom!' We would say—and this is what he intended: 'Become a pupil of the Sophia, the Isis Sophia.' Manuscripts of this book can still be found in many libraries. It becomes the impetus for the second path, for drawing near to the Isis Sophia through thought and knowledge. Two paths lead to the Isis Sophia—the cultic path and the path of knowledge.

This was a time when much hung in the balance. After Constantine—who was known as 'the Great'—made Christianity into one of the state religions, another emperor came along who was completely filled with the nature of the Mysteries and who sought to rediscover the path to the ancient Mysteries. This was Julian the Apostate. The Church calls him an apostate because it thinks he wanted to abandon Christianity and return to the old gods. But that was not the case. Rudolf Steiner speaks in detail about this; we can also read about this history ourselves. Julian wanted to find his way to the Old Mysteries in order to understand Christianity through them. But he was murdered. Rudolf Steiner says that Julian was murdered by the collegium of black magic we described earlier. He says: 'It is difficult to imagine what ... would have happened in Europe if the Christianity of Julian the Apostate had prevailed rather than the Roman Church; if his will to reconstruct the initiation schools had prevailed ...'[6]

During these centuries, life took on a kind of twofold intention.

Earlier, life had always been experienced as a unity, even in the offshoots of the Mysteries. The gods were in every house; people felt the gods close at hand. The gods were nearby in daily work and people called upon them. It still seemed as though heaven and earth were contained within the human being. But, as these instinctive perceptions of the spirit receded, human striving underwent a division. The feeling existed: 'The human being can move in two directions through all his activities, through his consciousness. He can move in the direction of the earth'— this was called the *Vita activa*—'and he can move in the direction of heaven, take up a religious life'—that was called the *Vita contemplativa*. A quite distinct doctrine developed during these first centuries that says that the emperor is responsible for the *Vita activa*; the pope is responsible for the *Vita contemplativa*. From Rome, the feeling developed that institutions like the Church and the state should direct and control the individual.

There was a parallel question in esoteric Christianity: How can the individual unite both forms of life? How can he simultaneously live a *Vita activa* and a *Vita contemplativa*? There was a feeling that this had been achieved in the Mystery of Golgotha. Through the fact that both natures were brought together in Christ Jesus, it was now possible for the human being to combine the two within himself.

On the level of culture, we must imagine that there was a great deal of heterogeneity in the way people behaved at that time. On the one hand, there is the sober, practical Roman character, directed to the physical world, unimaginative, with a profound talent for technology. The Romans owe their great victories not least of all to their technologically superior war machines and the battle technique of their legions. In fact, Roman times often seem quite modern. The Rome of antiquity was a modern, cosmopolitan city with a modern economy; it focused completely on what was practical and sober as well as on success. Caesar and his ilk were all very rich people; they handled money well.

On the other hand, the totally new and different religious life of the Christians swiftly ended up in a certain unworldly ecstasy. This began in Egypt and Syria with the Desert Fathers who sat in a kind of burrow in the earth; it continued with the appearance of something we can take as a real symbol, as a real imagination—the many pillar saints, the so-called Stylites. They erected pillars—often at a height of ten or twelve feet or more—upon which they placed a small platform. The pillar saint stood on this platform. There were three principles that all of them followed. The individual always stayed in the same place, always at the same spot; that was the reason for the pillar. He was not to wander around in the world.

He was to remain in one place for his entire life. Second, he was without shelter. He stood there in the glaring summer heat, in the cold of the night. And third, he had to stand. These were the three fundamental principles of the pillar saints. There are famous pillar saints like Simeon the Elder (*c.* 390–459), who stood on a 60-foot pillar. A small basket was lowered and disciples or admirers put bread or some such thing into it, and then he drew the basket up. There was also a Simeon the Younger, who stood on a pillar for 45 years.

There was a completely different bodily constitution at that time, and a different constitution of soul as well. These pillar saints stood there and prayed for decades, through summers and winters. This became rather like an image of someone lifting himself out of and away from the earth. In sharp contrast to this is pragmatic Rome with its earthly accomplishments, with its phenomenal agriculture and trade. It is astonishing to see how much of what was already being done in Rome is a precursor of our modern sense for life.

The Catholic Church grew into this whole world; the Christian church, Christianity grew into it. We must carefully differentiate between the cultus of the Catholic Church—the saints, the pious people, the religious people in the Church—and the institution of the Church, the official Church. Rudolf Steiner says wonderful things about this cultus: 'Spiritual science can ... well appreciate what a pity it is that what lies in the Catholic cultus is lost for many people. Spiritual science knows how to value the merits of the Catholic cultus in spite of cultural events ... Deep Mystery knowledge lies within this cultus.'[7] There are even more statements of this kind from Rudolf Steiner.

Along with this, we find the great saints and their orders—Francis of Assisi, Thomas Aquinas, Bernard of Clairvaux. Together they form a world unto themselves, and often had the greatest difficulty with the institution of the Church, the official Church. Rudolf Steiner notes that Thomas Aquinas was almost branded a heretic. And he reminds us of how the Franciscan order had to struggle to avoid falling prey to the Inquisition in order to come away whole. This means that the Church was familiar with the fact that not only the saint but any religious individual can come into conflict with the official Church and what it represents as an institution. Much of what we can criticize about the Church must be seen from this standpoint.

I said earlier that we can make use of the pious, naive, yet valid concept of a divine plan of salvation. In this divine plan of salvation everything is sensibly organized. We understand from this how empires like Rome arise; they represent the pole of sobriety, of connectedness to the earth, within the entire organism of humanity. Rudolf Steiner says it was right that an official Church arose that did not want to allow the individual to find his own way but, instead, always wanted to manage the soul quality of the individual. This is how the will arose in the individual to find his own path to the Christ. Here is the justification for the Church—that through its existence, individuals were compelled to find their own individual path in the same way that many of the saints had done.[8] Anyone who investigates the history of great religious figures knows that some were recognized immediately, others were condemned, and that there was always a battle over individual access to the Christ.

During this period when the *Vita activa* and the *Vita contemplativa* were torn asunder, the great event that transformed western culture appeared through Benedict of Nursia and his founding of the cloister on Monte Cassino. The cloister's basic principle was *ora et labora*, pray and work. It was already written in a circle at that time:

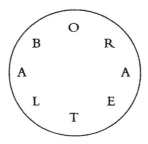

Ora et labora passes over and into itself. Sceptics will say: 'Prayer happens only once and then *et labora et labora et labora*'—then it is just work, work, and more work. But this picture is intended to be an image of the idea that work and prayer together make up human life. While the Desert Fathers may have cultivated a few cabbages or similar crops for their own use, the creation of the whole western cloister system has its source, its main impulse, in Monte Cassino. There were precursors; there were other small beginnings alongside it. But it is not without cause that Benedict of Nursia is called the 'Father of western monasticism'. Augustine had written only one rule for the course of the day; Benedict institutes and writes the first complete *Regula*. For all practical purposes, he creates what we call the great monastic republics that endured throughout the Middle Ages.

If we study the history of the early Middle Ages and the high Middle Ages in an unprejudiced way, we have to conclude that the whole culture of the time originated in the cloisters. The religious community was located there, but there was also a school for spiritual training and an academy for the sciences and the arts. Old manuscripts were copied in the cloisters. Music manuscripts also found their way from the Orient into the West. Music and crafts were developed and taught; agriculture was practised. The cloister was a complete city; today we would call it a campus, a university town with many buildings. It was the centre of culture.

Behind it all stood the concept: 'In the human being the *Vita contemplativa* and the *Vita activa* are one.' You work on the earth—that is a *Vita activa*; you pray and have a religious service—that is your *Vita contemplativa*. Both, bound together in the course of the day, of the year, make up the human being. From this emerge the many cloistered communities, the orders—the Franciscans, the Dominicans, the Benedictines. The great personalities live within these communities—Francis of Assisi, Bernard of Clairvaux, Thomas Aquinas. The knightly orders arise during the high Middle Ages: the Order of St John; most importantly, the Templars; the Teutonic Knights; and smaller orders as well.

Much of what was cultivated in the esoteric schools of the first millennia flowed into the communities formed by these orders and by the great knightly confederations. It often seems tangible that after his resurrection, the Christ passes through the Mysteries and into the esoteric schools, reforming them. From there, this stream flows over into the cloistered life we have just characterized; and all of this leads to a first great culmination from the seventh or eighth century on. The Grail Mysteries, the Templar Mysteries—later the Rosicrucian Mysteries—come into being; the great orders of the Cistercians, the Dominicans, the Franciscans arise; the so-called heretical streams of the Cathars also arise; and the mysterious pilgrimage paths like the one to Santiago de Compostela, the *camino*, come into being.

Of all these communities, the deepest and the most comprehensive is that of the Holy Grail. From a certain point of view, we can say that all of the other communities are further developments of the Grail. This is what Rudolf Steiner expresses when he calls the Templars the emissaries of the Grail, or when he says the Rosicrucians are the continuation of the Grail.

What is meant by the Grail? The Grail is the secret image of the whole of evolution; it is the concise image of what is found in *Occult Science, An Outline*. A bodily vessel is formed that includes an individual ego and, from another direction, something comes to meet this ego-being. Thus the Grail is always experienced as the human ego that then recedes, creating of itself a vessel for the Christ Spirit to fill. It is clear that this is an earthly aspiration; it is an image of evolution, an image of the plan for salvation. But never-ending battles play out around this image.

We have a glimpse into one of these conflicts through Rudolf Steiner's reflections on the Youth of Sais. Rudolf Steiner compares him with the figure of Parzival, and says 'the Youth of Sais should not have posed a question.'[9] He dies because he questions, because he lifts the veil. On the other hand, Parzival 'should have asked a question!' He fails at first because he does not ask. Initiation before the Mystery of Golgotha always came to people from the outside. A person was called by the initiates. The initiates perceived through the aura the higher being of a person, whether that person had matured enough for initiation. Then he was called and prepared; it was often the case that he was schooled for many years. In ancient times, a person was not permitted to decide for himself whether he wanted initiation or even whether he was mature enough for it. The Youth of Sais is the image for this. He was not mature enough, and he died because he was suddenly drawn unprepared into imaginations that he could not withstand.

After the Mystery of Golgotha, the situation is precisely the opposite. A person has to learn to take the step for himself that leads to initiation; he must ask. Parzival fails in this. Had he asked, he would have undergone a tremendous experience. Here I quote Rudolf Steiner's words: 'As Parzival rides away from the Grail Castle after failing to ask about the wonders of the Holy Grail, one of the first people he meets is a woman, a bride, who mourns her recently deceased bridegroom as she holds him in her lap.' (This is Sigune and the dead Schionatulander.) 'In fact, this is the image of the mourning mother with her son that later served so often as the motif of the Pietà! That is the first hint of what Parzival would have learned had he asked about the wonders of the Holy Grail. He would have learned about the new form taken by the relationship between Isis and Horus, the mother and the Son of Man. And he should have asked.'[10]

When we look at Michelangelo's *Pietà* in St Peter's, we have the feeling of viewing something infinitely significant. This image truly represents the metamorphosis of Isis with the Horus child into the Christian situation. At one time, the unprepared person would have been killed by imaginations for which he was not yet strong enough. Today, we must take the initiative ourselves to seek these imaginations out. No matter how artistically meaningful the *Pietà* in St Peter's is, no matter how powerfully it touches the heart through the grace of the mother, through the dead body, it is nonetheless only the veil. We must break through the veil by asking: 'What is triggered in me when I hear that hidden in the *Pietà*, as in the Isis with the Horus child, is the secret of how the spiritual is connected to the physical?' When we look back once again at the old initiation, we can ask this question: 'What would the Youth of Sais have had to have gone through in order to be justified in lifting the veil?' He would have to have gone through the three great steps of schooling necessary in all the Mysteries.

Each of the three steps requires a long schooling, a preparation, a catharsis of the soul. The first step was the approach to the 'brink of death'—properly stated, the encounter with the Guardian of the Threshold. The brink of death is reached at the abyss before which the person stands in full consciousness.

The second step was the experience of the elemental world. The individual entered into a realm of darkness which lit up and then became dark again until the next step.

The third step was always seeing the sun at midnight; the true being of the sun was seen from out of the third darkness of the soul. Physical matter becomes transparent; the solar system is recognized as a living organism; the sun beings are perceived as creative gods. The Cosmic Word spoken by the Cosmic Being is heard to resound.

Had the Youth been prepared, he could have experienced what is described here:

> When the individual undergoing initiation into the Isis Mysteries had arrived at the shore of cosmic existence and had seen the beings which constitute, for example, the physical and etheric bodies; when he had stood opposite the silent goddess from whom warmth and light flowed to sustain the innermost part of the human soul, he said to himself: This is Isis! This is the mute, the silent goddess whose countenance can be revealed to none who only see with mortal eyes, whose countenance can only be revealed to those who have worked their way through to the shore ... so that they may see with the eyes that go from incarnation to incarnation, eyes that are no longer mortal. For an impenetrable veil shrouds the form of Isis from mortal eyes.[11]

Rudolf Steiner introduces this passage by saying that what occurred at that time in initiations like these can only be spoken of 'with stammering words'.[12]

This 'seeing the sun at midnight' goes back to the Zarathustra Mysteries. First developed by Zarathustra, it spread across the whole earth and then into the Mysteries of the Holy Grail. 'Seeing the sun at midnight' was one of the great central Mysteries of the Grail. It made it possible to answer the question: 'How is something below formed so that it can receive what is above in order that both can be united—like a human ego that can take up a divine ego?'

The Parzival initiation led to this experience. In it, the soul of the candidate was purified through a whole series of practices, of soul exercises. Each one of these candidates was a Parzival. This was also the name of a real person who even had significant incarnations in his past. He had been the Youth of Sais; later, he was the Youth of Nain who was a follower of the Christ, a disciple in Jerusalem; and he was the great Manes.[13] He now returns as a human being in order to set in motion the whole Grail initiation—which had been created by Titurel—and in order to be the first to undergo the Grail initiation. Now he was instructed: 'You have purified your innermost nature; you have erased all evil qualities in yourself. But take heed for a moment of the imaginations around you. You will perceive the odour of lilies. You have become lily white, pure, a "Cathar".' (Rudolf Steiner applies this expression to this time that predates the Cathars themselves.) 'But you will also note an unpleasant odour, and that comes from the fact that you have only cast out all these bad qualities. What becomes of them then? Should all this bad and evil now remain in the world? You have to learn to take the evil back into yourself through a second step of initiation; and, this time, you have to transform it into something good. When you have achieved that, you will have the imagination of the rose. And then, instead of the unpleasant smell of the lilies, you will sense the wondrous scent of the rose.'[14]

It is as though the whole Parzival initiation were an answer to what must have seemed a difficult riddle to Jesus when He visited the Essenes: they purify themselves, and they chase Lucifer and Ahriman out into the rest of humanity. The Grail initiation is like an answer to the misdeeds of the Essenes. We cannot purify ourselves by releasing evil into the world; when we purify ourselves, the evil has to be transformed into something good.

The knightly order we call the Templars emerges from this attitude. Significant monastic impulses are connected with this knightly order. The superficial aspects of its history are well known. Some knights take part in the conquest of Jerusalem and then return home. In 1128, a great Council takes place in Troyes, in France. Bernard of Clairvaux is present, and the

Templar order is solemnly instituted. Its rule originates with Bernard of Clairvaux. This is the greatest esoteric order ever to exist. There was no equivalent esoteric element in the Order of Saint John or in the Teutonic Knights. The Order of the Templars was unique in this respect. Much has been written and said in mainstream literature about the Templars, most of it untrue. Nonetheless, Rudolf Steiner pointed to the Templars again and again. Their intent was to reconnect the ancient sacred Mystery knowledge with the Mystery of Golgotha and, above all, to make Paul's Damascus experience a reality for European society.

Paul had seen how the hierarchies work on the human sheaths—the etheric and astral natures—until they are developed to the point they can take up the ego which can then receive the Christ. The Templars wanted to accomplish this same thing for European society. At that time, Europe was the known world. Marco Polo had not yet been in Asia; there were a number of legendary realms. Naturally, America had not yet been discovered. They wanted to make the Mystery of Golgotha a reality for the world, right down into the social realm. They wanted, as Rudolf Steiner said, to include the sites of the Mystery of Golgotha in the unfolding domain of Europe. One of their great and wise esoteric insights centred on how the nature of the stars is related to the nature of the earth. Today we speak about etheric geography; for them, it lived in the experience of how heaven and earth are related.

Then, they formed Europe socially. It is often a surprise to discover how many markets, how many cities, how many roads were begun by the Templars, even for those who have studied the Templars for a long time. Based on their imaginative vision of the world of the stars, they set this starry world into the structure of life in Europe—above all, into its social structure.

The Templars were closely associated with one of the great orders. Bernard of Clairvaux was a Cistercian. Monastic life had fallen into some decay around the end of the first millennium. The early monastic impulses had endured for a few centuries and then died out. Attempts at monastic reform began in the ninth and tenth centuries, and the Cistercian order arose from this movement. These reform efforts began with an anchorite, a hermit, Abbot Robert. Then came the first significant reformer, an Englishman named Stephen Harding. He had been a Benedictine, but when the Normans invaded, he fled and became the first great abbot of the Cistercians. Very soon after, Bernard of Clairvaux arrived and the great spirituality of the Cistercian order came into existence.

If the Templars strove for—and, in some measure, founded—a

Christianization of the social order of Europe, the Cistercians were responsible for a Christianization of the land. It is worth noting here that the Cistercian order was the great agricultural order. At that time Europe was more or less a swamp, flooded in many places. The Cistercians took on something quite physically challenging. Whereas the Benedictines would always go up to the mountaintops, the Cistercians always went into swampy valleys and begin to drain them. They built dams, dried out meadows. Large portions of what we today refer to as Europe's agrarian culture—animal husbandry, the cultivation of fruit, pasture lands—date back to the Cistercians.

We need to take note of one spiritual fact in regard to all these knightly and monastic orders. Through his spirituality, the human being makes his way into the spiritual world—by sensing, perceiving, feeling; there are many ways. First, he seeks access to the hierarchies. If he works in solitude—in the mystical sense—he comes to the angels, to the archangels, and then to the archai—but no further than this. This means that he does not reach the Christ-being. For this reason, Rudolf Steiner says that the most important statement in Christianity will increasingly be: 'Where two or more are gathered in My name, there will I be among them.'[15] Rudolf Steiner adds: '. . . when a person is alone . . . the Christ is not present'. For the Christ is a being of 'all humanity'.[16] The Christ is only present when an 'I' stands opposite a 'thou', when one person faces another person. When the social element weaves among two or three, then He can be present.

What was still an elementary feeling led to the deeply significant reason for forming the monastic orders, the communities of knights. People knew: 'We must be with one another for the Christ; then He can also be there for us. We should not be alone.' When a person is alone, the only reality in which the Christ can live—love—cannot develop in him. Love can only exist between one person and another. When a person is alone, it is not even possible for him to love himself, because self-love is no love at all. Love is only possible when people are with one another; this was the reality in all of these communities at that time. In the monasteries they called one another 'Brother'—or, in the convents, 'Sister'—based on a deep understanding of these words.

The next great step in the development of the orders was taken when the Dominicans were founded in 1216, a century after the Cistercians reached their first great blossoming. An element that can be called the 'Christianization of consciousness' lived in the Dominicans. The Templars carried the Grail impulse into the social life; the Cistercians carried it into the cultural life of the land—right down into their manual labour; and the Dominicans carried the impulse into the human being's life of consciousness. They preached; they had a lofty education. Study was an essential part of monastic life—theology in general, then scholasticism in particular and, of course, there was the Inquisition. We must not judge this from the perspective of today; instead, we must experience how they jokingly called themselves *domini canes*, 'the dogs of the Lord'. By this they meant they were like the sheep dogs around a herd of sheep, protecting them from the wolf. That feeling was justified because the Dominicans lived intensely in the consciousness that the human being can only find a normal path to the Christ through clear thinking, not through atavistic clairvoyance. Atavistic clairvoyance was regarded as the wolf. In this way, the Dominicans experienced themselves as 'the dogs of the Lord', protecting the herd from the atavistic wolf.

Thomas Aquinas is undoubtedly the most eminent Dominican. Rudolf Steiner said significant things about Thomas in his 1909 Rome lectures. Thomas was not only a thinker, he was a mystic. He was thoroughly clairvoyant, so clairvoyant that, like Dionysius the Areopagite, he perceived all of the hierarchies.[17] Then Rudolf Steiner adds something else about a precept he frequently discusses during these years, 'the principle of spiritual economy'.[18] It is based on the fact that particularly valuable ether and astral bodies are not simply dissolved after death; instead, it is possible in the spiritual world to duplicate such ether and astral bodies and place them at the disposal of people yet to be born.

This, above all, is what happened with the bodies of Christ Jesus. Rudolf Steiner speaks about how first the ether body of Christ Jesus was duplicated, how people—like Augustine—received it, and how the astral body of Christ Jesus was also duplicated. One of those who received such a replica of Christ's astral body was Thomas Aquinas.

This astral body of Christ Jesus is the astral body of the Nathan Jesus in whom the Zarathustra-being lived from the twelfth to the thirtieth year. It is an astral body that contains all the secrets of the life of Jesus and, at the same time, all the secrets that were impressed into this astral body by the Zarathustra individuality.

Today it is not easy for us really to assess the figure of Thomas Aquinas. His philosophical work is difficult to understand. And yet Rudolf Steiner says that not a single new concept arose in intellectual history after Thomas Aquinas. With Thomas, the world of cognition came to a powerful culmination.

Rudolf Steiner once listed the Grail, the Templars and the Rosicrucians together; he calls the Templars the 'emissaries of the Holy Grail'.[19] He says the Rosicrucians then consolidated what they inherited from the Grail stream and the Templars. The will is present in the Rosicrucians to bring Christianization right down into matter. It is often thought that they were alchemists, therapists and doctors, but these professions were only the results of their activity. What actually concerned the Rosicrucians was bringing what had revealed itself to them as the secret of Christ Jesus into connection with earthly matter.

Here a particular law—which they knew—played a large role. Stated in modern terms, this law would say that atoms and thoughts consist of the same substance. What is spiritually connected with the atom is identical to what is spiritually connected with thought. The Rosicrucians were of the opinion that a person could only correctly deal with matter if, at the same time, he conducted himself in the right way spiritually. They thought every Rosicrucian actually had two places of work, the laboratory and the oratory, so that *ora et labora* were brought together in a whole new way. The train of thought leading to the transformation of one metal into another, for instance, was only possible through prayer, and was completely impossible for a layman. The Rosicrucians worked magic on matter, but this element of magic was nothing more than the result of a deep, inward spiritual life.

Here we arrive at the threshold of the modern age. In Rosicrucianism, aspects of life surface that are absolutely valid for us today and will be for centuries to come. With Rosicrucianism, an esoteric work begins in which the modern human being can participate. Rosicrucian schooling is an esoteric element that the modern person can pursue publicly. It is not necessary to withdraw in solitude to a hut or a cloister; instead, its practice can be taken up where the person is in life. He creates a moment of inner peace—even if only for a few minutes—and at the same time he creates an inner cloister, an inner cell, in which he is completely alone and sovereign. Based on these practices, the anthroposophical movement feels itself to be an heir to Rosicrucianism.

In this regard, a last great step in Christ activity begins with Rosicrucianism, particularly through its founder, Christian Rosenkreutz, who had a significant incarnation in the fifteenth century. In Rome, Rudolf Steiner relates for the first time that replicas of the ego—the ego organization—of Christ Jesus enter the world, and that Christian Rosenkreutz was the first to receive a replica of the Christ Ego. Through Christian Rosenkreutz the possibility arises for the human being to connect himself with the Christ through his will for knowledge and through his ego—a possibility that exists for the whole stream of Rosicrucianism, from the time of Christian Rosenkreutz into the present, and on into the future.

What first appears in the Epistles of Paul as a promise for the future begins to become a reality in the modern age through Christian Rosenkreutz, a reality for all those who want to follow him. This reality is that the human being can say in all honesty: 'Not I, but the Christ in me.'[20] The whole Christian Mystery is contained in this sentence. For it demands the elimination of all egoity; it demands the years and perhaps decades of life we need before we can really say 'Not I ...' And it demands that we live our lives so that we can free ourselves.

'The Christ in me', according to Rudolf Steiner, is the true ego being of the human being. At first, the human being experiences nothing of this ego being during his daily life where he merely has a sense of it. The human being comes to know the ego only gradually, when he has really cleared the results of the Fall of Man from his soul, when he has cleared away everything that would lead him to egoity, to selfishness. This work never stops. Through this inner soul process we will be able to say in our next life and the lives after that—with an ever-renewed sense of certainty—'Not I, but the Christ in me.'

Lecture 9

Mystery Impulses in the Life and Work of Great Christian Women

Virginia Sease

In these lectures, we have been presented with a vast panorama: Desert Fathers and pillar saints, Boethius, Bernard of Clairvaux, and Thomas Aquinas, to mention just a small part. And we have been able to experience from a sweeping perspective how the individualization of the Christ-impulse has had an effect down through the centuries.

In connection with this, I want to turn our attention now to the women in the most intimate circles around the Christ where we find two sisters, Mary Magdalene and Martha, who are identified as the sisters of Lazarus. Martha's place here is clear and beyond question. But down through the centuries there have been great controversies surrounding Mary Magdalene. Who is this figure? What is her role in this circle around the Christ? These controversies continue on in our time as well.

During the last 30 years, an extensive body of literature has been published about Mary Magdalene and the question of her identity. I want to offer a glimpse of a few of these points of view, some of which may even seem contradictory. We will begin with the biblical account of the woman with the ointment.

It is related that Jesus was in Bethany in the house of Simon the leper. A woman carrying an alabaster vessel filled with precious oil enters this gathering of men. According to some estimates this oil was so precious that an average farmer would have had to spend an entire year's wages in order to buy a container of it. This woman takes the oil and anoints the head of Christ with it. The men reproach her for the waste, saying the oil could have been sold and the money given to the poor. Christ responds: The poor are always among you; however, she has done this in recognition of My death. Christ says about this woman, who is unnamed: 'Wheresoever this gospel shall be preached in the whole world, there shall also this, that this woman hath done, be told for a memorial of her.'[1] Christ presents us with a paradox: her name is unknown, but we are to remember her. The image itself—of Christ, the Anointed One—is an image from the Mystery rites in which the king was anointed. And it was this woman who performed the rite. Luke in his Gospel assumes that she is a sinner who performs this act in order to receive forgiveness of her sins.

The Christian Community theologian Emil Bock says the three figures we are considering here—the woman with the ointment, Mary, the sister of Martha and Lazarus, and Mary Magdalene—are one person. A similar view has also guided the whole of Christian tradition from the time of Gregory the Great in the sixth century and throughout the centuries since. We find an example of this in the eleventh century with Gregory VII as well. Who is this unnamed woman really?

There are several Marys associated with the life of Christ. There is the mother of Jesus whom Rudolf Steiner says we should refer to simply as the Mother of Jesus—as she appears in the Gospel of John—to differentiate her from her sister who is also called Mary. Today it is unusual for two daughters in a family to have the same first name; and this was also the case at the time of Christ. Then there is Mary, the wife of Cleophas—she is always named among the Marys. And further, there is Mary Aegyptica (also Egyptiaca), the Egyptian Mary. A rich collection of legends exists about her. One tells that she dwelt in Alexandria and underwent a life-changing experience there, after which she lived for 47 years as a penitent in the desert east of the Jordan.

All these individuals and accounts are a part of the picture we come to when we examine the life of Mary Magdalene.—I am talking here about Mary Magdalene as a collective concept for various characteristics and qualities. Let us look now at who bore witness to her. Augustine is one such witness. Augustine carried a replica of the ether body of Jesus woven into his own ether body. This is a manifestation of the spiritual economy we spoke of earlier, which makes it possible for one of the bodies of Christ Jesus—the ether body, the astral body or, in our time, the ego—to be woven into the body of another. In the case of Augustine, this spiritual economy affected the ether body, which preserves memories. We may assume, therefore, that Augustine could see—that he could observe—the events of the Mystery of Golgotha with a special clarity, at least through the replica of the Christ ether body if not through his other capacities. And it is Augustine who calls Mary Magdalene the 'apostle of the apostles'. This is a significant description.

Mary Magdalene experienced the crucifixion on Golgotha directly; it is told in the Gospels how she stood near the cross. The only others who stood near the cross were John the Evangelist and Mary, the Mother of Jesus. Why is emphasis placed on proximity to the cross—'near the cross' or 'not far from the cross'? This has to do with the laws of the Roman Empire. It was extremely dangerous for friends or relatives of the one being crucified to be near the place of the cross. Public displays of grief were not permitted; in fact, they were forbidden—and the price for such a display was the mourner's own life. The Romans forbade these displays of emotion because they wanted to eradicate everything connected with non-Roman cults, with non-Roman personalities. It was extremely courageous of Mary Magdalene to have stood at the cross with the other two.

Afterwards, Mary Magdalene is then the one who goes to the tomb, and she is the first to see the Risen One. She arrives there and sees two angelic figures. This vision is connected with the degree to which the human constitution has been developed. Figures of angels can always be seen clairvoyantly around those who have recently died. They are actually the ether body and the astral body of the person immediately after his death, but they appear to the clairvoyant as angelic figures. These angels ask her: 'Why weepest thou?' Then the Christ Himself appears to her in His resurrection body as phantom body, and she fails to recognize Him outwardly until He calls her name. This is a remarkable moment: He calls her name. This is comparable only with the awakening of Lazarus, where Christ calls: 'Lazarus, come forth!' He calls her name: 'Mary!' Her higher capacities are awakened, and she replies: 'Rabboni, Master!' The details of this episode point to the fact that Mary Magdalene had already gone through many steps of initiation; she is a woman who has attained a certain level of initiation.

Then the words resound: 'Touch me not!' She is the first to see the phantom body of the Christ. His ether body was so powerful that He could also reassemble the parts of His physical body so that it could appear. We have mentioned this earlier.[2]

History records that it was Gregory the Great (†604) who attributed the traits of a sinner to Mary Magdalene. He also added some characteristics of Mary of Egypt who had lived the life of a penitent. Furthermore, Gregory assigns Mary Magdalene her place among the individualities who were revered throughout the Middle Ages as the three great penitents: Peter, who denied the Lord; Paul, who persecuted the Christians; and Mary Magdalene, the sinner. According to this ambiguous history, Gregory the Great's interpretation honours these three great penitents—Peter, Paul and Mary—while casting a shadow of sin on their greatness and their tasks.

In addition, the effect Gregory's handling of the liturgy had on the whole culture of the time is still evident. The liturgy used in early Spanish and early Iberian worship was eradicated through reforms Gregory instituted in the seventh century. These reforms were far-reaching and affected everything, including music. The wonderful musical modes from the early Iberian period were eradicated by the insertion of Gregorian chants which were imposed on all the cloisters. Unfortunately, early Iberian music was not noted down and we can only sense its quality in the few fragments that remain today.

The sister of Mary Magdalene—Martha—is also mentioned in the Gospels. It is told that Jesus comes into the village of Bethany where a woman by the name of Martha takes Him into her house. Martha's sister sits at the feet of Christ and listens to Him. Martha complains about this because her sister is supposed to help when a guest arrives. The words of Christ are: 'Mary hath chosen that good part, which shall not be taken away from her.'[3]

Interpretations of this event over the past two millennia have been a bit one-sided. It has been said that Mary's attitude of *Vita contemplativa*—she sits there and takes everything in—was the only right thing to do; and Martha's *Vita activa* was wrong. This interpretation became a great burden for the whole culture of women, encouraging the thought that women who are busy with housekeeping have less worth than those who are meditating.

Nevertheless, Martha plays a pivotal role among these women as the one who recognizes the Christ. In order to grasp this image more clearly, we must be aware that the visit recounted in the Gospels—when Jesus came to Martha's house and Mary sat at His feet—is not actually His first visit there, but one event of several during which Mystery instruction was given to the small, intimate circle around the Christ. Martha recognizes the Christ. This recognition of the Christ occurs immediately before the awakening of Lazarus, a fact that is rarely emphasized. I cite these next lines from the Gospel because of their significance for the whole history of the Mysteries. When Martha and Mary go to Jesus Christ and ask Him to come because Lazarus is dying, He delays and does not come immediately. Martha does not accept this, pleads for Him to come, and later she even reproaches Him:

> Then Martha, as soon as she heard that Jesus was coming, went and met Him: but Mary sat still in the house. Then said Martha unto Jesus, Lord, if thou hadst been here, my brother had not died.[4]

She pleads that He should come. Then Christ speaks to her:

I am the resurrection, and the life: He that believeth in me, though he were dead, yet shall he live. And whosoever liveth and believeth in me shall never die. Believest thou this? She saith unto Him: Yea, Lord, I believe that thou art the Christ, the Son of God, which should come into the world.[5]

Martha is the only one besides Peter who verbalizes this recognition of Christ Jesus during His lifetime.

It is worth noting that Martha's role has traditionally been dismissed. This also began with Gregory the Great who effectively pushed two significant female figures aside by maintaining that Martha's life had no value and that Mary Magdalene was the great sinner. Then, much later, Martin Luther stressed Mary Magdalene's significance by diminishing Martha, saying: 'Martha, your work must be punished and seen as nothing ... I will have no work, for the work of Mary is the faith.'[6]

After the resurrection, Christ Jesus, in the resurrection body, teaches the disciples for eleven years. This was only known through tradition until, in the eighteenth century, a Gnostic manuscript that had long been held privately surfaced and was then acquired by the British Museum in 1785. It is the so-called Askew Codex, which contains the text of the *Pistis Sophia*.

The *Pistis Sophia* is a text written in the language of Upper Egypt on approximately 180 parchment pages. It had been found in the same way as other such materials—the Nag Hammadi documents, for example, or the Qumran scrolls. A seeming contradiction is revealed even in the name of this Gnostic text: *Pistis*, meaning faith, and *Sophia*, meaning wisdom. These two contradictory words are brought together in a single expression. It is *Pistis Sophia*, 'faith wisdom', whose voice is heard throughout this text. When Christ speaks in it, He speaks in a manner that is like the *Pistis Sophia*.

Mary Magdalene is singled out in the *Pistis Sophia* as the pupil closest to the Risen One. For example, Christ says to her: 'Mary, You who are blessed, whom I will make complete in all the Mysteries on high, speak openly, You, whose heart is more directed to the kingdom of heaven than are the hearts of all your brothers.'[7] According to the *Pisitis Sophia* document, Mary Magdalene is the most intimate pupil of the Risen One.

Martha, too, is frequently addressed in this text. The apostles are also addressed, John most often, but others as well—Peter and Thomas, for example. But Martha is honoured by Jesus; every time He responds to her, He brings the answer in a kind of formula, saying: 'Splendid and well done, Martha, You who are blessed . . .' Through this teaching, Martha—along with the others—is given a charge of proclaiming the works of Christ. The text reveals that she was also given another mission: 'Martha stepped forward again and said, "My Lord, I am sober in spirit and comprehend the words that you have said. Now command me to proclaim their interpretation openly." ' In this Gnostic language, sober means: 'There is no obstacle here. I am ready to receive something.' 'He answered . . . and spoke to Martha: "I command you, Martha, to proclaim the interpretation of the words which the Sophia said in her hymn." '[8] Martha's mission is to proclaim the wisdom of the Sophia.

In his *Legenda Aurea* [The golden legend], Jacobus de Voragine, the thirteenth-century bishop of Genoa, collected many stories, especially those describing the continued activity of this most intimate circle around the Christ. I will mention only a few aspects of these legends—not because the legends themselves are interesting, but because our task here is to follow the dissemination of Christianity's influence. What was it in the atmosphere of the Mysteries that contributed to spreading Christianity among the people?

We find in the *Legenda Aurea* the story of how the disciples were persecuted after the Ascension, and how six of them fled as a group. They were Mary Magdalene, Martha, Marcelle (the servant in Martha's household), Lazarus, Maximin (who had baptized the three siblings), and Cedony (a blind man whom Christ had healed, but who is not well known). According to the legend, the six are cast adrift from Jerusalem in a boat without rudder, tackle or sail. They arrive in Marseilles. What course did their journey follow? From Jerusalem, they went to Naples—which was the usual route travelled at that time—then to Rome, to Genoa, and then over to Marseilles. Of course, we are to understand that this legend is an image. But, even as an image, it left a strong impression on European tradition and influenced the whole complicated picture of the Lazarus individuality who, after the awakening, became John the Evangelist, John the Apocalyptist. Up to this point the story focuses on Lazarus.

In this tale, esoteric knowledge is permeated with elements of reality and legend. Nevertheless, it is known that each of the three—Lazarus, Mary Magdalene and Martha—exerted a wider influence in the world. Lazarus is said to have centred his work in Marseilles where he became bishop. Martha founded a cloister for pious young women. Another legend set in Tarascon says that Martha, an energetic woman, became famous for vanquishing a dragon in the south of France. How did she overcome this dragon? She defeated it with the cross and holy water. This, once again, is to be understood as an image. She did not kill the dragon; she overcame it. Naturally, the dragon is an image of the soul. How do we tame the dragon in our soul? Martha shows us how. Then the legend tells us what became of Mary Magdalene; in fact, the remainder of the story's focus is primarily on her.

In the twelfth century, as early as 1140, the city of Vézelay in France became the centre of a cultus around Mary Magdalene. The lintel and the archivolt of the west portal in the cathedral there depict many scenes and images from her life. The following story is told about her—these stories portray images that can awaken qualities in the soul of the listener.

A husband and wife started off to Jerusalem to find out if something significant had truly happened there. During the journey, the wife dies in childbirth. The husband has to leave the wife and the child behind on an island. Desolate, the husband—symbolically called Peregrinus, the pilgrim—goes on to Jerusalem and is taught there for two years by Peter. Beforehand, however, he had asked Mary Magdalene to accompany him inwardly. He then returns to the island and sees a child scampering around on the beach. The child is frightened by him and runs to its mother who lies there dead. The pilgrim brings the child away from the woman, and then the woman opens her eyes: She is his wife and the child is his child.

Mary Magdalene has accompanied him inwardly during the whole journey and has brought about this awakening.

We may think this is just an interesting tale, but its depiction of the magical powers Mary Magdalene exercised has had an enormous effect down through the centuries. The influence of Mary Magdalene continues quite strongly with the Platonists; for example, Alanus ab Insulis wrote a hymn to her. Petrus Venerabilis (Peter the Venerable) composed songs about her, and even Abelard wrote a beautiful hymn dedicated to her.

We come now to the year 900 and somewhat beyond, to approximately the middle of the tenth century when Christianity in Europe was facing an event we have also faced in our time. The tone of the whole century preceding the year 1000 was coloured by a growing anticipation of the turn of the millennium. People noted: The millennium is coming—in 50 years, in 40 years, and then in one year—a new millennium begins! Rudolf Steiner remarks that wherever the decimal system is involved—especially when it concerns the change of millennia—luciferic and ahrimanic forces have a particularly strong effect; there is a greater possibility for their work to take place. Interestingly, around the year 1000 the expectation arose that the world would come to an end, and a deeply chiliastic mood prevailed.

At the beginning of the twentieth century, Rudolf Steiner said that around the year 2000 the situation would be 'exactly the opposite'.[9] I have often puzzled over what the opposite of the end of the world could mean. I think it is connected to our great faith in science and, for the most part, our belief that humanity today is more knowledgeable and aware. For example, we generally think that air pollution is quite terrible; but we also think someone will come along and invent something that will solve the problem. Because we live in an age of mighty inventions and somehow, as a result, are possessed of a quite materialistic optimism, we think humanity cannot possibly come to an end. We tell ourselves that it is simply impossible—that surely something will be invented to solve our problems.

At the end of the third millennium, i.e. at the turn of the millennium a thousand years from now, this will be completely different. The situation will have become so difficult that whole nations of people will long for the end of the world.

Now let us turn our attention back to the end of the first millennium. The most prominent figure of that era was Charlemagne. We see there, for example, the Carolingian renaissance in the ninth century that fused Christianity, the Germanic element and the influence of Rome. Later, in the eleventh century, we encounter the beginning of the great age of Chartres, the pilgrimage path to Compostela, and the earliest stages of scholasticism. Between these two periods came the tenth century, shaped by the enormous cultural influence that streamed from Otto the Great. He was naturally open-minded, and he contributed much to European culture. A significant individuality appeared at this time in what was perhaps her first incarnation since the pre-Christian era, Hroswitha von Gandersheim (born c. 935).

Hroswitha von Gandersheim became a nun at a time when cloister life was quite different from what we find in the later Middle Ages. It was not a secluded, ascetic life; the cloisters were really the centres of culture. Entering the cloister at Gandersheim as a young girl, she grew up amid the wealth of its cultural traditions. Naturally she learned Latin and began to compose Latin verses and dramas. Her work was completely forgotten from the thirteenth century until around 1500—some three hundred years later—when it was rediscovered by the humanist Conrad Celtes. He called her a 'German Sappho'—which is a great compliment. She is considered the first German poetess, the first dramatist in the whole Christian world, and the first woman in Central Europe to write history. When we look at her dramatic work—of course, all of it originally written in Latin—what strikes us as remarkable is that she wrote dramas at all. In fact, there had been virtually no dramas written anywhere since Seneca, i.e., for more than nine hundred years. The writing of dramas resumes in earnest with Hroswitha.

In the form of her works we find intimations of the reincarnation of the spirit of Plato. Hroswitha von Gandersheim's dramas were written in a dialogue form reminiscent of Plato's dialogues with his pupils.

What was the Platonic dialogue? The dialogue consisted of the teacher posing a question and the pupil responding. We might think of it as a bit like catechizing, but it was the beginning of conversation, of discussion. We also find this form in the *Pistis Sophia*. Christ poses a question to the apostles, they respond, and then He broadens and elevates the answer. This represents an important beginning of the art of dialogue.

What is interesting about Hroswitha von Gandersheim is that she never depicted great dramatic moments on stage. She chose the most dramatic stories, but portrayed them through the dialogue, through the word. We recall here that Rudolf Steiner told actors that dramatic action, movement, must really arise out of the formed word.

Later—in the thirteenth century—Thomas Aquinas tried to Christianize logical thinking. This was the question that lived in his soul as he lay dying: How is it possible to Christianize thinking? But for Hroswitha von Gandersheim in the tenth century, the question was: How can the arts be Christianized? Her ideal was the infusion of Christ into the arts.

Her model was the Roman dramatist, Terence. She loved, as she said, the sweetness of his language, although his dramas are rather bawdy, especially in his comedies. But Hroswitha wrote her dramas based solely on her admiration for his language. Avoiding comedy, she points out how the chastity of the soul wins the victory. Her work represents an education of the soul through the literary arts. The literary historian Hugo Kuhn wrote of Hroswitha's dramas: '... through their content, they refute Terence, [and are] a Christian victory over him in his own field.'[10]

In her drama *Theophilus*, Hroswitha took up the Faust theme for the first time in the Germanic world. Theophilus is portrayed as a striving individual; because of his striving, he is redeemed at the end. He is even saved by the 'Eternal Feminine'. At the end of the play, we hear how, through Mary's mercy and guided by the Mother of God, the soul of Theophilus escapes 'from the prison of the body', and ascends 'joyful into heaven'.[11] It remains an open question whether the drama was ever staged in her time.

Now we make a leap of five hundred years. Christian impulses have been developing in Europe from the year 1000 to 1525—the magnificent Gothic cathedrals, everything to do with great works of church music, and the pilgrimage paths. In the south, in Spain, there were no early feminine Christian mystics like those we find in Germany—women like Hildegard von Bingen and Mechtild von Magdeburg. At the end of the fifteenth century, in 1492, America was discovered; in Spain, the Moors were driven out by Ferdinand and Isabella, and the Jews were expelled.

This brings us to Teresa of Avila. Seven years before the expulsion of the Jews, her grandfather renounced his Jewish faith and was converted to Christianity. At that time, such a renunciation of faith was conducted before a tribunal. But after a person had renounced his faith publicly and was baptized, he was considered a Christian. Nonetheless, we can say that Teresa of Avila was descended from a grandfather whose roots were in Judaism.

We know quite a bit about Teresa of Avila because of her auto-biography—her *Vida*—composed five years before her death. She did not write it based on a mere desire to tell her story, but because she had to prove to a tribunal of the Inquisition that she had not committed heresy during her lifetime. Teresa had spent her life in a cloister and had struggled constantly for an inner deepening of the soul. She was not alone in her struggle at that time in Spain. That is the interesting thing. There were many movements in sixteenth-century Spain more interested in an inner deepening of spirituality than in the outer ceremonies of the Church. These groups achieved a certain kind of illumination and received from the Church the designation *Allumbrados*, the Illuminated Ones. For the most part, they ended up burned at the stake.

For Teresa of Avila, so-called inner prayer was the way to the Christ in her own soul. She cultivated this not only on a path of faith, but also on what was potentially a path of knowledge. This was during the first century of the age of the consciousness soul; and she pursued a path of knowledge to the extent possible at that time.

She said, for example, that continuous inner prayer is important, but also knowledge in the moment. It is important always to be awake when the moment of knowledge comes in the soul attitude of inner prayer. In addition to founding 19 cloisters and reforming the Carmelite order, Teresa also collaborated with St John of the Cross in a very fruitful friendship. And she wrote her greatest work, *The Castle of the Soul*, which is actually a path of schooling.

There were seven chambers, seven levels, in her *Castle of the Soul*, also translated as *The Inner Castle*. Its language makes it difficult to understand.

But it is worthwhile to read this text and to work through it if we want to
see how this very clever and alert woman attempted an inner schooling
five hundred years ago. It is a clearly constructed text, a work of art
intended to achieve transparency of the soul. She first goes through the
chamber of self-knowledge. As she describes it, the soul is in a position to
comprehend much more than we might think.[12] This is a very modern
thought. Next is the chamber of endurance, then the chamber in which
the human being releases herself from the entanglements of the world.
Then she writes about how the human being comes to a 'meditation
without any interest', how she becomes objective during meditation. It is
not a matter of thinking much, but of loving much. Then there are the
last three chambers which all have to do with transformation. She continually introduces the image of the silkworm as an image of the soul. It is
constantly in a state of transformation; it never becomes inwardly lazy.

One great theme that characterizes Teresa of Avila—we see it vividly
enacted in the establishment of the cloisters—is her high regard for both
Martha and Mary Magdalene. She writes:

> Martha and Mary [Magdalene] had to be together to offer lodging to
> the Lord and to keep Him always with them, otherwise He would be
> poorly entertained and left without food. What would Mary, who
> always sat at His feet, have given Him to eat if her sister had not
> hastened to her aid? However, His food is that we, in every way, gather
> souls so that they may be saved and praise Him for eternity.[13]

The *Vita activa* and the V*ita contemplativa* are wed here.

Rudolf Steiner spoke several times about Teresa of Avila, addressing
the subject of her visions somewhat clinically. Through her kind of vision,
he says, a person goes deep within himself so that he is somewhat closed
off from the world and broods within his own soul. But Rudolf Steiner
also stresses other characteristics of this individuality, for example: 'When
we ... consider the description of the mystical experiences of St Teresa ...
we inwardly sense a sweetish aroma, if we understand these things eso-
terically.'[14]

In esoteric experience, the sense of smell points inward to the mystical
union with God. Then comes a small reproach of a sort: 'If they [mystics
like Teresa of Avila] were to penetrate into what was external, they would
immediately come into the spiritual world, into the hierarchies. Instead,
they penetrate deep within themselves where they grope their way into
the materiality within their own skin!'[15] This was the real danger they
faced.

But Teresa is an individuality whose bodily members were strong because of her past lives. In his course on pastoral medicine, Rudolf Steiner says about Teresa of Avila:

> She comes from an earlier incarnation in which her soul became particularly strong, quite strong. She incarnates as St Teresa. She takes hold of her ether body with intensity, even before she takes hold of her physical body through incarnation. It becomes stronger, inwardly, qualitatively more intense than is normally the case with human beings. She carries in herself this inwardly strengthened ether body, strengthened in an inwardly qualitative way ... which thus extends beyond the physical body and binds itself strongly to the astral body and the ego, because they are also intrinsically strong from an earlier incarnation.[16]

Now I would like to point to a historical pattern and penetrate it more deeply in connection with our theme. Rudolf Steiner indicates that the three pre-Christian millennia are mirrored in the three post-Christian millennia. We have spoken about the events of the three pre-Christian millennia from various perspectives. Rudolf Steiner calls the time from 3000 to 2000 BC the 'Age of Abraham'. He describes how the potential was built into the physical organization of Abraham to develop the seed of logical thinking. Abraham was in a position to free himself from the old clairvoyance; he had only the one connection to Yahweh, to the God that held sway in the world around him. This was a consciousness of God that could develop in time out of human capacities. Abraham had been visited by Melchizedek, the great Sun-initiate in the Atlantean epoch, and had experienced a kind of initiation through this meeting with Melchizedek. Melchizedek was called the 'Light Purifier' before the time of Christ. In his description, Rudolf Steiner brings together the impulses of Abraham and Melchizedek; the depiction is not as clear in the *Pistis Sophia* where Melchizedek is also addressed as the 'Light Purifier'. Abraham's millennium thus brings about a step forward for human beings in relation to their consciousness of God.

The millennium from 2000 to 1000 BC is referred to as the Age of Moses. The great experience of this period was the voice of God resounding through a natural phenomenon, through the burning bush— but not the usual sort of bush! Tradition says that the tree of knowledge and the tree of life were bound together, and from their union arose the possibility for the voice of God to say: 'I am the I AM.' This experience came to Moses from without. We also recall the Egyptian initiation of

Moses during which Moses was endowed with a replica of the ether body of Zarathustra. This means he had a memory body that was totally familiar with the nature of time.

The Age of Moses lasted until 1000 BC. At the transition into the next millennium we saw the picture of David and the very first intimations of conscience. The period from 1000 up to the turning point of time is referred to as the Age of Solomon. At the close of this period, Jesus and the Christ enter. But before that, during this Solomonic period, we see that the great and wise Solomon could think through how the Temple should be built, yet could not build it himself. For that he required another talent, namely, that of Hiram. The organization of Solomon's bodily members was already so perfect that each bodily member—all seven of them—had its own name. Yet Solomon needed Hiram's help.

Then comes the turning point of time. We can view the time from the Mystery of Golgotha until around AD 1000 as a reflection of the Solomonic age. The effort at that time was towards an understanding of the Christ Mystery through a wisdom that could still be accessed until around the year AD 333, when the possibility dried up. But the influence of the apostles and their insights continued to affect what the early Church Fathers and the Gnostics understood, and for a thousand years the effort continued to understand the Christ Mystery through an inherited wisdom.

From AD 1000 to 2000, the Age of Moses is experienced in reflection. Instead of experiencing the identity of the 'I am the I AM' Who spoke to Moses by way of natural phenomena in the surrounding world, the human being now experiences this within himself. The human being strives within himself, through his own mystical efforts, to understand the divine. This is the great period of the *unio mystica*.

Hroswitha von Gandersheim stands at the end of the first post-Christian age, around the year 1000, at the end of the mirroring of the Solomonic Age. Teresa of Avila, with her inner deepening, stands in the middle of the next age, the mirroring of the Age of Moses. Now—since the year 2000—the mirroring of the Age of Abraham has begun. In Abraham's time the human being received a physical constitution that could shield him from clairvoyant ability to perceive God. Today, human beings will undergo an inversion of this; we will develop capacities through which we can and will experience the divine clairvoyantly.

This development, now present only in embryonic form, comes at the same time as another great cosmic event. For five thousand years—from the beginning of the Age of Abraham until our own time—humanity had been in the so-called Kali Yuga, in a dark age. Kali is perceived to be a great goddess, especially in the oriental tradition, the Indian tradition. This is not just an abstraction; the darkening brought about by this goddess should not be viewed as only negative. A darkness had to come so that human beings could find their way to earth. But this path quickly led to the hardening of the earth and, if the Christ had not come, this hardening into matter and darkness would have ruined humanity.

The age of Kali Yuga is now past. Human beings will develop the capacity to receive more and more insight into the spiritual world. We will develop this capacity through our physical constitution, where the seeds of it already exist.

Logos and Anti-Logos—Sorat, the Sun Demon, and the Counter-world of the Trinity

Manfred Schmidt-Brabant

Myths about the evolution of the world and the origin of creation are found among many peoples and cultures. One motif that runs through these myths is the introduction of evil into evolution at the moment creation was set in motion by a divine being or beings.

This motif is probably most familiar to us through two great images in the Christian imagination of creation. One is the image of the Fall of Man—the seduction of Eve by the snake, and then the seduction of Adam that led the two to eat from the tree of knowledge of good and evil. They had been forbidden to eat from this tree, but they acquired the ability to distinguish good from evil after they were seduced by the snake. In the Oberufer Paradise Play, which contains many truths, God says:

> ... how has Adam wealth so fine:
> he has become almost divine.[1]

The gods had a capacity of discernment that human beings did not possess until Adam and Eve ate from the tree. This capacity came too early to humanity and, for this reason, they were expelled from Paradise.

Shortly afterwards, the second great evil breaks into humanity: Cain slays his brother Abel. They are the first two children of humanity, and one slays the other. Murder stands at the very beginning of the history of earth and humanity.

Of course, these are pictorial imaginations; no one really thinks that there was actually a snake wound around a tree. Nonetheless, these images correspond to knowledge that came from the Old Mysteries. Moses carried within himself the secrets of time—of genesis—through the ether body of Zarathustra. Various interpretations throughout religious history have claimed that the Books of Moses (the Pentateuch) were probably written by multiple authors. But there is a unified spirit present in these books, in their depictions of the beginning of the earth.

Participants in the Old Mysteries still had a very spiritual knowledge of the beings, the processes and the spiritual realms we today call evil. They knew about beings we call Satan, the devil, demons; they knew about events like the Fall of Man and others; they knew about the spiritual realms belonging to evil that we call hell and other cultures refer to as Gehenna, and so on. We must recall that at that time all this was experienced—even by those who belonged to the Mysteries—quite differently from the way we speak of evil today. Until the end of Atlantis, the workings of evil were seen as objective, cosmic processes of the divine, just as we think of natural catastrophes as objective processes—a bolt of lightning that hits a house and burns it to the ground; tornados that lay waste to whole cities in America; or an earthquake. Only very gradually, after the end of Atlantis, did the modern feeling for the existence of evil begin to awaken faintly in humanity.

During the ancient Indian period, people left the spirit world of Atlantis—they had actually stepped on the earth only after the great flood—and they experienced the whole earth as *maya*. They were not yet prepared to recognize it as a reality that had the potential for errors and evil. Through steps taken within the Mysteries, they gradually came to accept the fact that they had entered the world of reality as though across an abyss. Thus, the hallmark of the entire ancient Indian culture—one could say, the general theme of all the Mysteries of that time—was the secret of the abyss.

The situation in the Ancient Persian period proceeds a step further. The name of a great initiate—Zarathustra—arises here. Of course, Zarathustra incarnates again and again. The important step he takes now is to see two great principles as cosmic forces: the principle of good, Ahura Mazda, or Ormuzd; and the principle of evil, Ahriman. The former is the principle of light; the latter is the principle of darkness. These powers are outside the human being, but they have effects in the human world, in the earthly world.

These two cosmic forces begin to differentiate in the third post–Atlantean period—the Egypto-Babylonian period. Now good gods and evil gods are identified. Above all, this is represented in the central theme of Egyptian initiations and their cults—the theme of Isis and Osiris.

In his explanation of this theme, Rudolf Steiner attaches great importance to the fact that Osiris is both the son and the husband of Isis. Isis brought forth Osiris. Then a quite dramatic story begins. There is another divinity, Typhon—also called Set—who is a figure similar to Ahriman. Typhon murders Osiris, divides him into 14 pieces and scatters them all across Egypt. The weeping Isis travels the country gathering up the various parts of Osiris, but she is unable to find his genitals. She revives Osiris, so that he lives once again, but he cannot procreate. Prior to all this, Isis had already conceived the Horus child through a beam of light from Osiris. Horus avenges Osiris by murdering Typhon. Osiris becomes the great god of the underworld who takes care of human beings between death and a new birth. Those who are worthy may unite themselves with Osiris after death, and will carry the name of Osiris. However, Horus becomes the creator of the human being who will live on earth in the future.

Here, for the first time, processes affecting human life enter, as it were, into the Egyptian Mysteries; but these processes were still supra-human, divine processes. Only later were they experienced in the cults as being relevant for human beings. The first real step towards something new comes with Moses. Through Moses, the law is given to the human being so he could either be in accord with it or at odds with it. The human being becomes capable of doing good or evil. Until then, people were more or less moved to act by supersensible forces in their subconscious. Now, they are capable of doing good or evil based on the ego in them that the laws of Moses address.

The Ten Commandments are the central piece in what is actually an extensive catalogue of social conduct. Anyone who has studied the Books of Moses (the Pentateuch) knows that they contain well over six hundred indications about conduct. Similar compendia existed elsewhere in this period, even among the Babylonians and the Sumerians. They appear, for example, in the laws of Hammurabi written on a stele now found in the Louvre. But none of this represented what later became known as the laws of good and evil. These were still only rules of conduct. For example: 'If you murder a slave not your own, you must replace him with another or three oxen.' Or, 'If you murder another man, you must marry his wife.' There were also processes for compensation, down to the smallest detail. For example: 'If an ox has been loaned to you and you injure one of its eyes, you must give a sheep to the owner of the ox.'

The Ten Commandments introduce the concept of human responsibility. For the first time we find a very lofty generality directed at the ego: 'Thou shalt not kill.' In the work of Hammurabi, this is still prescribed in terms of 'If you kill a sheep ...'; 'if you kill a man ...'; 'if you kill two men... '; 'if you kill a slave ...'; and so on. Now in the Ten Commandments it simply says: 'Thou shalt not kill.' The human being is left entirely to his own devices; he enters into the conceptualization of a deed that he must define for himself. Today, it is difficult for us to imagine what

arose in the feeling realm of human beings through the Ten Commandments Moses brought down from Mount Sinai. We know that
when someone tries to keep the Ten Commandments, the interpretations
suddenly become more complex. 'Thou shalt not steal.' What does that
mean in economic life, with taxes, with deductions? How often in this
century has a question arisen about the meaning of 'Thou shalt not kill'?
What does this mean in regard to whether you should become a soldier?
Does this only apply to killing humans?

Earlier instructions were graphic down to the most concrete detail,
even with Moses. Among the rules of conduct, for example, there is the
famous one: 'You must not cook the flesh of a young goat in the milk of
its mother.' All of kosher cooking originates with this statement. Even
today, pious Jews still take great pains to avoid bringing any kind of milk
product into contact with a meat product. Meals consist either of a milk
product or a meat product, but not both. This can be interpreted even
more specifically. We have friends in Israel who are immersed in their
culture; they have, for example, two sets of dishes because meat cannot be
placed on a dish used to hold cheese or else the dish will have to be broken
and thrown away. Thus these friends have a set of red dishes and a set of
blue dishes. Someone who leads a pious life by observing these rules has a
sense of what is correct or incorrect, good or evil, that is completely
different from someone who finds himself suddenly confronted with the
direct statement from God: 'Thou shalt not kill.'

The true placement of the individual between good and evil appears
for the first time in Christianity. In the New Testament, the human being
is situated for the first time in the realm of free choice between good and
evil. Satan is mentioned in the New Testament 28 times, the devil is
mentioned 62 times, hell is mentioned 15 times, and evil is mentioned 48
times. An enumeration like this can point to how the human being is
confronted with alternatives by such a powerful statement from God:
'You can decide between good and evil. It is up to you to decide.'

We can understand, therefore, why early Christianity constantly
struggled with the question: Where does evil come from? This question
has not disappeared even today—not in modern theological discussion,
not in the discussions of other religions, not in spiritual science.

The Church Fathers were of the opinion that evil itself was without
substance. Each held a certain opinion about the nature of evil. Thomas
Aquinas says: 'Evil does not exist as an idea within God.' Origen expresses
it this way: 'Evil is turned by God to the good of the whole.' Augustine
says: 'Christ makes use of evil for good.'

Here a theme surfaces that Rudolf Steiner also addresses when he speaks about the fall of Lucifer; he says Lucifer's fall was a sacrifice made in order to prepare for the coming of the Christ. Plotinus, the Neoplatonist, says that primordial evil is physical matter that appeared as the last emanation of essential good; this essential evil is non-existence and has no substance of its own. Satan is the great riddle with which they all struggled. It was said that Satan is the leader of the forces of darkness. The Church Fathers describe him as a creature that emerged pure from the hands of his creator, an angel that stood on one of the highest levels of the heavenly hierarchy. But he rebelled against God and won lower angels for his rebellion.

But this led to further philosophical problems for the Church Fathers. What is the basis for the fall of bad angels? Where does evil come from? Did evil pre-date Satan? Satan became evil, but did evil exist before him? These are not just the focus of fanciful theological debates. They were matters that entered deeply into the inner life of people at that time and, above all, led to spiritual and historical arguments, wars, even catastrophes.

Here the argument with Manichaeism arises. In the third century, Mani, a Persian, took up Christianity as well as the old Persian teachings of light and dark, and established a strict dualism. For him, the process of the world is an on-going battle between light and dark, between good and evil, between spirit and matter. Even after Manichaeism was condemned by the Church, it continued underground and resurfaced in the Middle Ages among the Bogomils and the Cathars.

We are reminded here of a terrible catastrophe—the annihilation of the Cathars, the murder of so many people. This event is traceable directly to the Cathar's cultivation of this old dualism—although the whole matter was much more complicated. They held the view that light battles dark. Thus the battle centred on the question: Where does evil come from? This battle has been going on for two thousand years and is often fiercely fought.

Our modern idea of evil—of the devil, of hell—has its principal source in the vivid imagery of the Middle Ages. We see the devil and even hell depicted in the capitals of pillars in Romanesque churches. Demons of all sorts are carved in the exterior decoration of Gothic cathedrals. There is a rich flood of images from Bruegel, Hieronymous Bosch and others. It is impossible to go through a museum in Europe and not see wonderful angels next to devils that are just as wonderful.

The artistic conceptualization of evil actually began around AD 1000.

The so-called Iconoclast controversy took place over a long period in the first millennium. We recall in the Pentateuch: 'Thou shalt not make unto thee any graven image or any likeness of thy God.' Even after the Mystery of Golgotha, when people knew that Christ had appeared in human form, they still hesitated for a long time to depict Him. They opted instead to use a symbol or an image like two fish. The crucifix originated in the fourth century and the first one is in the basilica of Santa Sabina in Rome. Only gradually were a few images of Him made.

In the eighth century, Emperor Leo III issued an edict forbidding the veneration of images throughout his whole empire. Iconoclasm then comes to a mighty culmination under Constantine V, also in the eighth century. The Council of Hiereia in 754—the so-called 'Iconoclastic Council of Constantinople'—approved the eradication of all images with religious content. This resulted in a great wave of destruction that coursed through Europe. Every image with any religious content at all was destroyed. Some of the cloistered monks refused to destroy their lovingly painted little icons. Hundreds, even thousands, of monks were murdered because of these images. Only somewhat later did the Empress Irene rescind the ban; but even Charlemagne issued a strong edict against every form of image worship. A new flood of images breaks through for the first time in the Romanesque period.

Thus the first millennium appears to be more like a thousand years of judging evil by means of the intellect. It is still the age of the intellectual soul and when these deliberations began they were as a purely intellectual activity. Whole volumes could be filled with the arguments of the Church Fathers and those that come later—disputations on evil, on the devil, and their relationship to God. Then the inner life asserted itself, for an imaginative fulfilment of the inner life begins with images of good and evil. This assertion of the inner life is obvious to anyone with even the slightest knowledge of Europe's art treasures. It is especially striking if account is taken of how much art was later destroyed in yet a second wave of Iconoclasm. An infinite splendour is still visible in what remains. These images—particularly those in which a genuine Mystery knowledge plays a role—have formed our consciousness, and rightfully so. For example, there is Master Bertram in Hamburg with his creation myth that clearly depicts an anthropomorphic snake with a human head in the Garden of Eden. Bertram's depiction led Rudolf Steiner to say that this imagination corresponds to the essence, so to speak, of what people of that time confronted in a spiritual way as the Fall of Man.[2]

The materialistic nineteenth century loved to talk about the dark

Middle Ages. But, in fact, these dark Middle Ages exerted a strong power of imagination on the soul. When people spoke of the many devils—when they painted them and depicted them—it was based on their perception of the evil forces active in the world.

We can speak of three aspects to the medieval perception of evil in the Middle Ages. The first is the controversy over Iconoclasm. The second is the increasing demonization of heretics, a process that requires we understand it. There was a feeling that Christ had brought light and freedom to the human soul. People sensed the presence of an old, atavistic clairvoyance in heretics—and this was very often true. It was believed that this old atavistic clairvoyance came from the devil. This is why the Dominicans felt themselves to be *domini canes*, 'sheepdogs of the Lord', who guarded the flock against the wolf of the old clairvoyance.

People were excommunicated from the Church in the first millennium; but soon after began the tragic history of the great destructive crusades that continued with the burning of witches. It is easy to say: 'Those superstitious people! They actually thought there were old witches who could cast spells; and they burned these poor old women!' However, careful accounts were kept at that time with lists of the witches that were burned. Few of them were old women. Records exist that reveal the identity of those who were burned as witches, and there are religious figures and children among them—the three-year-old daughter of the mayor, the son of the goldsmith, the canon. We think: 'But people then could not have been so blind that they would take a small child, a prelate, or a craftsman for a witch.' These lists show that the accused and the dead run right through every strata of society.

Rudolf Steiner solves this conundrum when he says those who were destroyed were suspected of being clairvoyant. Clairvoyance could occur in a child, a young boy, a young man, a religious figure, the nobility. People sought to wipe out anyone suspected of being able to see more than the outer reality. The intent was to exterminate those who could see—perhaps clairvoyantly—what lies beyond the superficial workings of the world. Behind this development was a highly placed collegium with a particular dogma or doctrine that said esoteric perceptions should only be available to a few for the exercise of power. They thought dogmas and historical traditions were good enough for the masses.

The third aspect that needs to be mentioned here is a particularly painful chapter. Lust for power had given rise not only to an unjust demonization of the old clairvoyance or thoughts that deviated from the norm, but has since ancient times taken the form of a genuine devil worship, black magic, genuine black sabbaths. I mentioned this earlier in connection with Herod when I spoke about the terrible black magic cults behind his infanticide, and the same forces that lay behind Salome. The further we delve into the Middle Ages, the more material there is that points to the existence of genuine devil worship. We touch upon something here that leads directly into the present. Throughout the world, black sabbaths, devil worship, black magic continue to exist, even today—and this has crept into our culture, most visibly through rock music. A survey was conducted a few years ago among older German schoolchildren that brought a shocking statistic to light. A significant percentage of these school-age children had taken part in black sabbaths or devil cults. This is just as bad in the rest of the western world, in America. There are syndromes that afflict adults who were forced in childhood to eat human flesh in a black magic cult. The whole matter is kept tightly under wraps. It is not reported in the news, in the *Frankfurter Allgemeine* or in the *Süddeutsche Zeitung*; but every now and again, something about it surfaces. This is an evil stream from the decadent Mysteries that continues to flow through history. Naturally, it was known in earlier times that such circles existed, and justified attempts were made to destroy them root and branch.

The actual battle with evil, however, became possible only in the present time. All epochs have their great tasks which are actually Mystery themes. We have already identified one of them. The mystery theme of the period of ancient India was the 'mystery of the abyss'. Then there was the ancient Persian epoch with the 'mystery of number'; then the Egypto-Babylonian period with its theme of the 'mystery of affinities', of alchemy, of the elective affinities of matter. Then came the Graeco-Roman period with the 'mystery of birth and death'. The task of our own time—the battle with evil—only surfaces after 1413, with the beginning of the fifth post-Atlantean epoch—the 'mystery of evil'. The 'mystery of the Word' and the 'mystery of divine bliss' will follow in the sixth and seventh cultural epochs respectively.

These themes are embedded in the organism of the divine plan and they are true for all rhythms of seven. Old Saturn stood under the signature of the 'mystery of the abyss'. Earth, in the fourth planetary position, stands under the sign of the 'mystery of birth and death'. The sign of the 'mystery of evil' will not occur until Jupiter, the next condition after Earth.

This fifth post-Atlantean epoch did not actually begin until the twentieth century. Earlier centuries were precursors and the Middle Ages continued to play a role in them. But then two events took place. The first is the end of the Kali Yuga. For five thousand years, a divine being had the task of veiling humanity from the spiritual world so that, as a whole, it could learn to develop the human ego on the earth. This epoch ended in 1899 as had been predicted by the sages in ancient India, marking the beginning of an epoch of openness. The expression *New Age* was not invented by the current adherents of esotericism; it already existed at the turn of the last century among those who knew that a new age was beginning, an 'epoch of light', a time in which the human being can find the means within himself to ascend to the gods.

Associated with this new age was the great emancipation of the human ego that began towards the end of the nineteenth century. We are still engaged in that process. Previously, human beings had been strongly defined by group affiliations—their ethical behaviour was defined by society, family, religion, state. People were told what was good and what was evil. From the nineteenth century and into the twentieth, a kind of anti-authoritarian revolution began. People shed one taboo after another. They began to reject any external authority in moral matters, and sexual licence carried this right into the past few decades.

What replaces this external authority today? The human being looks at the past and says: 'I will not let myself be told what I have to do! Who says so?' Each human being has to judge for himself. Rudolf Steiner wrote his great fundamental work of philosophy, *The Philosophy of Freedom*, based on this very idea. In it he says individual ethics, or 'ethical individualism', will arise.[3]

How do people today find the basic principles of good and evil? The twentieth century actually begins with this riddle, and so we can say that anthroposophy led to the first understanding of the relationship of good to evil. For almost two millennia, people had always contrasted good with evil, and had always gotten into difficulties as a result. If something was good, its opposite had to be evil, even though that conclusion was often not at all reasonable or logical.

Aristotle arrived philosophically at another way to come to terms with this problem. Among his voluminous texts, he also wrote an ethics, the *Nicomachean Ethics*, in which he pursues the question: What is right? What is virtue for human beings if we are not supposed to think in terms of good and evil? His answer was: Virtue is the human capacity to maintain the middle ground between too much and too little, a capacity guided by reasoned insight. Bravery is right; but excessive bravery is foolhardiness and too little bravery is cowardice.

Economy is right; but excessive economy is stinginess, too little
economy is waste.

The idea that evil is a deviation towards either of two sides arises for the
first time with Aristotle. We become evil by going in either of these two
opposite directions. In time, this idea went underground in the history of
philosophy and intellectual history. Even today, good and evil remain as
opposites in most people's minds. Good and evil are in our blood, deeply
embedded even in the language we use.

Rudolf Steiner says, however, that we must view this question not as a
duality, but as threefold. Thus, within anthroposophy the image arises of
evil as either of two possible deviations from the third way—a true,
human, Christian middle. These deviations are designated with the names
of beings: Ahriman, the ahrimanic deviation, and Lucifer, the luciferic
deviation. In the context of the basic theme we are examining here—the
relationship of the spiritual to the physical—we can understand the first as
a deviation towards too much spirit and the other as a deviation towards
too much of the physical.

Anyone who has read the work of Rudolf Steiner knows that it
contains extensive descriptions of this great polarity as it is reflected in all
phenomena. There are ahrimanic illnesses and luciferic illnesses; there is
an ahrimanic deviation in life and a luciferic one. Even in the human
polarity between inwardness of soul and outwardness of the senses, the
outer senses tend towards what is ahrimanic and the inner soul tends
towards what is luciferic.

One of the most significant historical processes gradually develops as
a result of this tendency to deviate to one side or the other of the
Christian middle. The Christ-being made His way through the world
after His resurrection; the reformation of the Mystery centres is one
effect of the Christ on historical events. But Christ's path of suffering
also continued. When Christianity became a state religion, the Christ-
being experienced it as though it were a crucifixion. We have lost an
understanding for the terrible materialism of our age; we are no longer
so sensitive to it. But this nineteenth-century materialism was like a
second crucifixion for the Christ. The Christ continues to undergo a
similar sort of crucifixion when human beings fail to act out of a spirit
of love.

All of this has a consequence which resulted in anthroposophy's great
proclamation of the Christ. Rudolf Steiner says that initiates observed the
fact that the Christ-being drew close to the earth again in the twentieth
century and entered its etheric sphere. We speak about this as the

reappearance of Christ in the etheric. Christ can be found by humanity in the etheric realm.

After the Mystery of Golgotha, some of the Mysteries became followers of this Mystery of Golgotha. Other Mysteries remained at a distance, especially the Asiatic Mysteries that continued under the leadership of a luciferic inspiration and did not participate in the Mystery of Golgotha. Something similar happened with western initiates who took no part in the Mystery of Golgotha and instead sought out ahrimanic beings. Both these kinds of anti-Christian Mysteries are widespread today, and can no longer be identified merely by their locale. Asiatic, anti-Christian Mysteries are found all across the earth as far away as California; western, anti-Christian Mysteries are found all over the earth as far away as Tokyo.

These anti-Christian Mysteries are active in the world through various societies that have two fateful intentions for civilization. The eastern initiates in these Mysteries see the reappearance of the Christ in the etheric realm and they do not want to accept it. They hold the view that it would be better for souls to leave the earth, that individuals are better off in the world of the stars. These eastern initiates are the source of every impulse to make the earth as uninhabitable as possible, so that souls no longer have the desire to incarnate. Their aim is to do away with repeated earth lives. Everything of this sort launched from the East is directed toward creating such chaotic, inhuman, miserable conditions that souls who witness this turn back before incarnating, preferring instead to remain in the spiritual world.

The impulse that emerges from the so-called western initiates in the anti-Christian Mysteries is completely different. They also see that human beings could look to the Being of the Etheric Christ, and they want to put another being in His place—a strictly ahrimanic being. Therefore, they present another impulse—to make the earth so habitable, so pleasant, that souls will not want to leave after death. These initiates want souls to renounce the normal course of their existence—that they pass after death through the world of the stars and undergo the transformations there that make a new earthly life possible. This renunciation means that these souls would remain connected with the earth after death, and reincarnation would stop for them. We live in an age when these Mystery battles take on frightening forms, but they are forms closely associated with the enormity of the human task. It literally comes down to undermining repeated earth lives or else strengthening them. This battle is a central theme of anthroposophy.

A reciprocal relationship plays into this process. Through their Christ-initiation, the Templars had already discovered the law that governs it—natural phenomena and social phenomena are simply two sides of the same coin. Anyone who wants to work in the world must always work on both aspects, the natural and the social.

The Templars had a specific ideal. They recognized that human nature requires a *Vita activa* and a *Vita contemplativa*. After the Fall of Man, the human being had gradually become incapable of practising a *Vita activa* and a *Vita contemplativa* on his own; the Templars realized that the human being had come under the direction of the Emperor and the Pope. They had the will to free the human being from this supervision, to place him on him own two feet—so to speak—in an active social and religious life. To this end, they trod a path of selflessly handling the gold of the world. They knew that gold is the nature side of wisdom, of the Sophia, in the social realm. Their organization functioned as a cohesive state throughout Europe for two centuries—other states were merely fragmented fiefdoms, greater or lesser counties, and so forth. With this imperium, they founded a way of dealing with gold that was based on a spiritual insight into a kind of selflessness. They are often called the first bankers because they managed gold throughout all of Europe. A traveller could deposit his gold at a Templar castle and receive a receipt, a cheque; he could then travel straight through Europe, redeem the cheque for gold at another Templar castle, and use the money for business or payments. But this describes only what is known of their external practices. Behind these practices stood a social service that was to bring new impulses for the social life.

At this point, one of the most gruesome figures in world history, the French king Philip the Fair, steps in. He was the reincarnation of a black magic initiate from Mexican Mysteries that had carried out a horrendous slaughter of prisoners. By the hundreds and thousands, these prisoners were sacrificed, cut open, on the Mexican pyramids so that stone gutters had to be built in order to drain the blood away. Philip reappeared later in European civilization where he was filled with a manic lust for gold. He believed he was entitled to possess all the gold there was. This was not only physical greed—a king is normally wealthy enough. It was driven by the knowledge that someone who possesses gold in an egotistical sense has power over other people; when gold is managed selflessly, others are liberated. Philip the Fair set in motion the great opposition to the Templars' destiny.

He sought to acquire all the Templar gold for himself by destroying the Templar order. The Pope was the king's creature, and between 1307 and 1314 he set in motion the great trial that resulted in the destruction of the

Templar order. The last Grand Master, Jacques de Molay, said from the stake: 'In a month's time I will bring you before the throne of God.' A month later Philip the Fair died in a hunting accident.

The Templars' deeds are like a model of what anthroposophy is trying to accomplish through the threefold social order. Rudolf Steiner makes quite clear that this means recreating a society in which the human being can be free in his spiritual life, in his religious life; free in the organization of the rights life; and free to exercise brotherhood in economic life.

In these discussions, we have also come to know the problem of evil from other perspectives. Jesus, through His encounter with the Essenes, had the experience: 'There is no purpose served in overcoming evil in ourselves if we then chase it out into the world.' This theme arises again with Parzival. The descriptions we have of the Grail initiation of Parzival show that the stage of purification in which the individual overcomes evil in himself must lead to a next step in which evil is taken up again, internalized and transformed into something good. This is also the principal theme of the Rosicrucians. The Rose Cross itself is the symbol for the transformation of evil.

The Rose Cross meditation is a basic meditation. It involves imagining how the chaste, green sap within the plant brings forth the pure rose, and how in the human being the drives and passions are connected with the red blood. The entire meditation, which can be found in *Occult Science, An Outline*, asks us to imagine how the lower drives—not the drives themselves, but what is evil about the drives—are burned up in the black cross and thereby transformed into the roses of spiritland.[4] This is also how the great law—that atoms and thoughts are two sides of the same thing—lived in the Rosicrucian Mystery.

Let us look at what lies behind the world of appearance as the great, fundamental principle of evil. An imagination has been developed and often described in the following way. The beginning of the Gospel of John relates that the Logos created the world: 'All things were made by him; and without him was not any thing made that was made.'[5] The Logos creates the world; the Logos creates it, as it were, in the void. But as a result of the Logos creating the world in the void, the void becomes being. The void takes on the nature of being. However, because people thought of the divine in terms of the Trinity rather than the unity of the Logos, they had the feeling that the divine deed of creation itself calls forth a kind of counter-Trinity.

People noted three elements in this counter-Trinity. They said that the abyss, hell, stands opposite the Father. Hell was experienced as a being.

There is a wonderful literary passage in the apocryphal Gospel of Nicodemus in which Satan converses with Hell.

> Satan arrived, the heir of darkness, and spoke to Hades: 'Insatiable, all-
> devouring One, hear my words! There is One among the Jewish
> people Who is named Jesus and calls Himself the Son of God. He is,
> however, merely a man. At my instigation, He was crucified by the
> Jews. And since He is now dead, be ready to imprison Him here. For I
> know He is just a man ... Prepare yourself so that, when He comes
> here, you can capture Him firmly in your power.'
>
> Hades responded: 'Heir of darkness, Son of Ruination, Devil ... If
> He has freed others from the grave, how and with what force can He
> be overpowered by us? I recently devoured a dead one by the name of
> Lazarus, and very soon after one of the living ones did violence to me,
> tearing this Lazarus from my bowels with mere words. I assume it was
> the same one of whom you speak. If we take this one up now, I fear we
> will risk losing the others ... for not as a one who is dead, but as an
> eagle, He flew away from me ...[6]

This story shows the kind of striking imagery through which hell was seen
as a being. This being was also painted as the maw of hell. As an abyss, it is
the counter-image of the Father.

The counter-image of the Son is Satan, especially as depicted in the
Sorat-being in the Revelation of John. This is a being that emerges from
the depths of the cosmos, has no relationship with our evolution, that is
foreign to and an enemy of our evolution. It is also a being with no
understanding for the fact that other beings create an ego and that one day
this ego will be capable of saying, 'Not I, but the Christ in me.'[7] Thus, this
being—Sorat—wanted to destroy the whole of evolution. He did not
succeed, but instead had to be satisfied with what was left over, with the
dregs of humanity that ended up in the whirlpool of counter-Christianity.

A being that has been depicted in various ways is seen as the
counterpart of the Holy Spirit; it is referred to in Revelation as the
'Whore Babylon'.[8] What occurred in Babylon was the misuse of spiritual
capacities for personal, egotistic reasons. But, of course, the Apocalyptist
thought: 'The whole of Babylon is the earth. Babylon is the humanity
that behaves in such a way that it misuses spiritual treasures, the humanity
that serves only the lower ego through everything spiritual, especially its
spiritual capacities.'

The initiate painters arrived at the right image for this based on the
Book of Revelation. This Whore Babylon carries the counter-Grail. In

her hands, the task of the Holy Spirit—to create the chalice that will take up the Christ—becomes the vessel of horror that she carries. We think here, for example, of the wonderful engraving by Dürer. There are many other illustrations of this Whore Babylon, and in each it is evident that people at the time knew precisely what was meant.

There is something else associated with this image of the counter-Trinity—the image of the Antichrist. This Antichrist is mentioned in the New Testament, but was never experienced as a satanic, devilish being. Instead, it has always been known that the Antichrist is a human being; the Antichrist is human. The famous passage from the second epistle of Paul to the Thessalonians says: '... first the great breach of faith, the separation from the spiritual world must occur; the human of chaos must be revealed, the son of the abyss and of the ruination, the spirit of contradiction ...'[9]

Through the Antichrist, hostility and contempt towards all knowledge and towards reverence for the divine world are revealed to the world. He seizes hold of what should be a temple of God and presents himself there as the god. The image of the Antichrist has been a part of history since the New Testament. There are all manner of images, Mystery plays from the Middle Age, like *The Antichrist*. Of course, it belongs to human nature that people describe one another as the Antichrist—for example, Luther called the Pope the Antichrist and the Pope called Lutherans the emissaries of the Antichrist.

Something else lies behind this. It would be wrong to think that the Antichrist is a human being who will one day appear. This is an image, an imagination. The Antichrist is the human being in each of us that does not want the Christ. Rudolf Steiner's *Occult Science* ends with very serious words that draw attention to the fact that forces of evil are related to our sensory impressions of this world. He says that an evil humanity will arise, an evil human will arise.

> These two things, sensory impressions and the soul-spiritual element, create divergent streams of development to some degree. Through the forces that belong to the sensory stream, the forms of 'evil humanity' arise. The necessity for a human soul to incarnate in such a form will occur only when a person has created the conditions for it himself ... Supersensible knowledge must seek the development of human forms and the development of soul destinies along two completely different paths; and a confusion of the two ... would be a remnant of a materialistic attitude which, if present, would interfere with the science of the supersensible in an adverse way.[10]

These are the final words of *Occult Science* and thus, so to speak, the final words in its depiction of evolution.

Shortly before his death, Soloviev, the great philosopher of the Sophia, wrote a well-known story of the Antichrist. He sets the story in modern times; it takes place in 'the United States of Europe'. There had been another war with the East, with Asia, and it is now over. A brilliant young man emerges, conquers all hearts with his brilliance, and finally he is chosen Emperor of Europe. This person is spiritual, of course; he is socially sensitive, a vegetarian, and a lover of animals. There is a scene in which he—as though in a trance—is led one night to an abyss. Out of this abyss climbs a figure with icy eyes and a metallic voice that says to him: 'You are my dear son. Do everything in your own name. I want nothing from you.' This is a kind of fundamental ahrimanic inspiration. The man returns home and, in the course of one night, writes a great pamphlet that solves the social questions of the whole world.

When he is chosen emperor, he takes care that economic parity arises everywhere. He finds a way for the poor to have something to eat and for the rich to keep most of their wealth. In the end, he tries to unite all religions, and he demands of all religious people that they worship him. Then three men of the cloth—a Catholic priest, an Orthodox priest and a Protestant minister—resist this. The whole thing ends—although the story is unfinished—when Christ appears in the clouds and shatters the Antichrist.

Whenever this story is interpreted—and many scholars have done so correctly—it is said: 'This Antichrist is quite a good man. He solves social problems and economic questions, and he is actually noble and good. There is only one thing he cannot do: he cannot love another being. He only loves himself.' Soloviev describes in a wonderful way how the Christ appears to the Antichrist and offers him His hand. He shows why the Antichrist is, so to speak, inwardly torn asunder. No, he loves only himself! This is his principle. He puts himself where the temple of God should be—into the body—and considers himself a god.

A certain lecture of mine has raised a question—one that also arose in Rudolf Steiner's time: If the Christ is present only when two or more are gathered in His name, what happens when a person is alone? When a person is alone, he can direct love to other people. When he does his exercises, his concentration exercise, his meditation, he is, of course, alone at the beginning. But through these exercises he makes himself capable of developing selflessness, the element into which the Christ can immerse Himself.

Rudolf Steiner once said that the Christ could be mistaken in the spiritual world for Lucifer, because Lucifer also appears in radiant beauty. But we will always recognize the Christ-being through one thing: His complete and absolute selflessness. Of course, this selflessness can also be practised in silent prayer. We can silently pray the model prayer to ourselves, the Lord's Prayer, and say to ourselves: 'Don't I pray, "Give us this day our daily bread"? I do not pray that I be given "*my* daily bread"; it is "our daily bread". "Forgive us our trespasses" means that this fundamental prayer contains what should be in all prayers—that I take up the concerns of the rest of humanity. Others do not need to be there physically. When I pray the Lord's Prayer in this way, I include in this "us" real people whom I know, about whom I hear—in Kosovo and elsewhere—so that this comes to exemplify "Two or more in His name".' Statements like this must be understood on the basis of the principle they represent.

If we can understand them in this way, then we will understand how, before the appearance of the Christ, a great imagination arises that also appears in the Book of Revelation and then became reality: the battle of Michael with the dragon. Of course, there is the one image: the dragon—a figure of satanic forces—forced into the abyss by Michael. But the dragon is also in us. If we turn to Michael, we turn to that being who can hold the Antichrist, the dragon in us, at bay. If we take the image of Michael into ourselves—which we can do—this etheric image in us battles the inclination to self-love, selfishness, the dragon nature in us, and everything that is merely human.

In fact, the Antichrist can more properly be identified as the 'Anti-Jesus'. The entire preparation of Jesus and the figure of Jesus Himself lead to taking up the Christ—a humanity prepared to take up the Christ. The 'Anti-Jesus' in us is that part of the human being that rejects the Christ, that does not take Him up.

If we examine this image carefully, we understand how the Christ battles evil, for this is what Michael does. Michael, the countenance of the Christ—this was how it was experienced in earlier times—is Christ revealed to the world of evil. When Christ appears there, He appears as Michael and battles evil. Christ Himself is characterized in the most wonderful words: The Christ sees only love, not sins. What Christ observes in the world are the deeds of love.

The Representative of Humanity—the sculpture at the Goetheanum carved by Rudolf Steiner—portrays the Christ, but He is not engaged in battle with Lucifer and Ahriman. Lucifer falls simply through the Being of

The Representative of Humanity

Christ; Ahriman binds himself with the light that radiates from the Christ. The Christ strides forward in endless selflessness. He strides forward in such a way that we understand that He stands with us always before the abyss of evil. He stands at the abyss of evil as an image of how the human being should deal with evil.

This is one reason evil must exist. The human being is to join the world of the hierarchies through the spirit of freedom and the spirit of love. He must find freedom in order to act out of it in love and, as a result, escape the two deviations of evil.

'If it were impossible for the human being to sail into the abyss of evil,' says Rudolf Steiner, 'it would likewise be impossible for the human being to attain what we call love on the one hand and freedom on the other. This is because, for the esotericist, freedom is inseparable from the concept of love . . . It was the intent of wise providence to give the possibility of freedom to humanity as it developed through the system of planetary evolution; and the only condition for this gift was that the human being freely choose between what is good and what is evil.'[11]

Religion and Knowledge in the Age of the Consciousness Soul: New Religions in the East and West

Virginia Sease

I would now like to go more deeply into the reflection of the Age of Abraham we spoke of earlier and consider how it will take shape from our time onwards. The period of darkness, the Kali Yuga, has been over since 1899; we are now in a period of light. The mirroring of the Age of Abraham began a hundred years after the end of the Kali Yuga, in the year 2000. During this age, the human being will create within his constitution the capacity to win back his clairvoyant faculties.

But first, permit me to make a few brief preliminary remarks. Many statements by Rudolf Steiner are based on the outcome of his spiritual research. On more than one occasion, something Rudolf Steiner presented was later confirmed by independent scientific means. We saw an example of this in our discussion of the Essenes. His statements about them date from 1910—from even earlier in lectures to private circles—and much of what he said has been corroborated by the great discovery of the Nag Hamadi library in 1947.

We are now in the Michael Age. Michael has always been connected with the sun; the esoteric expression for him is the 'Sun–intelligence'. Before this Michael Age, Gabriel was the regent of humanity; he took his forces from the moon. The Gabriel epoch began in 1510 and lasted until 1879 when he was succeeded by Michael. Every archangelic regency has its own tasks connected to the development of humanity.

We know from Rudolf Steiner that over the course of approximately four hundred years, Gabriel had the task of building up in the human being the foundations for a new organ that will also bring with it certain capacities. In order to understand how something like this is even possible, we must look far back in the evolution of humanity to the Atlanteans, the inhabitants of old Atlantis.

Circumstances then were completely different. The earth was semi-liquid, shrouded in mist. The human being was situated in his body so that the etheric head extended outside; it was not as connected with the physical head. As a result, a kind of external brain took form that the human being used like an antenna in order to find his way. It was simultaneously an eye, an ear and a navigational and perceptual organ. Over time, this developed more and more inwards until, after a long time, the enclosed brain we have today came into existence.

The organ that was once on the outside and is now enclosed is referred to as the pineal gland or the epiphysis. It lies in the brain in the region of the speech centre. In 1861, the French surgeon Paul Broca discovered the effect of the speech centre and showed that speech creates this organ. The organ is there; but without speech it does not develop completely. The activity of speech brings about the completion of the organ. Rudolf Steiner establishes that a change also has taken place over the last four hundred years in the human epiphysis which lies in the frontal cavity near the base of the nose. Today this organ is so developed that human beings will be able to make use of it from now on. Rudolf Steiner says something remarkable about this to a private circle of esoteric pupils:

> ... if we were able to examine a corpse from today and one from the thirteenth century, for example, we would find differences in the development and the convolutions of the brain in the place we are discussing. The archangel Gabriel gradually prepared this organ in human beings so that they would be able to take up the message of the archangel Michael, who replaced him as regent in 1879.[1]

Gabriel is regent over birth. We recall here Gabriel's Annunciation to the Virgin of the impending birth. During the centuries of his regency, Gabriel worked on the formation of this organ in the period between conception and birth. The task of this organ is to enable the human being to take up real, spiritual thoughts; in other words, to open himself to clairvoyance.

We can look back in time and see how during the first centuries human beings came ever closer to an understanding of the Christ Event through certain formations that developed in them. This was first made possible up until about AD 600 through the ether body of certain human beings—not just a few—who were able to take up a replica of the ether body of Christ Jesus. In later centuries, throughout the Middle Ages and even into the fifteenth and sixteenth centuries, it was possible for the human astral body to take up a replica of Christ Jesus' astral body, which brought with it the grace for the capacity to understand. This process is now gradually taking place with the ego organism as a replica of Christ Jesus. This is one possibility. But the other possibility already exists as potential for all of humanity. That possibility lies in the building up of this organ called the epiphysis, so that the human being begins to work with its potential.

How does he build up this organ? The epiphysis is built up through thought-penetrated spiritual work. When the human being accomplishes this, he will be able to experience the Christ-being from this incarnation onwards, not only as an historical fact but also in the etheric realm. This will be the case for souls who have their incarnations during the next centuries as well. The task of this organ is to create a substance that will bring the human being the capacity for greater insight. As a result, it will become possible for human beings to look back during their next incarnation to see what they experienced in their incarnation in the twentieth century.

What is particularly interesting about this is that it can happen only if the organ is not created from materialistic thoughts but through spiritual-scientific thoughts carried by the spirit. These thoughts carried by the spirit are written in the Akasha Chronicle, in cosmic memory. After death, the person enters these realms and is capable of reliving his experiences through what is around him there—not the materialistic ideas, only the spiritual ideas. Then the person continues after death either in a very social situation in the spiritual world—if he has done a lot of spiritual work—or in a lonely, even isolated situation.

In the next life, we will only be able to remember what we actually thought. We will not be able to remember what we have not thought. This is a fundamental principle of this new possibility. The human being will have time to make use of this organ during earthly life; this is part of the potential. But there will not be a lot of time as we have already noted. We must get to work on this now, because, as with all human faculties, if an organ goes unused, it gradually becomes dried up—shrivels, falls away and decays—which is what could happen with the epiphysis in the future.

In the end, people who do not make any use of this organ over the course of several incarnations will be unable to keep pace with the rest of humanity; they will become 'displaced'. When evolution then moves into the Jupiter condition, they will be taken along by spiritual beings— or, more crudely put, dragged along—as a small colony unto themselves. They will have no place in the normal development of humanity, and they will be exposed to other forces, counter-forces. This, of course, sounds quite dire. Humanity still has time, but it is a task of spiritual science to make humanity aware that such events lie ahead.

The Gabriel Age was a period of secretiveness. Everything was quite hidden. It was the great period of secret societies of all kinds, right up to the end of the nineteenth century and a bit into the twentieth as well. Today, there is a lot of literature about these secret societies. Nevertheless, this is the point where Rudolf Steiner went his own way. He formed the Anthroposophical Society as a completely public society. As early as the beginning of the twentieth century, he wrote and spoke openly about the greatest Mysteries. Revelation belongs to the Michael Age. This means that everything has to be accessible to all of humanity. It is the task of this Michaelic Age to make the spiritual visible. For example, eurythmy is visible speech, visible sound—and this is connected to the task of this epoch.

There is a discernible regularity in the sequence of incarnations. Today, people are capable of knowing themselves—in accord with the words of the Greek Mysteries, 'Man, know thyself.' This is true for everyone in our time. Anyone can test the state of his own incarnation. Is it an incarnation marked more by genuine faith, by the power of faith, or is it an incarnation characterized more by knowledge? Is there more of an inclination to faith or to knowledge? It can also be discerned whether a person has more of an inclination to turn outwards, to make use of the capacity to love, or is more centred in his ego, more inclined to go solo. While in times past it was permitted to let these inclinations simply be, this is no longer appropriate. Now these contradictory tendencies must be brought into harmony.

When we look around us at the age in which we live, we see innumerable efforts to establish new religions. In this age of light, human beings have the need quite literally to reconnect—*re-ligio*—with the spiritual world. There is a standard that may be applied to these religious movements. It can be found in the answer to the question: Does the religious movement bring the human being closer to the possibility of reaching the Christ in the etheric realm, closer to understanding Him, or is this not the case?

Naturally, our task here is not to judge any religion or religious movement. Based on a strong inner sense of conscience, a person may recognize that a religious situation is right or wrong. But it is difficult to see into the karma of these things. Often the relationships within a religious context are formed out of relationships from earlier incarnations. There are groups of people who had earlier karmic relationships, who come together again in our time in order to take up a particular task with one another again. That is why it is so difficult to decipher something like this merely as an observer.

When we look at our age, we oftentimes see that technical or spiritual elements are not just confined to one place. We are connected to one another through technological achievements and also in spiritual realms. Today this is a vast field of study. Let us look now at two different areas of the world in order to consider two different aspects of this. First we will look at America.

America, like every large country or continent, is a powerful confluence of nationalities, religions, ethnic groups, races, and so forth. During our pre-birth existence, we choose our country of birth, our family, and so on according to our karmic needs. According to Rudolf Steiner, there are two main groups that have chosen America as their country of birth.

The first group is in the minority. Rudolf Steiner offers the example of the great philosopher and essayist Ralph Waldo Emerson, and describes in the karma lectures how Emerson had a long and old connection to Europe. From the time of Tacitus, Emerson was a friend of the individuality who would become Hermann Grimm. Rudolf Steiner notes that it is characteristic of the incarnation of Emerson—he was born in 1803 and died in 1882—that he had a thoroughly European education. This is actually characteristic of all souls who seek an American incarnation along these lines. A European education—this might sound quite nationalistic or even a bit arrogant. But it has a deeper foundation. What it means is that this one grouping of souls was immersed in everything that developed in Europe throughout earlier centuries, throughout the Middle Ages, including the Christian context.

The other grouping of souls is a larger one. These are souls who before, during or immediately following the Mystery of Golgotha were incarnated in an oriental setting and had certain experiences there. In many civilizations at that time, this oriental culture was fairly decadent. These souls experienced an overpowering spirituality, but in a very abstract way that rejected the earth. As a result of this, these souls spent a long time in the spiritual world, a longer time than would normally be the case between births. They incarnated on the North American continent and could not adapt to their bodies because of this earlier spiritual tendency to abstraction, to rejection of the world.

Corporeality in North America, South America and Central America is determined by the forces of the earth, by its electromagnetic forces. Rudolf Steiner describes them as the forces of the geographic double; our corporeality is quite affected by them. These souls could not rightly find their way into this corporeality and then sought a substitute for spirituality. They pushed aside thoughts connected, for example, with suffering and illness. They wanted nothing to do with them.

Thus it is not surprising that a religion—Christian Science—arose in America that addressed precisely this quality. According to the teachings given by its founder, Mary Baker Eddy, body and illness do not exist when they are thought about correctly. People have judged this teaching rather harshly, but that is not my purpose here. Instead, I only want to point out how the modern form of Christian Science is connected with earlier incarnations. Mary Baker Eddy was under the impression that she received a calling as a result of a fall she took. Interestingly, she founded her church in 1879. Millions of people belong to this movement, and it is not limited to North America. It is a worldwide movement.

Mary Baker Eddy was an exceptionally well-educated woman, a prolific author, and—according to the testimony of Christian Scientists— she effected many healings. Her work gave rise to other groups which had an especially strong influence in the western world on everything to do with the power of personal conviction. We think here of the ground-breaking book by Napoleon Hill that has been translated into many languages, *Think and Grow Rich*; or *The Power of Positive Thinking* by Norman Vincent Peale, and so on. My purpose in mentioning them is not to criticize them, but to point out how souls try to adapt to their current incarnation. Each person has his own individual path, and many people who begin in something like Christian Science later pursue completely different paths.

We also come across people who work quite individually. They undertake their tasks as solitary individuals, as those who are working alone. These people are part of the American phenomenon, but it is not so easy to see how they are connected to the European and the oriental aspects. The evidence leads us to think they tend more towards the minority group, towards medieval European Christianity.

There was one such woman in America who remained entirely alone. She had a number of experiences when she was a young woman, and based on these experiences she thought that normal middle-class life could not be what human life is really about. There had to be something else to it. Over the course of 15 years she prepared herself inwardly without knowing why. What she did during those 15 years—and this is my interpretation of it—was practise the eightfold path, but without recognizing it for what it was. She practised these qualities and then, in 1953, she set out on a mission to remain a wanderer until she sensed that humanity had learned the way of peace. She was not connected to any religion and she called herself simply Peace Pilgrim. She made known neither her birth name nor her place of birth.

I had the opportunity in 1964 to experience her personally when I was invited to hear her speak in a Los Angeles church across town from where I lived. I had never heard of her before. I am describing this here because it is part of the picture. Her talk was in a large church building. She spoke anywhere she was invited—whether it was in a synagogue, a school, a university, in a prison or in a hospital. In this case, it was in a large room in a Protestant church with seating for 250 people. That day, there were about 20 people present. She had silver-grey hair and was dressed simply in a navy blue blouse, slacks, and a tunic. The tunic had pockets in the hem for everything she needed: a comb, toothbrush, pencil and paper.

She spoke about her mission and about her vow. Inwardly, she had made the following vow: 'I will remain a wanderer until mankind has learned the way of peace, walking until given shelter, and fasting until given food.' This sounds a lot like St Francis of Assisi in a modern form. Of course, in time she made friends with people who offered her invitations, but she would sleep in train stations or in the gutters, whatever was available. She viewed her walk as a continuous prayer.

She also gave interviews, and much of what she said in these encounters has been written down. Wherever she was, she spoke to anyone—to people on the street, people she would meet in train stations. When I saw her in 1964, she had already travelled 25,000 miles on foot; on the back of her tunic was written, '25,000 miles on foot for peace'. She lived a long life and died suddenly in an auto accident.[2] She is a singular figure in our time; she did not want to draw attention to herself. Her aim was not that others would form a connection to her, but to her mission. I asked her if she had ever heard of Rudolf Steiner, and she said, 'Yes, absolutely.' It was not possible to ask her any further questions. She answered with, 'Yes, absolutely,' and fell silent again.

Let us turn our attention now to Japan. When we look at Japan, we might ask ourselves what it means that so many souls incarnate there. It is curious that Rudolf Steiner does not say much about Asia in general or about the Pacific Rim, for example. But he does speak about Japan. At the beginning of the last century, during the opening decades of the twentieth century, Japan was not as well known as it is today. However, it can now be said that Japan was perhaps the most important Asiatic country in the history of the twentieth century, and it continues to be a very important place on this earth.

Many of the souls currently in this Japanese corporeality—souls must always be distinguished from their corporeality, they should not be confused—are souls who lived during the period of the folk migrations in

Europe, especially in southern Europe. If we consider the hordes of people at that time—when Europe was in motion—and how the most varied tribes and folk groups met, we of course have to take into account that they fought and killed each other, and tried to exterminate one another root and branch. We also must think about this enormous activity of movement and the forces of bravery and courage these souls had to develop. All of this belongs to our discussion. It is not known how many of them became acquainted with Christianity during this turbulent period of folk migrations, how many found a relationship to it, or just where they experienced this unspoiled early European Christianity that we have described here. But our Japanese friends believe that very many souls had this experience. Then these souls spent time in the spiritual world and are reincarnated now in Japan.[3]

The two main religions currently practised in Japan are Buddhism and Shinto. Buddhism is there primarily for the momentous events in life. It is intimately connected with rituals—birth, marriage, death, the most serious events in life, but also illness and the blessing when crops are planted, for example.

Shinto, one of the oldest religions in the world, is more involved with well-being in life, and has always been the national religion of Japan. It dates far back into pre-Christian times, and has been connected solely with Japan from the time Japan first became aware of its own culture. One of the differences between Shinto and Buddhism—which entered Japan in the middle of the sixth century BC—can be found in the word Shinto itself, which comes from the Chinese *Shen-tao*, the path of the gods. Shinto is a belief system that does not lead directly to the divine beings it honours. If you were to ask about a god, you would receive an explanation based on the name of the god. For example: that is the god of the cloud that gives us shade and sometimes rain; but it could also be the god of the cloud that protects the plants so the heat of the sun does not burn. It depends.

The Shinto belief is that the Japanese islands were the first divine creation. They attribute Japan's creation to Amaterasu, the sun goddess, whose origin was the sun. Shinto is the only major religion that has a feminine goddess rather than a god as its central figure. Until the end of the Second World War, it was said that the Japanese emperors were descended from her, that they came from divine origins. Human beings, however, descended from *kami*. *Kami* means 'divine force' and encompasses not only human spirits but nature spirits as well. There are many shrines dedicated to *kami* spirits.

During the Second World War, the world had to turn its attention to Japan. Suddenly the world awoke to it. At the end of the war, not only had the country been destroyed, but the moral stability of the people had as well. In a 1945 radio broadcast, Emperor Hirohito signified a major change when he announced that he no longer had the divine right to rule.

A Japanese man by the name of Mokichi Okada lived at this time. He was born in 1882 to a very poor family of five. His father was a junk collector, later an antique dealer. His mother—carrying her child on her back—followed her husband, pushing the cart filled with the things he collected. Mokichi Okada was a sensitive and very intelligent boy. He graduated from school at the age of 13, almost two years earlier than usual. His ambition was to study art. He entered the art academy with a scholarship. A year into his studies he suffered an eye illness that required a long period of treatment and eventually he overcame it. At 18, he became ill again, struck down by tuberculosis. The doctors had given up on him and told him that he would not live very long. He recognized this and thought: Fine! If I am not going to live, then I will try something different. I will try to heal myself. I will change everything I do. He altered his whole lifestyle, became a strict vegetarian, took long walks, and began—not to meditate, but to observe his own thoughts. He regained his health, helped his father at home, and later studied western philosophy. In 1905, after the death of his father, he started his own business and was very successful. Then he began to collect fine art. Today, this collection is in Atami and is considered one of the best art collections in Japan.

In 1923, there was a powerful earthquake in Japan in which 150,000 people died. Anyone who has ever experienced a large earthquake knows that the soul is just as shaken as all the material things rattling around it. This was the case for Okada. As a result, a very serious pursuit of the spiritual character of the earth was set in motion in him. It became for him a personal mission; he was already inwardly engaged in meditation, but he continued to lead his normal daily life and conduct his business affairs. Then, one day in 1935, he experienced a kind of inner enlightenment. He believed a spiritual being, a hierarchical being, united itself with him in order to work for the good of humanity through his corporeality. He called this being a 'bodhisattva'. In the context of anthroposophy, however, that is a bit misleading; 'bodhisattva' is a technical term in Asiatic theology. Okada used the name 'Kannon' for this being.

As a result of this power of enlightenment, Okada realized that he had the capacity to heal when he was in harmony with an individual's karma.

During an intimate conversation with 'Kannon', this being said the whole world should be illuminated by this spiritual light.

There were people who were friends of Okada's, but he did not want to be their spiritual leader. And then, in 1941, he experienced Pearl Harbor. His first assessment was, 'If we [Japan] do not lose [the war], a real Japan cannot emerge.'[4] This was meant in a Michaelic sense—that the old blood ties should no longer play a role. Afterwards, when he expressed his pleasure that Japan had not won the war, someone asked him indignantly: 'Are you Japanese?' He replied: 'No, I am not Japanese.' Startled, the man asked, 'Then what country *do* you belong to?' Okada answered: 'I belong to the whole world.'[5] Then Okada set out to explain his ideal of universal love that reached far beyond ties to a single country.

In 1950, Okada established a church where people could draw close to this power of love and receive teachings. The priesthood of this church receives a special training through which it too is able to effect healing by means of a spiritual power of light.

That same year, Mokichi Okada claimed that a transformation had occurred in the spiritual world. Since that moment, much more light, much more light power became available to people. Now, laying on of hands was no longer appropriate; instead, assistance with healing could only occur through the power of light. He called this way of working *Johrei*, which means 'power of light'.[6]

Mokichi Okada died in 1955. In 1988, Manfred Schmidt-Brabant and I were invited by friends to the centre of the *Sekai Kyusei Kyo* movement—the 'Church of World Messianity'—in Atami. We were invited to speak with the movement's central leadership. There are currently millions of followers not only in Japan, but in North and South America, and in other countries. A few of the seven leading personalities at that time, who were also priests, had studied the works of Rudolf Steiner intensively and had three major questions to ask us. 'Who was Jesus? Should Jesus be seen only as part of the Hebraic world?' The second question was: 'Who was the Christ and what is the relationship of Christ to Jesus?' A long conversation resulted from this. The third question was: 'Who bestows the healing light force that we can then take up? Who is the bestower?' These questions reveal a religion with its origins in modern Japan, with its own complex structure, that goes its own way—but one that concerns itself with questions about people and humanity, even though it would not be described as Christian.

Until the present time, religion—or faith—had always been considered separate from knowledge. Today, religion and knowledge must find their way to one another. For example, it is not enough merely to believe the spiritual researcher; we must also seek to test the results of that research for ourselves. Rudolf Steiner always refers to this as the necessary application of a 'healthy human understanding'. On the other hand, Rudolf Steiner also made it possible for a new sacramental element to come into the world with the Christian Community.

The sacraments have undergone a great change throughout the course of human history. This is, of course, a vast field of study; I will mention only two main aspects. The first of these is the experience in antiquity of the Father God within the physical body; even when there was no connection with the Hebraic world, there was still an experience of the Father God within physical corporeality, within the blood. This is why there were sacrificial offerings—sacrificial blood offerings—either of animals or humans. Blood ruled through the forces of the moon and the earth. A transformation took place at the turning point of time with the Last Supper, where the blood sacrifice is transformed into the offering that springs forth from the powers of the sun—the bread and the wine. Bread and wine are created from the forces of the sun along with the labour of human beings. Bread must be baked; wine or grape juice must be pressed from grapes. This is the new way.

One quite future-oriented theme in the work of Rudolf Steiner is the power of sacrifice in the absence of any physical substance. Rudolf Steiner associates two elements, knowledge and the power of sacrifice without physical substance. He says, for example, 'The meditant should take up every meditation as a sacrifice, like sacrificial incense that rises to the gods'[7]—'as a sacrifice', but in a quite specific sense, as what is called the sacrifice of the intellect. This means that the person restrains his own beliefs in order to avoid being filled by beliefs arrived at through his intellect. If he were filled with these intellect-based beliefs, his thoughts could not be placed at the disposal of higher spiritual beings.

In 1923, Rudolf Steiner related a startling outcome of his own research. He said that a literary work, an epic drama, from sometime during the first four Christian centuries had been lost. He describes it as 'the greatest work brought forth by the New Testament, [which was] simply and utterly destroyed by the later Church so that nothing of it remained in subsequent centuries'.[8] The content of this very early work was concerned with the fact that the teachers of the Mysteries at that time saw how the intellect should be developed further in order to bring freedom and independence to the human being; but they also saw how this development removes the possibility of clairvoyance. Here is the story in short. There was a young hero who offered a sacrifice by declaring his readiness for the *Sacrificium intellectus* so that he could achieve clairvoyance for the cosmic significance of the Christ. This story pointed far into the future.

Rudolf Steiner mentions that this attitude of sacrifice will have to rise up in every human being who wants to be learned and wise, because sacrifice is a law of the spiritual world. 'Sacrifice must exist; without sacrifice there is no growth, no progress. We need to sacrifice our intellect and bring it to the Christ so that He may array it in the crown of pearls He weaves for Himself from the sacred sacrifices He has brought for the evolution of humanity.'[9] But something must exist before it can be offered up. If we want to sacrifice our intellect, it must already exist, and be cultivated as well. We must always keep this in mind by way of caution. It is not good enough to say: Well, if I do not develop an intellect, I will become clairvoyant. Instead, it is the sacrifice of the developed intellect that contributes to a person's ability to be more open to the truths of the spiritual word.

In the Mystery Drama *The Guardian of the Threshold*, the spiritual pupil Maria stands before Lucifer, the great representative of egotistical forces. Maria makes a vow for the future that any element of self-love will be removed from her own knowledge. The sacrifice of the intellect that Maria offers in this moment is a vow in order to rescue Johannes Thomasius from the clutches of Lucifer. Maria says:

> ... Never will I in the future
> Let myself be found by that bliss
> That humans feel when thoughts ripen.
> For the service of sacrifice will I set my heart,
> So that only my spirit can think, and in thinking
> Sacrifice to the Gods the fruits of knowledge.
> For me, knowledge will then become consecrated service.[10]

This can be the future goal of our efforts: 'For me, knowledge will then become consecrated service.'

The Creation of the New Christianity in the Supersensible Cultus of the Nineteenth Century, and the Karma of Love as the Earth's Future

Manfred Schmidt-Brabant

What I said in my first lecture also applies to these closing remarks. I indicated then that the findings of spiritual science are models for thinking; we cannot take them in a concrete, objective way because spiritual facts have to be translated into a language that refers to objects of the sense world. But patterns may become visible in these presentations that can lead our thoughts—as well as our experiences and our observations—in a certain direction.

When spiritual science speaks about a being—an angelic being, for instance—we cannot avoid the fact that we carry in us ideas of angelic figures from western art. Of course we know an angel is a purely spiritual being. But through the objectivity of spiritual-scientific descriptions we can discover patterns—ways of behaving—that make it possible in experience, feeling and thought to enter into the realm of this pattern and thus of this being.

We have observed great arcs of history, and now the question arises: What is the place of anthroposophy within this history of the Mysteries? I have already pointed out that Rudolf Steiner speaks of three calls. In the seven cultural epochs from the Ancient Indian to the final, the seventh, there are three decisive points for the continuing evolution of humanity. The first call to humanity resounded with a thunderous voice from Mount Sinai in the commandments of Jehovah. The second call in the desert came through John the Baptist as he spoke to those who wanted to hear: 'Repent ye: for the kingdom of heaven is at hand.'[1] And the third call is the one proclaimed out of spiritual worlds as anthroposophy.

Here, something essentially universal is meant by anthroposophy—not an institution, not a society, not even the terminology we use. What is meant is a soul impulse, which may be living in millions of souls—according to a comment made by Rudolf Steiner. This general spiritual science with its terminology seeks to serve this soul impulse, as do the

Anthroposophical Society, facilities like the Goetheanum or even the Studienhaus Rüspe, our hosts for this conference. These are earthly means of accommodating something that lives as a spiritual impulse in human souls. In order to understand the origin of this spiritual impulse, we must once again look far back into the past.

We observe the evolution of the earth in great epochs, like Atlantis and the Lemurian age before it. Before these there were two epochs, the Hyperborean and the Polaric during which the earth was still fiery, gaseous. It was during the Lemurian epoch that a certain condensation took place. 'Lemuria', as one calls the continent for short, was where Australia, New Zealand, the Pacific are today. The principal regions of Lemuria existed where there is now water.

This Lemurian time period is characterized by a certain occurrence. The moon was originally bound together with the earth. This is also recognized in science, which even speaks about a 'trench', an extremely deep cleft where the moon separated from the earth in primal times when matter existed in a completely different way. But the forces that harden matter, that form it, come from the moon. When the moon was still in the earth, these moon forces threatened to bring to a halt and harden all development that requires movement and plasticity. This is the so-called moon crisis in evolution. At that time humanity existed in an earlier form, without individuality, but still as a soul being. Naturally, the physical body looked different; ensouled human beings had an ether body, an astral body and the configuration necessary for the soul. But the physical body threatened to become hardened. Thus began a great exodus; humanity emigrated to the planets. Human souls departed spiritually into the regions of Jupiter, Venus, Mars, Saturn, Mercury; they also went to the region of the sun.

Then—in the process of evolution—the moon separated from the earth. The formative forces now worked only from the outside; evolution became more flexible again, and could continue. A thread of human bodily development, the strongest that could withstand the moon forces, had remained on the earth. Spiritual science speaks of a 'primary couple' that guaranteed the further evolution of the physical body. After the moon departed the earth, the souls eventually returned from their planetary exile. This is when humanity actually began. When the souls returned—first a few, then more—and took hold of the physical body, an ego was bestowed on them by the elohim. At that time, the ego of human beings was placed into souls from the realm of the exusiai—the spirits of form, the elohim—and these souls gradually connected themselves with it.

When we speak about Adam—whom we meet later as John the Baptist—we are speaking of the oldest, the first, soul-ego thus endowed. First this slender branch had to develop further, had to spread out among the descendants; there had to be more and more bodies so that more and more souls could descend.

What was peculiar about this return was that one large group of souls descended very quickly during the Lemurian time, and also in the Atlantean period. Other souls remained where they were in the spiritual world connected to their planetary sphere for a longer time, and descended into earthly incarnation only later, at the end of Atlantis or even during the post-Atlantean cultures. This is the basis for the fact that, even before anthroposophy, people have spoken about 'old' and 'young' souls. What is meant by an old soul is one who descended very quickly and, therefore, has had many incarnations. Young souls are those who remained above longer and have had very few—perhaps four, five, six—incarnations on the earth.

As souls went to the various planetary regions and to the sun—which is understood here as a planetary region—there were some in this exodus who remained connected with the sun for a long time. This means they were connected for a long time with Michael, the archangel of the sun; and they were, of course, connected with the Sun Spirit, with Christ. This group of souls who found a temporary dwelling place on the sun now went through a process that had two aspects. There were souls who descended very quickly into incarnation, who ascended again, entered into another incarnation and then ascended yet again. The remaining group stayed above in the sun, where the two groups met. When the souls ascended from one incarnation, they met their old soul comrades from the sun who had not yet descended into an incarnation, but who—from their vantage point of spiritual existence—had accompanied evolution. At that time, there was a continuing and lively discourse between souls who were beginning to collect earthly experiences and those souls who were collecting spirit experiences based on their extended stay in the sun sphere. Friendships developed between the old souls already below on the earth and the young, disembodied souls who were still above in the region of the sun.

This continued throughout the entire time, especially in Atlantis and up to the Old Indian-Persian and then Egypto-Babylonian cultures—approximately when history begins. A particularly young soul came down to the earth for the first time in the era of Gilgamesh.

The objection can be raised: 'What kind of stories are these? Why are you talking about this? It is all very interesting, but in the world around us there are cars and streetcars, the conflict in Kosovo is taking place. What is the point of these old stories?' The point is that they are not old; they are quite timely. There is something characteristic here that is connected to human nature.

When we sleep, the soul-spiritual element frees itself from the physical body and the ether body. What remains in the bed has the character of a plant. It lives, breathes, but is not in motion, and it is not permeated by spirit, because soul and spirit are gone. Where have they gone? They go back through time. When we leave the physical element of space, we immediately enter time. We do not enter a spiritual space; we enter time. Rudolf Steiner gave a detailed description of this pattern—or, more simply, this behaviour: in sleep, we revisit at lightning speed all of our incarnations back to the point where our ego originated from the hands of the elohim.

We can actually sense many of these complicated sounding truths even with a pious soul that is naive. Every night, we return to God. Every night, we return to the Creator Who made us. This simple image corresponds precisely with a description that shows in detail how the ego can hasten back; time is not subject to the same limitation as space. In the spiritual world, we can go by means of spirit vision through entire periods of time. Thus, every night we go back through all of our incarnations—through the Atlantean, the Lemurian, the historical incarnations; and every night, every time we sleep, we renew the reservoir of our individuality.

When we speak of such things and begin to take account of them as models of thinking, feeling and willing, the soul itself becomes aware. Usually, we do not bring back any of this night-time experience because it takes place outside the spheres where dreams are formed. But many people who are sensitive experience a little of how something works its way into their dreams that comes from completely different times.

Thus these souls who were especially connected with Michael and the sun—including the young ones who descended as late as the age preceding the Mystery of Golgotha—now made their way through their incarnations. Of course, they have quite different behavioural tendencies, as one might say today. There were the souls who had already been on the earth for a long time—we can perhaps have a naive sense of this—who were already a bit weary of the earth. So many earth lives with so many destinies, battles and disputes!

These old souls actually long to return to the spirit. When they entered

during the historical period before the Mystery of Golgotha, they had a
tremendous inclination towards everything connected to Platonic
philosophy. They felt drawn by a philosophy that points people to an
ideal world. We think of Raphael's painting *The School of Athens*.
Regardless of who he actually is, the figure who might be Plato points to
this world. These old souls are thus called the Platonists, the Platonic
souls. After the Mystery of Golgotha these souls experienced a certain
confusion. There are indications that they were incarnated during the
third to the seventh century AD. They entered into the disputations I have
mentioned. What is the nature of the Christ? What is the nature of the
Father? Are they the same or are they merely similar? They were confused
because they could not understand who the Christ is; after all, they had
experienced Him earlier as a Sun-being. Now He was a kind of unknown
god to them. After death, they encountered further confusion—they did
not find Him! They lived with the question: Where is the Christ?—the
One who had, in fact, gone to the earth.

This was one group of souls, many of whom later found their way into
the anthroposophical movement. But we are speaking here of millions of
souls. The other group was the young souls. They were not at all weary of
the earth; they were eager for the earth. They descended—one often has
the impression they were like young puppies who grabbed at everything—and they took part in the heathen Mysteries. They lived with the
other gesture from the *School of Athens*. In the centuries before the
Mystery of Golgotha, this group of young souls found itself especially at
home in Aristotelian philosophy where the conceptualization of the
earthly realm is schooled. Thus, these young souls are often called the
Aristotelians.

After the Mystery of Golgotha, they entered into a different inner
situation than that of the old souls.[2] They were not yet weary of
paganism, but were instead utterly filled with everything that had lived in
the pagan Mysteries. They became Christians, however, and sought to
grasp Christianity by means of these pagan Mystery practices, so that they
had the feeling: 'This is something for the future. What we understand of
the Christ works its way into the future. We will really understand Him
only in the future.' They were among the souls who thought quite a bit
during these centuries, not always as scholars or theologians but as people
who over and again expanded the intellect.

During these centuries, questions connected to the Trinity and to the
relationship of the Christ with the Father were discussed to an astonishing
degree. There are delightful depictions in which someone from the third

or fourth century says: 'It is awful! When I go to the barber shop, the barber greets me with the words, "The Father is greater than the Son!" When I go to the inn, the waiter says to me, "No! The Son is identical to the Father." ' An eyewitness from that time confirms what Rudolf Steiner later said, that these thoughts and discussions lived among the people.

The destinies of these souls continue into the Middle Ages when some of these Platonic souls entered into the Cistercian order we have discussed, into the order of Bernard of Clairvaux and others; but some also joined the many heretical movements. An uncertainty lived in them: 'What does it mean that the Christ is on the earth? He is after all a Sun-being.'

From this point of view, if we read about the religion of the Cathars, the Bogomils, the Waldenses, and so forth, we note that heresy was simply the uncertainty of knowledge. Naturally, people took positions because of this uncertainty and they died for it. For example, the Cathars on Montségur who, by the dozens—144, in fact—voluntarily allowed themselves to be burned. But here the overarching question is: How is this possible? It is especially in the Dominican order that we again find the young souls inclined towards the Aristotelian view and Thomas Aquinas, the reincarnated Aristotle himself. Many of these Aristotelians lived in the Templar order as well.

The communities of souls who went through the eons—above, below and together—are characterized by the fact that they were never all on the earth at the same time. When old souls were down below, the young ones were above; when the young ones descended, the old ones were again above. Encounters occurred only rarely and there was no collaboration— as when the Cistercians were below, and then ascended as the Dominicans descended.

Nevertheless, there was a community of souls in the spiritual realm; in the existence after death and before birth these souls met one another over and over. They experienced something in the cosmos that connects the planets with the hierarchies—the Cosmic Intelligence. The Cosmic Intelligence is the sum of all the patterns of behaviour among the hierarchies, but it is also a being.[3] The Cosmic Intelligence is a kind of emanation of the Isis Sophia. We have already looked at the mysterious nature of this being, the Isis Sophia, who says: 'I am what was, what is and what will be. I am space and time, and thus the whole cosmos as wisdom.'[4] Thus, of course, there is always the feeling that this Isis Sophia is a form in which the Holy Spirit itself appears, but in a lofty hierarchical position as a so-called spirit of wisdom, as a kyriotetes-being. The Isis

Sophia, a hierarchical manifestation of the Spirit God and an emanation from this world of wisdom, was the Cosmic Intelligence.

The Sophia gave the leadership of this Cosmic Intelligence over to a being who stood in relationship to her as a son to a mother. This being was Michael. Michael had gone through his human existence as an archangel during the Old Sun phase of the earth. When beings undergo their stage of human existence, they are always endowed with an ego from the realm of the elohim who, for their part, also evolve upwards. At that time the Sophia was an elohim, an exusiai, a spirit of form. She was the highest of the elohim, and Michael was the greatest of the human beings at that time. Sophia bestowed an ego upon him; his ego came from the source of the Sophia's being.

All of this lived in the Old Mysteries, where Michael was revered as Marduk and where these relationships were still deeply understood. In this way, the Sophia handed over to Michael what she had bestowed on the world as the Cosmic Intelligence. He ruled this Cosmic Intelligence from the sun throughout the eons of earth evolution. The souls who are connected with the sun and with Michael had experienced all of this.

The sun was not only the place of Michael; it was also the place of the Christ. As the Christ-being moved to the earth through the Mystery of Golgotha, the Cosmic Intelligence gradually came to follow Him. It departed from the sun; it fell away from the administration of Michael. Finally in the seventh, the eighth century, the Cosmic Intelligence arrived on the earth—which means it came to human beings. It became the human intelligence. At the same time, it was in danger of being taken hold of by Ahriman. The Cosmic Intelligence—which is administered from the sun—threatened to become the prey of Ahriman. All of this was experienced by the souls in the spiritual realm after death and before birth, thus between lives. Together, old and young souls, Platonists and Aristotelians, turned to their old leader, Michael.

Down below, there were mighty souls like Bernard of Clairvaux or Thomas Aquinas or Albertus Magnus, mighty souls from all realms who were already fully clairvoyant in the physical realm—we have already heard this about Thomas Aquinas—and who had already seen the hierarchies from the physical world. Based on their long experience, these souls addressed something like a petition to Michael. This petition—or question—asked whether or not everything that now lived among human beings as the Cosmic Intelligence, but distributed in the heads of individuals, could or should be spiritualized again in order to return it to Michael and snatch it away from Ahriman. The whole matter was taken up in a kind of supersensible council during the thirteenth century where it was set forth before the being of Michael as in a mighty intuition.

Spiritual science shows how this petition received a positive response from Michael. The great supersensible Michael School—this is what Michael's school is called—takes place in the region of the sun. Throughout long periods of time, from the fifteenth to the end of the eighteenth centuries, these souls were gathered around Michael—the last of them who then ascended were from the circle of the Aristotelians. There were many souls. In response to the question of just how many, Rudolf Steiner said—and this is well documented—that around seven million took part at that time in this Michael School.

What was taught there was how the character of the Old Mysteries had to transform itself through the Mystery of Golgotha into a new kind Mystery for the future. We recall that Christ as the Risen One had gone through the Mysteries, into the esoteric academies, and had reformed them—of course, in light of the Mystery of Golgotha, His own deed. It had been a deed of such importance that we must conclude: Michael now taught what the deed of Christ had been. He summarized it, since the Christ had worked in many different places. This work of Christ is a wondrous area of study, a vast research, because we have many reports from the first centuries. It is possible to see throughout the whole Mystery world, throughout the remnants of the Mystery world, how something suddenly emerges everywhere—reaching into Asia, Africa and the West—that demonstrates that a new element is entering here.

Michael summarizes all of this in his supersensible school. He brings a picture of the whole nature of the Mysteries on earth, and how the Mysteries were changed by the Mystery of Golgotha. Thus, what was prepared in this supersensible school gives us reason to say that a new kind of Mystery must come into being.

But now comes the culmination. We can actually imagine this a bit through a comparison. A supersensible school, naturally without a podium or desks and chairs; souls live in one another, but in something like an alternation, a differentiation. In earlier years, when someone did not understand anthroposophy quite right, we—I am from Berlin—said: 'He sat behind a pillar so he only got half of it.' And in fact it is true that souls participated in varying ways. But then something like a mighty, celebratory ritual closing took place. For almost 30 years, from the end of the eighteenth century into the first third of the nineteenth century, the whole supersensible school was brought to a close in a supersensible cultus.

Although Rudolf Steiner speaks quite extensively about this, and we will see that it cast a significant reflection, it is extraordinarily difficult to imagine ourselves in this situation. What happened was that everything that had been taught was now summarized in great cosmic imaginations. In relation to the transformation of the cultus by Mark and Ormuz, you will recall that I said 'imaginations remain.' The imaginative world is actually more real than the objective one. A desk eventually breaks, disintegrates. Imaginations can endure in the spiritual world.

Thus a kind of being consisting of cosmic forces and cosmic substances was formed from mighty cosmic imaginations. In connection with this cultus, it is important to see that higher hierarchies were present; the Christ-being Himself took part in it; Michael was there, as well as all the souls who took part in the supersensible school. The being that arose was a human Sophia, an Anthroposophia, as Rudolf Steiner calls anthroposophy in especially solemn moments; a being like a human being, but of a purely spiritual nature. Rudolf Steiner often described what anthroposophy is in reality. Here we must turn our glance back to the supersensible cultus, for Anthroposophia is at home as a true being there, and from there she works into our world.

Rudolf Steiner gives another name to this being: the new Christianity. We too can say that this human Sophia—which is to enable human beings to take up the human Logos—is a new form of Christianity. It was a needed addition to what had developed earlier. There is a fascinating reflection of this. The French Revolution took place on the earth. Friedrich Schiller, who had at first celebrated this revolution, was pained to see how the whole affair dissolved into a reign of terror and blood complete with guillotines. He wrote about this, describing how we can rightly shape social relationships so that human beings do not fall victim to oppression. These essays are his famous *Letters on the Aesthetic Education of Man*. What he means by aesthetic education is the education of the ideal human being.

He describes how—from the perspective of the physical—we are all subject to the drive for materiality. It takes hold of us so that we are in no way free. If we take a purely intellectual approach, we are subject to the drive for form. The intellect forces us to think its eternal truths. Only in the middle—between the intellect's drive for form and nature's drive for materiality—is there a space for human beings to play; there we are free and capable of developing a drive for play. What Schiller means by 'play' is a creative, free activity in which we are subject neither to the drive for materiality nor to the drive for form, but where our deeds are freely creative. His famous thesis is that a human being is a human being only where he plays; and only when he plays is he truly human.

Goethe was delighted with this because he immediately recognized Schiller's essay for what it was: a manual for educating the ideal human being in us. If, so to speak, we must philosophically educate the ideal human being we carry within us, then this book is a great help. But the book is written quite philosophically, and that was not Goethe's cup of tea. It was too Kantian for him. But Goethe's inner approval brought about a kind of opening to the spirit. Goethe was someone who was very open to the spirit. He had crossed the threshold to the spiritual world and, in his youth, had even received a highly unusual initiation based on Rosicrucian impulses. From this capacity of his soul he opens himself and perceives the supersensible cultus, not in perfect clarity but as though in parts—as though it were pouring into him from different floodgates, as if certain parts enter his soul. Goethe, who was living on the earth, wrote his *Fairy Tale of the Green Snake and the Beautiful Lily* based on his participation in this supersensible cultus. Time and again, Rudolf Steiner calls this fairy tale 'Goethe's secret revelation'. Goethe knew full well what this fairy tale meant for his biography, this fairy tale with three kings standing at their altars, a mixed king standing at a fourth altar, and the snake—wisdom— that sacrifices itself.

The fact that Goethe had been able to receive this fairy tale from the spiritual world led him to the point where he became open to another inspiration. I have already mentioned that Philip, the so-called Fair, had destroyed the Templar order because of a black magic lust for gold. The Templars were completely destroyed; many were murdered, and still others fled to Scotland and Portugal. These Templars who fled—and this is said with a good deal of caution—created a kind of successor organization. The Templar order as such was dead. But the secret knowledge of the Templars was passed along under other names in the successor organizations. Goethe, himself a Freemason and an Illuminati, was taken into such a Templar successor organization and was initiated there. He took the old Templar oath when he joined. This successor organization was called the 'Strict Observance'; it had continued up to the time of Goethe when it came to an end and was fully dissolved. It is as though the Templar knowledge was meant to reach Goethe.

Goethe's connection to this successor organization allowed him to take up something else. An uninterrupted stream of inspiration from the many murdered Templars flowed down to the souls below who were open to receive it. Thus Goethe, who was given an external impulse through this organization, receives many inspirations in his soul. There were so many, in fact, that Rudolf Steiner speaks several times about Goethe knowing the secret of the Templars. Goethe wrote this secret down as the second part of his *Faust*. The second part of *Faust*, Goethe's most mature work, contains what the Templars knew about the secret of Europe's future development.

The Sun ritual, the supersensible cultus, also takes place at three altars. For some time before the First World War, Rudolf Steiner led a regular ritual work that was then closed at the beginning of the war. This ritual work was celebrated at three altars, which had never before been done. Thus it cannot be said that Rudolf Steiner had connected his work with Freemasonry; there never was a Freemasonry ritual with three altars. Instead, this instruction is a partial realization of what was handed down from Mark and Ormuz, what passed through the ages—adapted and modified over and over again—as the ritual of esoteric Christianity, as the Grail ritual, as the Templar ritual, as the Rosicrucian ritual, and what now presents itself in the supersensible cultus and finds its reflection here on earth. In Rudolf Steiner's Mystery Dramas, we again find the three altars in the temple scenes.[5]

This is a theme that is like an accompaniment to earth evolution. In speaking about the Mystery Dramas, Rudolf Steiner said that it was natural to connect with Goethe's *Fairy Tale* as he attempted to present in dramatic form, in earthly form, what occurred in the supersensible cultus. The first drafts of Rudolf Steiner's Mystery Dramas are still written entirely in the language of Goethe's *Fairy Tale*.[6] Capesius and Strader are the will-o'-the-wisps; Maria is the Beautiful Lily; Johannes is the youth; Balde is the old man with the lamp; and so forth. These were the drafts— they have also been published. Then Rudolf Steiner brought the drama into a new form—this time rightly conceived. However, we still feel the whole atmosphere of what shone from the supersensible cultus into the earthly world through Goethe's *Fairy Tale*.

Now anthroposophy sets off on its way to the earth below. The souls who took part in the supersensible cultus descend into incarnation, and were born at the end of the nineteenth and into the twentieth century. And this will continue.

The third call sounds with these souls and through these souls.[7] What is the third call? The first was the Ten Commandments that came down from Sinai with a thunderous voice. The second call took place at the turning point of time: 'Repent, for the times are changing.' It is the task of anthroposophy to re-establish the link between the physical and the spiritual, between the world and the earth on the one hand and the spiritual hierarchies on the other. Anthroposophy's task is the reconnection of the spiritual with the physical. This is expressed abstractly, but it is the third call. Naturally, it resounds in a thousandfold form; but it has a central core.

Rudolf Steiner pointed to what differentiates anthroposophy from many other esoteric streams that had a justified place in esoteric Christianity through their schooling and initiation. How can we determine if someone is an anthroposophist, if someone has a relationship to anthroposophy? There is a lovely passage where Rudolf Steiner says that God is neither omnipotent nor omniscient because He shared omnipotence with Ahriman and omniscience with Lucifer. However, He kept love completely for Himself. 'God'—in this case Christ is meant—'is pure, genuine love'.[8] When someone grasps this difference between power and knowledge on the one hand and love on the other, then he is a Christian. Even if he has never heard anything about the Mystery of Golgotha; if he never heard anything about the Gospels; if, outwardly, he has never experienced any of this—if he knows the difference between power and knowledge on the one hand and love on the other, then he is a Christian.

When is a person an anthroposophist? Rudolf Steiner already raised this question in 1912 in some important lectures. The content can be summarized in the following way. The core of anthroposophy—the new element it brings whereby it illuminates everything else anew—is 'reincarnation and karma'.[9] Whether a person can approach anthroposophy is dependent upon whether or not he can find an approach in his life to reincarnation and karma.

I have described the significant decisions facing humanity and the effects they have right down into our civilization. It is a matter of nothing less than preserving the continued process of repeated earth lives. We can also speak more to the point and say: Ahriman wants to snatch souls out of a normal passage through repeated earth lives and put them in his dark, earthly realms. Lucifer wants to snatch souls away from the earth and tear them away from normal reincarnations, to put them in his spirit realms where the human being would not be able to develop further.

The Christ-being wants to continue leading human beings through regular incarnations. What happens in these reincarnations? We accomplish everything on the earth that we brought with us, and arrange for new things. Then, after death, we ascend and go through the planetary world, the world of the hierarchies. We encounter the angels, the archangels; we traverse the region of the sun, Mars, Jupiter, Saturn, until we come to a place that is called the 'cosmic midnight'. From there, we descend again through the planetary regions to the earth—which always means through an encounter with the hierarchies—and enter into a new incarnation. Along this path, we have transformed our destiny into a new one. We have incurred debts as well as rendered services; we have learned things and missed others. From all of this, we create the next incarnation so that it offers us the possibility to make good our debts, to learn new things, and to put in service to others the experiences we had and the capacities we acquired during our lives.

This means that there is no greater connection between the spiritual and the earthly world than the passage through incarnations. Above and below, cosmic midnight and our earthly foundation are in continuing connection. When we live here with a biography in a physical body, with a profession in the physical world, we carry an uninterrupted element of what is spiritual into this world by way of our supersensible being. When we ascend after death and go out to the spiritual beings, to the planetary spheres, we take earthly experiences with us that can only be had on this earth.

Through this new beginning that comes with the supersensible cultus, something is to take place that had been lost after the Old Mysteries surrendered their full effectiveness. If we were to look into the Egyptian or Babylonian Mystery sites, or into others, we would see that there was no split of the sort that exists today when we say: Here we have science; here is something of art; there is a religious event. Instead, science, art and religion were a unity in the old Mysteries, and had to be a unity so that the life of the Mysteries could exist. What does this mean? Knowledge, art and religious process were one and the same thing. We see that art and religion belong together when we look at the temple buildings and the statues of the gods. These were art and also the subject of religious veneration—the means to arrive at an experience of the gods.

But all this was science as well. When these people saw the statues of the gods, when they experienced the temple building, and especially when they participated in the various cults, they discovered something about the world. They discovered things that were fundamental and brought them closer to the truth. They discovered more than we are able to speak of today when we analyse the ancient teachings, the Egyptian *Book of the Dead,* and so forth with our intellect. It is precisely because science was penetrated by art and religion, because art was carried by science and religion, and because religion was carried by wisdom, by knowledge and art that this trinity could lead people into the spiritual world. As the Mysteries came to an end and had to withdraw for the sake of human freedom, this unity dissolved into its parts. Today, science has nothing more to do with art, and religion leads its own independent life.

Bringing science, art and religion back together is one of anthroposophy's great tasks—throwing light on religion by way of science again, enlivening science through art, filling art once again with religious feelings—so that all three can draw closer to one another. This is a process that will require time.

A vast transformation will take place in this process. We posed the question: What is God's plan of salvation? What is to become of the world? It should transform from a 'cosmos of wisdom' to a 'cosmos of love'.[10] What the divinity exhaled as a complete cosmos full of wisdom must be transformed so that it returns to the divinity as a cosmos of love.

The esoteric schools have always expressed this in a very specific formula. They have made a threefold step out of this great step from one thing to another. They have expressed this threefold step in the words 'wisdom', 'beauty' and 'strength'. By 'strength', a cosmos of love was meant; it was a code word, if you will. Wisdom will become love by passing through beauty's world of revelation; here beauty does not mean a beautiful picture or a beautiful girl, but the *Gloria*, the appearance of the world—taken up and formed by human beings.

This was described as follows. This stream of wisdom enters the earth out of the past; then it comes to a certain standstill, appears as the glory of the world. And the human being must take up the glory of the world through what he does artistically, and guide it over into the cosmos of love. Thus science, art and religion must work together.

Everything at this central point is art. We like to associate the word 'art' with activities that stem from anthroposophy. We speak about the art of education, not the science of education; the art of healing, not medical science. Of course, there is a science of education and a medical science, but the activity of the human being becomes art in the transformation of the old wisdom into an element for the future. Science transforms itself by way of art into religion.

In these New Mysteries, the old phrase *ora et labora* receives a new meaning. At first, the thinking human being with his *Vita contemplativa*, and the working human being with his *Vita activa*, are placed as though side-by-side in the life of the cloister. But the complete human being is comprised of prayer and work together.

From the present onwards the old phrase must be reformulated. It must be: *ora est labora, labora est ora*—'Prayer is work; work is prayer.' Each must unite with the other so the separation ceases to exist. We often express this by saying: 'The work of the human being must regain a sacramental character.' Or: 'Meditation must regain the character of work.' When a person meditates, he creates something in the world. Meditation is a sacrifice, but it is also an activity. It is significant that they merge: the *Vita contemplativa* becomes a *Vita activa*. It is precisely in anthroposophy that this becomes quite clear. It is not possible to pursue a path of schooling, a contemplative meditative path, if it is not taken up as actively as we take up the rest of the world.

In the long run, we can no longer do any work in the world, any social work, any manual labour, spiritual or agricultural work if the work itself does not acquire a contemplative character, if the *Vita activa* does not simultaneously become a *Vita contemplativa*. This is the dawning of the new Mystery future before which we stand—the gradual union of the spiritual and the physical as a full reality.

All of this is playing itself out now, has played itself out, and will continue to play itself out further in the face of a great event. We have looked at the destiny of the Christ Who has passed through the centuries. There would be much to add here about where the Christ-being stepped in, where He had influence. Modern history—history since the Mystery of Golgotha—is unthinkable without the many effects of this Christ-being. The goal for all of this was the event that has played itself out in the present to bring a historical epoch to a close.

When the human being dies, he pursues the same path he takes when he sleeps. He first follows his incarnations backwards to his divine source. But people have always asked: Where does a person go when he dies? Up to now, on the path backwards—which is, at the same time, the path to the spiritual world—a powerful image has stood before every human being, a spirit image that is also filled with a significant reality. Moses stood before each human being with the tablets of the law, and next to him was the cherub with the shining sword. The human being had to hear: 'An eye for an eye, a tooth for a tooth.' Whatever you did, you have to make good again, regardless of what you have to endure along the way. The law of karma was carried out with a certain inexorability, like a law of nature. Thus, in order to fulfil the law, everyone who died saw the cherub with the shining sword and Moses with the tablet: 'Thou shalt not . . . !'[11]

That has now come to an end. It was always known among initiates and esotericists that this law comes to an end and that another being, namely, the Christ enters in the place of this mighty image, and takes over this role of karmic judge. Moses withdraws, the cherub withdraws, and

Christ passes judgment. But He judges differently. He does not judge by weighing 'an eye for an eye, and a tooth for a tooth'. He passes judgment based on the cosmic law of love. Karma must be cleared away. If I have been guilty during my life, I have to make compensation in a subsequent life—but how? Earlier this compensation followed spiritual laws with a certain inexorability. Now this compensation is formed through the Christ so that it serves the human being's path of development. The Christ says: You must make up for these things, but in such a way that you progress in your own development. The karma of the law transforms into the karma of love. However, it is also true that the Christ still stands there as the great judge. Thus esotericists, even the Rosicrucians, said: When this point in time comes, the Last Judgment begins. The Last Judgment will last until the end of the earth. Christ will judge the quick and the dead.

We have to acquire a sense for the fact that this lies ahead for every person. Christianity is not a matter of a religion or even a denomination; it is not a question of a particular culture. Christ is there for all humanity.

Rudolf Steiner frequently drew attention to the fact that the Christ is to be found in every religion, naturally not by that name. Christ is the translation of 'Messiah', which means 'the Annointed One'. It was anticipated among the Hebrews that an anointed one would come. The true name of Christ is 'I AM'. If we look into this, we find that an 'I AM' was sought in all religions, in all cultures, but it was formulated differently. The Christ is also there for every atheist and every materialist. He is the Being of humanity, the ego, the higher ego, of all human beings. This is what we mean when we say 'Not I, but the Christ in me' as my actual, true ego, my true being.[12]

I would like to close our lengthy journey through human history with the thought that this process will take a long time. Spiritual science will bring an understanding of the Christ-being to people from ever loftier perspectives, until humanity has understood the full meaning of the Christ and has, without reservation, given over its whole life to His impulse. Such a powerful perspective shows us how the human being must turn his gaze upwards to supersensible history if he is to understand the meaning of earthly history. Everything depends on making clear to the human being what it means to fulfil the words 'I am with you always, even unto the end of the world.'[13]

Notes

Editor's Note: The references to Rudolf Steiner's works listed below are to the original German editions, with a literal English translation of the title shown in brackets. The passages quoted in the text have been translated directly from the original German. The 'GA' numbers given refer to the catalogue number of the *Gesamtausgabe* or Collected Works in the original German as published by Rudolf Steiner Verlag, Switzerland. The dates of Rudolf Steiner's lectures are also given. To facilitate the identification of official English-language editions of the cited lectures, a bibliography of such books follows on page 191.

Citations are given in full the first time they appear in each lecture. Works cited only by title and GA number are by Rudolf Steiner.

Lecture 1

1. Published as *Paths of Christian Mysteries: From Compostela to the New World,* Virginia Sease and Manfred Schmidt-Brabant, trans. M. Miller and D. Miller (Temple Lodge: Forest Row, 2003).
2. *Das Christentum als mystische Tatsache und die Mysterien des Altertums* [Christianity as mystical fact and the mysteries of antiquity] (GA 8), 1st ed. 1902.
3. *Das Prinzip der spirituellen Ökonomie in Zusammenhang mit Wiederverkörperungsfragen* [The principle of spiritual economy in connection with questions of reincarnation] (GA 109); *Das Ereignis der Christus-Erscheinung in der ätherischen Welt* [The event of Christ's appearance in the etheric world] (GA 118).
4. Karl Josef Kuschel, *Geboren vor aller Zeit?* [Born before all time?] (Piper Verlag: Munich, 2001).
5. Johann Wolfgang von Goethe, *Faust*, Part 1, 'Study', l. 1236 f.
6. Kuschel, p. 25.
7. *Die Geheimwissenschaft im Umriß* [Occult science in outline] (GA 13).
8. *Wahrspruchworte* [Verses and Meditations] (GA 40).
9. *Die Geheimwissenschaft im Umriß* [Occult science in outline] (GA 13), chapter on 'The Present and Future of Cosmic and Human Evolution'.
10. Ibid.
11. John 10:34.
12. *Geheimwissenschaft* (GA 13), chapter on 'The Evolution of the Cosmos and Man'.
13. *Vorstufen zum Mysterium von Golgatha* [Preparatory steps for the Mystery of Golgotha] (GA 152), lecture of 5 March 1914.
14. Ibid.

15. *Christus und die geistige Welt: Von der Suche nach dem heiligen Gral* [Christ and the spiritual world: On the quest for the Holy Grail] (GA 149), lecture of 1 January 1914.

16. Hella Krause-Zimmer, *Die zwei Jesusknaben in der bildenden Kunst* [The two Jesus children in the visual arts], 3rd edition (Stuttgart: Verlag Freies Geistesleben, 1986).

17. Andrew Welburn, *Am Ursprung des Christentums. Essenisches Mysterium, gnostische Offenbarung und die christliche Vision* (Verlag Freies Geistesleben: Stuttgart, 1992), p. 176; English edition: *The Beginnings of Christianity: Essene Mystery, Gnostic Revelation and the Christian Vision* (Floris Books: Edinburgh, 2004).

Lecture 2

1. Cited in *Die Apokryphen und Pseudepigraphen des Alten Testaments* [The apocryphal writings and pseudepigrapha of the Old Testament], trans. and ed. Emil Kautzsch (Georg Olms Verlag: Hildesheim, 1992), p. 177.

2. *Christus und die geistige Welt: Von der Suche nach dem heiligen Gral* [Christ and the spiritual world: On the quest for the Holy Grail] (GA 149), lecture of 29 December 1913.

3. Alfons Kurfess states that the Oracula Sibyllina flourished from about the third century BC to the end of the second century AD, *Sibyllinische Weissagungen*, ed. Alfons Kurfess (Heimeren: Munich, 1951), p. 19 f.

4. Ibid, p. 183; trans. M. Miller and D. Miller.

5. Johann Wolfgang von Goethe, *Faust*, Part II, Act 2, l. 7454 f; trans. M. Miller.

6. *Goethes Werke* (Weimar edition), reprint Deutscher Taschenbuch Verlag, 1987, Part 2, vol. 15, p. 209 f.

7. *Vorstufen zum Mysterium von Golgatha*, GA 152, Dornach 1980, lecture of 27 May 1914 in Paris, note to page 140.

8. *Aus der Akasha-Forschung. Das fünfte Evangelium* [From research in the Akasha: the fifth gospel] (GA 148), lecture of 5 October 1913 in Oslo.

9. *Das Hereinwirken geistiger Wesenheiten in den Menschen* [How spiritual beings work into the human being] (GA 102), lecture of 13 April 1908.

Lecture 3

1. *Das Matthäus-Evangelium* [The Gospel of Matthew] (GA 123).

2. Andrew Welburn, *Am Ursprung des Christentums. Essenisches Mysterium, gnostische Offenbarung und die christliche Vision* (Verlag Freies Geistesleben: Stuttgart, 1992), p. 176; English edition: *The Beginnings of Christianity: Essene Mystery, Gnostic Revelation and the Christian Vision* (Floris Books: Edinburgh, 2004).

3. Ibid, p. 73.

4. Philo of Alexandria, *Vom beschaulichen Leben* [On the contemplative life]

cited in Emil Bock, *Cäsaren und Apostel* [Caesars and apostles] (Urachhaus: Stuttgart, 1958), p. 268.

5. *Das Lukas-Evangelium* [The Gospel of Luke] (GA 114), lecture of 17 September 1909.

6. *Von Jesus zu Christus* [From Jesus to Christ] (GA 131), lecture of 14 October 1911.

7. *Christus und die geistige Welt: Von der Suche nach dem heiligen Gral* [Christ and the spiritual world: On the quest for the Holy Grail] (GA 149), lecture of 2 January 1914.

8. Rev. 2:14–17, German translation by Emil Bock (Urachhaus: Stuttgart, 1998).

9. *Von Jesus zu Christus* (GA 131).

10. Christian Morgenstern, *Gesammelte Werke in einem Band*, ed. Margareta Morgenstern (Piper: Munich, 1965), p. 151; trans. M. Miller and D. Miller.

Lecture 4

1. *Der Christus-Impuls und die Entwickelung des Ich-Bewußtseins* [The Christ-impulse and the development of ego consciousness] (GA 116), p. 34.

2. *Bausteine zu einer Erkenntnis des Mysteriums von Golgatha* [Building stones for a knowledge of the Mystery of Golgotha] (GA 175), lecture of 24 April 1917.

3. *Die Geheimwissenschaft im Umriß* [Occult science in outline] (GA 13), chapter on 'The Evolution of the Cosmos and Man'.

4. Ibid.

5. *Aus der Akasha-Forschung. Das fünfte Evangelium* [From research in the Akasha: the fifth gospel] (GA 148).

6. Ibid., lecture of 5 October 1913.

7. Ibid., lecture of 4 November 1913.

8. Ibid., lecture of 22 November 1913.

9. Ibid., lecture of 5 October 1913; trans. M. Miller and D. Miller

10. *Von Jesus zu Christus* [From Jesus to Christ] (GA 131), lecture of 10 October 1911.

11. *Das Markus-Evangelium* [The Gospel of Mark] (GA 139), lecture of 17 September 1912.

12. *Aus der Akasha-Forschung* (GA 148), lecture of 17 December 1913.

13. *Zur Geschichte und aus den Inhalten der ersten Abteilung der Esoterischen Schule 1904 bis 1914* [On the history of the first section of the Esoteric School 1904–14, and from its contents] (GA 264), p. 424.

14. Exod. 3:14.

15. Exod. 20:13, 15.

16. Matt. 3:2.

17. *Das Markus-Evangelium* [The Gospel of Mark] (GA 139), lecture of 17 September 1912.

18. *Das Matthäus-Evangelium* [The Gospel of Matthew] (GA 123), lecture of 7 September 1910.
19. *Vorträge und Kurse über christlich-religiöses Wirken II* [Lectures and courses on Christian religious work] (GA 343), documentary supplements, p. 118.
20. Ibid, p. 510.
21. Adolf Müller, *Werdestufen des Glaubensbekenntnisses* [Evolutionary steps of the confession of faith] (n.p., 1932).
22. *Aus der Akasha-Forschung* (GA 148), lecture of 23 November 1911.
23. *Das Christentum als mystische Tatsache und die Mysterien des Altertums* [Christianity as mystical fact and the mysteries of antiquity] (GA 8), chapter on 'The Miracle of Lazarus'.
24. John 11:47.
25. *Geheimwissenschaft* (GA 13).
26. *Von Jesus zu Christus* (GA 131), lecture of 11 October 1911.
27. *Die Polarität von Dauer und Entwickelung im Menschenleben* [The polarity of permanence and development in human life] (GA 184), lecture of 6 October 1918.
28. *Vorträge und Kurse* (GA 343), lecture of 8 October 1921, morning.
29. Müller, p. 35.

Lecture 5

1. Wilhelm Braune, *Althochdeutsches Lesebuch*, ed. Ernst A. Ebbinghaus (Niemeyer: Tübingen, 1962), p. 89.
2. Varro, *Rerum Rusticarum Libri Tres*, ed. Fairfax Harrison, http://sailor.gutenberg.org/1/2/1/4/12140/12140-8.txt
3. Cited in Georg Luck, *Magie und andere Geheimlehren in der Antike* [Magic and other secret doctrines in antiquity] (A. Kröner: Stuttgart, 1990), p. 108.
4. Matt. 23:5.
5. Num. 6:22–6.
6. Matt. 26:40, German translation by Emil Bock (Urachhaus: Stuttgart, 1998).
7. *Metamorphosen des Seelenlebens*, 2.Teil [Metamorphoses of the soul life, part 2] (GA 59), lecture of 17 February 1910 in Berlin.
8. *Das Vaterunser. Eine esoterische Betrachtung* [The Lord's Prayer: an esoteric consideration] (from GA 96), lecture of 28 January 1907 in Berlin.
9. Rev. 2:17, German translation by Emil Bock (Urachhaus: Stuttgart, 1998).
10. On the two prayers, see J. J. Petuchowski and C.Thoma, *Lexikon der jüdisch-christlichen Begegnung* [Lexicon of Jewish-Christian dialogue] (Herder: Freiburg, 1989).
11. *Das Vaterunser* (from GA 96), lecture of 28 January 1907 in Berlin.
12. *Zur Geschichte und aus den Inhalten der erkenntniskultischen Abteilung der Esoterischen Schule 1904–1914* [On the history of the cognitive-cultic section of the Esoteric School 1904–1914, and from its contents] (GA 265), pp. 154 f., 449; trans. V. Sease.

13. John 1:1–14.

14. *Aus den Inhalten der esoterischen Stunden* [From the contents of the esoteric lessons] (GA 266/1), lesson of 5 December 1909 in Munich.

15. *Der Konstitution der Allgemeinen Anthroposophischen Gesellschaft und der Freien Hochschule für Geisteswissenschaft; Der Wiederaufbau des Goetheanum 1924/25* [The constitution of the General Anthroposophical Society and of the School for Spiritual Science; The reconstruction of the Goetheanum 1924/25] (GA 260a), 10th Letter to the Members, 23 March 1924, 'On How to Present Anthroposophical Truths'.

16. *Anweisungen für eine esoterische Schulung* [Indications for an esoteric schooling] (GA 245).

17. *Die Geheimwissenschaft im Umriß* [Occult science in outline] (GA 13), chapter on 'Cognition of the Higher Worlds'.

18. *Aus den Inhalten der esoterischen Stunden* (GA 266/1), lesson of 14 March 1908 in Berlin.

Lecture 6

1. *Menschenfragen und Weltenantworten* [Human questions and cosmic answers] (GA 213), lecture of 16 July 1922.

2. Manfred Schmidt Brabant and Virginia Sease, *The Archetypal Feminine in the Mystery Stream of Humanity: Towards a New Culture of the Family* (Temple Lodge: London, 2000).

3. *Wie kann die Menschheit den Christus wiederfinden?* [How can humanity find Christ again?] (GA 187), lecture of 29 December 1918.

4. Hanns Bächtold Stäubli, *Handwörterbuch des deutschen Aberglaubens* [The concise dictionary of German superstition] (W. de Gruyter: Berlin and Leipzig, 1927–1942).

5. Gen. 2:7.

6. Deut. 5:8.

7. Emil Bock, *Kindheit und Jugend Jesu* [Childhood and youth of Jesus] (Urachhaus: Stuttgart, 1980), pp. 100 ff.

8. *Das christliche Mysterium* [The Christian mystery] (GA 97), lecture of 29 July 1906.

9. Reported by Nicephorus Callistus Xanthopulus (*c.* 1320) in his *Historia Ecclesiastica* (i, 20).

10. *Heilfaktoren für den sozialen Organismus* [Healing factors for the social organism] (GA 198), lectures of 11 and 16 July 1920.

11. *Menschenfragen* (GA 213), lecture of 16 July 1922.

12. *Das Geheimnis der Trinität* [The secret of the Trinity] (GA 214), lecture of 23 July 1922.

13. Ibid., lecture of 22 August 1922.

14. *Bausteine zu einer Erkenntnis des Mysteriums von Golgatha* [Building stones for a knowledge of the Mystery of Golgotha] (GA 175), lecture of 24 April 1917.

15. Paul in 2 Cor.12:2 ff.
16. *Die Geheimwissenschaft im Umriß* [Occult science in outline] (GA 13), chapter on 'The Evolution of the Cosmos and Man'.
17. *Die Theosophie des Rosenkreuzers* [The theosophy of the Rosicrucian] (GA 99), lecture of 6 June 1907.
18. *Die Mission einzelner Volksseelen im Zusammenhang mit der germanisch-nordischen Mythologie* [The mission of individual folk souls in connection with Germanic-Nordic mythology] (GA 121), lecture of 12 June 1910.
19. *Die menschliche Seele in ihrem Zusammenhang mit göttlich-geistigen Individualitäten* [The human soul in its connection with divine-spiritual individualities] (GA 224), lecture of 13 April 1923.
20. *Grundelemente der Esoterik* [Basic elements of esotericism] (GA 93a), lecture of 8 October 1905.
21. *Vorträge und Kurse über christlich-religiöses Wirken*, II [Lectures and courses on Christian religious work, II] (GA 343), lecture of 8 October 1921, morning.

Lecture 7

1. Arthur Schopenhauer, *Preisschrift über die Grundlage der Moral* [Tract on the basis of morality] in *Sämtliche Werke* [Collected works], ed. J. Frauenstädt, vol. 4, p. 192 f.; cited in: Heinz D. Kittsteiner, *Die Entstehung des modernen Gewissens* [The origin of the modern conscience] (Insel: Frankfurt am Main, 1992), p. 21.
2. *Rhythmen im Kosmos und im Menschenwesen* [Rhythms in the cosmos and in the human being] (GA 350), lecture of 25 July 1923 in Dornach.
3. *Der Christus-Impuls und die Entwickelung des Ich-Bewußtseins* [The Christ impulse and the development of ego consciousness] (GA 116), lecture of 2 May 1910 in Berlin.
4. Johann Wolfgang von Goethe, conversation with Friedrich Wilhelm Riemer; cited in *Lexikon der Goethe-Zitate* [Lexicon of Goethe quotations], ed. Richard Dobel (Weltbild Verlag: Augsburg, 1991), p. 359.
5. John 8:6–11.
6. *Christus und die menschliche Seele* [Christ and the human soul] (GA 155), lecture of 15 July 1914 in Norrköping.
7. On *apocatastasis* see Virginia Sease and Manfred Schmidt-Brabant, *Paths of the Christian Mysteries* (Temple Lodge: Forest Row, 2003), p. 47.
8. Kittsteiner, p. 135 f.
9. Encyclical Quanta Cura, 8 Dezember 1864, in Heinrich Denzinger, *Kompendium der Glaubensbekenntnisse und kirchlichen Lehrentscheidungen* [Compendium of articles of faith and decisions on church doctrine], ed. and trans. Peter Hünermann (Herder: Freiburg, 1991), p. 796 f.
10. Thomas Aquinas, *Summa Theologica*, I, q. 79a.13; cited in Kittsteiner, note 1, p. 447.
11. 1 Kings 19:11 ff.

12. Daniel von Czepko, *Geistliche Schriften* [Spiritual writings], ed. Werner Milch (Wissenschaftliche Buchgesellschaft: Darmstadt, 1963), p. 198. trans. M. Miller and D. Miller.

13. Matt 25:40.

14. *Erfahrungen des Übersinnlichen. Die drei Wege der Seele zu Christus* [Experiences of the supersensible. The three paths of the soul to Christ] (GA 143), lecture of 8 May 1912 in Cologne.

Lecture 8

1. *Ägyptische Mythen und Mysterien* [Egyptian myths and mysteries] (GA 106), lecture of 2 September 1908.

2. *Aus der Akasha-Forschung. Das fünfte Evangelium* [From research in the Akasha: the fifth gospel] (GA 148), lecture of 6 January 1914.

3. Ibid.

4. *Die Geheimwissenschaft im Umriß* [Occult science in outline] (GA 13), chapter on 'The Present and Future of Cosmic and Human Evolution'.

5. *Bausteine zu einer Erkenntnis des Mysteriums von Golgatha* [Building stones for a knowledge of the Mystery of Golgatha] (GA 175), lecture of 24 April 1917.

6. *Menschenfragen und Weltenantworten* [Human questions and cosmic answers] (GA 213), lecture of 16 July 1922.

7. *Erdensterben und Weltenleben: Anthroposophische Lebensgaben* [Earthly death and cosmic life: Anthroposophical gifts] (GA 181), lecture of 23 July 1918.

8. Ibid.

9. *Aus der Akasha-Forschung* (GA 148), lecture of 6 January 1914.

10. Ibid.

11. *Die Mysterien des Morgenlandes und des Christentums* [The Mysteries of the East and of Christianity] (GA 144), lecture of 5 February 1913.

12. Ibid.

13. *Zur Geschichte und aus den Inhalten der ersten Abteilung der Esoterischen Schule 1904 bis 1914* [On the history of the first section of the Esoteric School 1904–14, and from its contents] (GA 264) Dornach 1996, p. 228 ff.

14. *Aus den Inhalten der esoterischen Stunden* [From the contents of the esoteric lessons] (GA 266/1), lesson of 27 August 1909.

15. Matt. 18:20.

16. *Geistige und soziale Wandlungen in der Menschheitsentwickelung* [Spiritual and social transformations in the development of humanity] (GA 196), lecture of 6 February 1920.

17. *Das Prinzip der spirituellen Ökonomie in Zusammenhang mit Wiederverkörperungsfragen* [The principle of spiritual economy in connection with questions of reincarnation] (GA 109), lecture of 31 March 1909.

18. Ibid.

19. Rudolf Steiner, *Über die Wanderung der Rassen* [On the migration of peoples] (Berlin, 1904); reprinted in *Gäa Sophia, Jahrbuch der naturwissenschaftlichen*

Sektion der Freien Hochschule für Geisteswissenschaft am Goetheanum [Gaia Sophia, Annual of the natural science section of the School for Spiritual Science at the Goetheanum], ed. Guenther Wachsmuth, vol. 3 (Orient-Occident Verlag, Stuttgart/Den Haag/London, 1929), pp. 27 ff.
20. Gal. 2:20.

Lecture 9

 1. Matt. 26:13.
 2. *Das Johannes-Evangelium im Verhältnis zu den drei anderen Evangelien* [The Gospel of John in relation to the other three Gospels] (GA 112), lecture of 7 July 1909 in Kassel.
 3. Luke 10:42.
 4. John: 11:20 f.
 5. John: 11:25 ff.
 6. Cited in *Große Frauen der Bibel in Bild und Text* [Great women of the Bible in picture and text] (Herder: Freiburg, 1997).
 7. *Pistis Sophia*, ed. Carl Schmidt (J. C. Hinrichs: Leipzig, 1925), Chapter 17:30, p. 18.
 8. Ibid., Chapter 80:175, p. 130.
 9. *Bilder okkulter Siegel und Säulen: Der Münchner Kongress Pfingsten 1907 und seine Auswirkungen* [Images of esoteric seals and columns: The Whitsun Munich Congress, 1907, and its consequences] (GA 284), 1993 ed.; E.A. Karl Stockmeyer, 'Über die Einheit von Tempel und Kultus im Zusammenhang mit der Goetheanum-Bauidee' [On the unity of temple and ritual in connection with the architectural idea of the Goetheanum], p. 167.
10. Hugo Kuhn, 'Hrosviths von Gandersheim dichterisches Programm' [Hrosvita of Gandersheim's poetic programme] in *Dichtung und Welt im Mittelalter* [Literature and world in the Middle Ages] (J. B. Metzler: Stuttgart 1959), p. 91; cited by Bert Nagel in Hrosvita of Gandersheim, *Sämtliche Dichtungen* [Collected literary works] (Munich, 1966), p. 17.
11. Ibid, p. 19.
12. See St Teresa von Avila, *Die innere Burg* [The interior castle] (Zürich, 1979).
13. Ibid, p. 212.
14. Rudolf Steiner, *Geisteswissenschaft als Erkenntnis der Grundimpulse sozialer Gestaltung* [Spiritual science as knowledge of the basic impulses for social formation] (GA 199), lecture of 8 August 1920 in Dornach.
15. Ibid.
16. *Das Zusammenwirken von Ärzten und Seelsorgern* [The cooperation of physicians and pastors] (GA 318), lecture of 9 September 1924 in Dornach.

Lecture 10

 1. *Spiel vom Sündenfall* [Play of the Fall of Man], told by Karl Julius Schröer (Breitkopf und Härtel: Leipzig, 1917), p. 18.

2. *Die Verbindung zwischen Lebenden und Toten* [The connection between the living and the dead] (GA 168), lecture of 16 February 1916.

3. *Die Philosophie der Freiheit* [The philosophy of freedom] (GA 4), Chapter XII.

4. *Die Geheimwissenschaft im Umriß* [Occult science in outline] (GA 13), chapter on 'Cognition of the Higher Worlds'.

5. John 1:3.

6. From 'Christ's descent into hell' in the Gospel of Nicodemus, *Neutestamentliche Apokryphen I, Evangelien* [New Testament apocrypha I, Gospels], ed. Wilhelm Schneemelcher (J. C. B. Mohr [P. Siebeck]: Tübingen, 1987), p. 415 f.

7. Gal. 2:20.

8. Rev. 17:5.

9. 2 Thess. 2:4, German translation by Emil Bock (Urachhaus: Stuttgart, 1998).

10. *Die Geheimwissenschaf* (GA 13), chapter on 'The Evolution of the Cosmos and Man'.

11. *Die Apokalypse des Johannes* [The Revelation of John] (GA 104), lecture of 30 June 1908.

Lecture 11

1. *Aus den Inhalten der esoterischen Stunden* [From the contents of the esoteric lessons] (GA 266/1), lesson of 5 May 1909 in Berlin.

2. Peace Pilgrim, *Peace Pilgrim: Her Life and Work in Her Own Words* (Ocean Tree Books: Santa Fe, 1992).

3. *Die Brücke zwischen der Weltgeistigkeit und dem Physischen des Menschen* [The bridge between cosmic spirituality and the physical in the human being] (GA 202), lecture of 12 December 1920 in Dornach.

4. Mokichi Okada, *The Light from the East* (MOA Productions: Atami, 1983), vol. 1, p. 297.

5. Ibid., vol. 2, p. 16.

6. Ibid., p. 170.

7. *Aus den Inhalten der esoterischen Stunden* [From the contents of the esoteric lessons] (GA 266/2), lesson of 6 February 1910 in Kassel.

8. *Initiations-Erkenntnis* [Initiation knowledge] (GA 227), lecture of 31 August 1923 in Penmaenmawr; *Esoterische Betrachtungen karmischer Zusammenhänge* [Esoteric observations on karmic connections], vol. 5 (GA 239), lecture of 5 April 1924 in Prague.

9. *Zur Geschichte und aus den Inhalten der erkenntniskultischen Abteilung der Esoterischen Schule von 1904 bis 1914* [On the history of the cognitive-cultic section of the Esoteric School 1904–14, and from its contents] (GA 265), lesson of 1 June 1914 in Basel.

10. *Der Hüter der Schwelle* [The guardian of the threshold], in *Vier Mysteriendramen* [Four mystery plays] (GA 14), scene 3; trans. M. Miller and D. Miller.

Lecture 12

1. Matt: 3:2.
2. See *Esoterische Betrachtungen karmischer Zusammenhänge* [Esoteric observations on karmic connections], vol. 6 (GA 240), lecture of 18 July 1924.
3. *Anthroposophische Leitsätze* [Anthroposophical leading thoughts] (GA 26), chapter on 'Heavenly History, Mythological History, Earthly History, Mystery of Golgotha'.
4. *Ägyptische Mythen und Mysterien* [Egyptian myths and mysteries] (GA 106), lecture of 2 September 1908.
5. *Vier Mysteriendramen* [Four Mystery Dramas] (GA 14).
6. *Entwürfe, Fragmente und Paralipomena zu den vier Mysteriendramen* [Drafts, fragments and paralipomena for the four Mystery Dramas] (GA 44).
7. *Die Mission der neuen Geistesoffenbarung* [The mission of the new revelation of the spirit] (GA 127), lecture of 30 November 1911.
8. *Erfahrungen des Übersinnlichen: Die drei Wege der Seele zu Christus* [Experiences of the supersensible: The three paths of the soul to Christ] (GA 143), lecture of 17 December 1912.
9. *Wiederverkörperung und Karma* [Reincarnation and karma] (GA 135), lecture of 5 March 1912.
10. *Die Geheimwissenschaft im Umriß* [Occult science in outline] (GA 13), chapter on 'The Present and Future of Cosmic and Human Evolution'.
11. Exod. 20:2–17.
12. Gal. 2:20.
13. Matt. 28:20.

Bibliography of Cited Materials from the Collected Works of Rudolf Steiner Available in English

Where a GA (Gesamtausgabe) number is absent, the work is currently unavailable in English

GA Volumes Available in English

GA No.   Title of volume in English, publisher, date(s) of lecture(s) cited

4   *Intuitive Thinking as a Spiritual Path* (Anthroposophic Press, 1995) or *The Philosophy of Freedom* (Rudolf Steiner Press, 1999).

8   *Christianity as Mystical Fact* (Anthroposophic Press, 1997).

13   *Occult Science, An Outline* (Rudolf Steiner Press, 2005).

14   *The Four Mystery Plays* (Rudolf Steiner Press, 1982), 'The Portal of Initiation', 'The Soul's Probation', 'The Guardian of the Threshold', 'The Soul's Awakening'.

26   *Anthroposophical Leading Thoughts* (Rudolf Steiner Press, 1973).

59   *Metamorphoses of the Soul,* vol. 2 (Rudolf Steiner Press, 1983), 9 lectures, Berlin, 17 February 1910.

93a   *Foundations of Esotericism* (Rudolf Steiner Press, 1983), Notes of 31 lectures, Berlin, 8 October 1905.

97   *Christian Mystery, The* (Completion Press, 2000), Landin (Mark), 29 July 1906.

99   *Rosicrucian Wisdom* (Rudolf Steiner Press, 2000), 14 lectures, Munich, 6 June 1907.

104   *The Apocalypse of St John* (Anthroposophical Publishing Co., 1958), 12 lectures, Nuremberg, 30 June 1908.

106   *Egyptian Myths and Mysteries* (Anthroposophic Press, 1971), 12 lectures, Leipzig, 2 September 1908.

112   *The Gospel of St John* (Anthroposophic Press & Rudolf Steiner Press, 1948), 14 lectures, Kassel, 7 July 1909.

114   *The Gospel According to Luke* (Anthroposophic Press, 2001), 10 lectures, Basel, 17 September 1909.

116   *The Christ Impulse and the Development of Ego Consciousness* (Anthroposophic Press, 1976), 7 lectures, Berlin, 2 May 1910.

121   *The Mission of the Individual Folk Souls* (Rudolf Steiner Press, 1970), 11 lectures, Christiania (Oslo), 12 June 1910.

123   *The Gospel of St Matthew* (Rudolf Steiner Press, 1965), 12 lectures, Berne, 7 September 1910.

131   *From Jesus to Christ* (Rudolf Steiner Press, 1991), 11 lectures, Karlsruhe, 10, 11 and 14 October 1911.

135   *Reincarnation and Karma* (Anthroposophic Press, 1992), 5 lectures, Berlin, 5 March 1912.

139   *The Gospel of St Mark* (Anthroposophic Press, 1986), 10 lectures, Basel, 17 September, 1912.

143   *Freud, Jung and Spiritual Psychology* (Anthroposophic Press, 2001), Cologne, 8 May 1912; Zürich, 17 December 1912.

144   *The Mysteries of the East and of Christianity* (Rudolf Steiner Press, 1972), 4 lectures, Berlin, 5 February 1913.

149   *Christ and the Spiritual World and the Search for the Holy Grail* (Rudolf Steiner Press, 1963), 6 lectures, Leipzig, 29 December 1913 and 1 and 2 January 1914.

187   *How Can Mankind Find the Christ Again?* (Anthroposophic Press, 1984), 8 lectures, Dornach, 29 December 1918.

199   *Spiritual Science as a Foundation for Social Forms* (Anthroposophic Press & Rudolf Steiner Press, 1986), 17 lectures, Dornach, August 8, 1920.

227   *The Evolution of Consciousness* (Rudolf Steiner Press, 1991), 13 lectures, Penmaenmawr, 31 August 1923.

245   *From the Contents of the Esoteric School 3* (Anthroposophical Publishing Co., 1954), .

264   *From the History and Contents of the First Section of the Esoteric School 1904–1914* (Anthroposophic Press, 1998), ed. Hella Wiesberger.

284   *Occult Seals and Columns* (Anthroposophical Publishing Co., 1924), Photogravure and half-tone reproductions, with introductory text (1907).

318   *Pastoral Medicine* (Anthroposophic Press, 1987), 11 lectures, Dornach, 9 September 1924.

350   *From Mammoths to Mediums* (Rudolf Steiner Press, 2000), 16 discussions with workers, Dornach 25 July 1923.

Additional Cited Works by Rudolf Steiner Available in English

From GA
No.   Volume title, publisher and date(s) of lecture(s) cited

(40)   *Truth-Wrought Words* (Anthroposophic Press, 1979).

(96)   *The Christian Mystery* (Anthroposophic Press, 1998), 28 January 1907.

(102)   *The Influence of Spiritual Beings upon Man* (Anthroposophic Press, 1961), 11 lectures, Berlin, 13 April 1908.

(148)   *The Fifth Gospel* (Rudolf Steiner Press, 1995), 13 lectures, Oslo, 5 October 1913.

(155)   *Christ and the Human Soul* (Rudolf Steiner Press, 1974), 4 lectures, Norrköping, 15 July 1914.

(175)   *Building Stones for an Understanding of the Mystery of Golgotha* (Rudolf Steiner Press, 1972), 10 lectures. Berlin, 24 April 1917.

(184)   *Three Streams in the Evolution of Mankind* (Rudolf Steiner Press, 1965), 6 lectures, Dornach, 6 October 1918.

(214)   *The Mystery of the Trinity and the Mission of the Spirit* (Anthroposophic Press, 1991), 8 lectures, Dornach, 23 July 1922.

(239)   *Karmic Relationships* (Rudolf Steiner Press, 1966), 7 lectures, Prague, 5 April 1924.

(260a)   *The Life, Nature and Cultivation of Anthroposophy* (Rudolf Steiner Press, 1963).

For more information on the works of Rudolf Steiner in English and German please contact these libraries:

The Library
Rudolf Steiner House
35 Park Road, London NW1 6XT
England
Phone/Fax: 020 7224 8398
Email: RSH-Library@anth.org.uk

The Rudolf Steiner Library
65 Fern Hill Road
Ghent, New York 12075
Phone: 518 672 7690
Fax: 518 672 5827
Email: rsteinerlibrary@taconic.net

Paths of the Christian Mysteries
From Compostela to the New World
Virginia Sease and Manfred Schmidt-Brabant

Over the past decades there has been an upsurge of interest in 'the Camino', the pilgrim's route to Santiago de Compostela in northern Spain. But where does this fascination in the spiritual exploration of the Middle Ages come from, and what is its significance? Virginia Sease and Manfred Schmidt-Brabant attest that we live in a time of spiritual quest, discovery and change. Humanity is becoming increasingly sensitive, and primal memories are beginning to emerge in people's consciousness. Within this dynamic context of inner transformation, the Camino's historic importance is being re-echoed in many human souls.

Rudolf Steiner stated that people have a need to live not only with external history but also with the esoteric, hidden narrative which lies behind it: the history of 'the Mysteries'. Now at the beginning of the twenty-first century, the authors suggest that it is increasingly necessary for us to live consciously with this veiled history of humanity's continual search for communion with the divine world.

Based on lifelong researches and contemplations, the authors present a survey of extraordinary breadth and depth. Focusing on the spiritual history of mankind, they begin with the cosmic origin of the Grail Mysteries and culminate with the Supersensible Michael Cultus and the Being of Anthroposophia. In the intervening chapters they study the School of Athens, early Christian art and its Gnostic impulses, the Grail Initiation in northern Spain, the role of the Cathars and Troubadours in the Manichaean stream, the Camino to Santiago de Compostela and the esoteric aspect of music for the pilgrims, the Music of the Spheres and the Elders of the Apocalypse, the Templars as emissaries of the Holy Grail, the initiations of Christian Rosenkreutz and his relation to anthroposophical art, the early Rosicrucian impulses in America and Europe, and much more.

256pp; 23.5 × 15.5 cm; paperback; £14.95; ISBN 1 902636 43 0